# THE
# STRATEGY
# JOURNEY

Book Preview was first published in 2018
Copyright © 2020 by Julie Choo and Graham Christison. All rights reserved.

Published by Stratability Academy
Registered as Stratability Global Ltd, United Kingdom

Cover image: Dana Adnan
Cover design: Julie Choo and Dana Adnan
Book layout and illustration design: Julie Choo
Illustration images: Dana Adnan
Instructional Design Editor: Nicola Palmer
Language of publication: English (US)

Stratability Academy publishes in a variety of print and electronic formats and by print-on-demand. Some materials included with electronic versions of this book may not be included in print or print-on-demand. If this book makes references to any tools or assessments, that is not included in the version you purchased, you may download or access this material at https://strategyjourney.com/tools.

For general information about our other products and services, or to place orders of this book for re-sale, please contact us at https://strategyjourney.com/contact or email us at info@strategyjourney.com.

ISBN 978-1-9164433-0-3 (ebook)
ISBN 978-1-9164433-3-4 (Paperback)
ISBN 978-1-9164433-2-7 (Hardcover)

# THE
# STRATEGY
# JOURNEY

How to transform your business operating model in the digital age with value-driven, customer co-created and network-connected services

**Julie Choo and Graham Christison**

 Strat**ability**

# Forewords & Endorsements

I have spent 25 years leading and driving innovation and change in Financial Services but following the global financial crisis in 2008 I felt there was a need to build a team who could re-architect the business, reset our business strategy, understand our point of departure and build a roadmap to take us on the journey to realise our vision. It took me 2 ½ years of searching for individuals across the globe with the right character, skill-set & experience that could help me on this journey. That's when I met Julie and Graham, unique individuals in their own right but bringing them together as a powerful, innovative and galvanising duo to drive, lead and transform the way we thought about setting, executing and delivering business strategy transformation.

THE STRATEGY JOURNEY book is a hugely important and timely guide to the business community. It demystifies the former 'black art' of making a strategy executable by connecting all the existing best practises in the transformation discipline together, adding key missing elements and 'joining-the-dots' through data to make the ensuing framework and methodology practical and accessible to both business executives and transformation professionals alike. The result is a pragmatic, engineered, data driven approach to devising and executing transformation that all businesses need to establish their digital future and to develop agility to react to environmental based threats such as what we experienced with COVID-19. As a seasoned senior executive and business founder with strategy execution experience built over many senior leadership roles in the Global Investment Banking and Financial Consulting sector, it's the best, most complete approach I have seen in my career.

It doesn't surprise me that Julie and Graham's unique talents & combined experience could create such an accessible and complete book given my first-hand experience of them and the fundamentals of the methodology. I have been the early sponsor of it from as early as 2014, when I introduced them to each other, as we embarked on driving and delivering a set of global transformation programs for an investment bank.

I have two final thoughts before you read further. "No one likes to create but everybody likes to edit" - Julie and Graham have created a wealth of text and content in THE STRATEGY JOURNEY that can be re-used and applied in your organization. And it's "Always better to invent the future than try to predict it" – using this book as a guide will allow you to invent the way you do, manage and execute strategy on your journey.

**Stuart McClymont**
**Managing Director at JDX Consulting - Head of Market Infrastructure Services**


As a busy CEO and Entrepreneur of a growing tech company and platform business, it is difficult to find the spare time to read and learn, even if we all know we should, especially when it can help the strategy of your business. This is why I really like THE STRATEGY JOURNEY, as it is full of illustrations, tips and case study examples that tell the story of WHY you would take on the challenge of building a business and evolving it through networks and communities, as I have been doing with my business - it speaks to me and should do with other similar entrepreneurs. The book is practical and teaches entrepreneurs to leverage the power of communities to turn their ideas into products and services for their tribes through co-creation. This is how many future businesses will grow especially in challenging times.

**Gina Bianchini**
**CEO Mighty Networks**

I hope you enjoy the book as much as I did! Since reading THE STRATEGY JOURNEY I have found myself referring to the book on a number of occasions. It was enjoyable to read but its true value will come in the future as an "Ace up my sleeve".

As a seasoned transformation director in many large organizations responsible for their global transformation programs, and now a CTO of a growing SME who has recently taken my organization from operating with paper and phones into the digital world, I recognize many of the tips and techniques in the book. I wish I had them and am indeed glad that I have them now in this "one stop shop" for Strategy, to inspire me to continuously evolve my organization's digital transformation journey.

If you need to design and build a new digital platform solution or a SaaS business and introduce apps as well as digital services into the architecture of your incumbent or more traditional business model, as I have been doing to transform my organization for today's digital economy, then this book is for you. The roadmap to the Digital Operating Model recommended by the authors is the real path so many businesses need to take if they are to fight against disruption, survive, and even begin to thrive in the challenging environment that we have today.

While reading the book, it became clear to me that THE STRATEGY JOURNEY has been written to cater for a wide target audience. This book would be a great tool for someone who is starting their first "Strategy Journey" but also a seasoned "Strategist" would get a lot out of the book. One thing (of many) I especially liked about the book is the way it covers both Technology and Business aspects well. It is full of practical tips and techniques, that will help any professional responsible for implementing digital transformation in and across their organization big or small.

I found THE STRATEGY JOURNEY to be a good balance of theory, case studies and the authors' experience. The book covers all the key Strategy principles in a clear, easy to read and condensed format. It uses case studies of well known brands to reinforce the importance of a specific Strategy principle. I have found in the past books on Strategy can be heavily theory-based, something you read them once, it can be difficult to stay engaged whilst reading, and you don't really use them again. THE STRATEGY JOURNEY is the complete opposite. It's a book that I will certainly keep within arms reach and reference *regularly*.

**Richard Weir**
**Chief Technology Officer (CTO), PayVantage Global, Singapore, Australia & New Zealand**


THE STRATEGY JOURNEY is a masterpiece. It weaves together novel elements with existing concepts and disciplines for a sweeping scope of subject matter, artfully 'joining-the-dots' from strategy to execution in a digital context. It does this in the language of the business and with a rare coherence and clarity. It is highly practical with each element usefully illustrated through real business examples to evidence the application of the content and show its value. Regardless of your role within an organization, this book will help you understand how business really works, where it is going, and importantly how to build the capability to achieve the business agility required for continual business transformation.

THE STRATEGY JOURNEY underscores the critical role business architecture plays across the entire journey from strategy to execution and in the orchestration of change. It highlights the importance of value led thinking, driven through co-creation processes between customers, the business and business architects, facilitated by a common shared language. This book is a must-read for every business architecture practitioner as the answer to our greatest challenge and opportunity lies within it: how to understand, speak the language, integrate into, and deliver relevant value within the bigger picture context of business and its strategic journey.

**Whynde Khuen**
**Founder of BizArchMastery.com, Founder S2E Transformation,**
**Partner & Co-founder of Business Architecture Associates, Fellow Institute of Digital Transformation**

I have been in the consulting business for 30 years and have probably forgotten more methodologies and frameworks than I care to remember. One thing I do remember very distinctly was a small format, 50-page booklet which was handed out by my first employer, one of the large global consultancies. Each page illustrated and explained one strategy tool. They were all in there, from the Boston Matrix to Value Stream Maps and from Porter's Five Forces to the SWOT Matrix. I thought it was super useful, but of course, these tools were just…. well, tools in a toolbox. What enabled me to create value in my assignments was the much broader understanding of a transformation journey and how to succeed on such a journey. This really wasn't taught in business school, but rather at in-house training at the large consulting firms of the day. And of course, on the job over time.

And this is what I really enjoy about THE STRATEGY JOURNEY. It does not only explain a framework for strategy, transformation, and some tools to you – which it, incidentally, does very well – but explains the entire journey and all the different aspects you need to consider. It talks about the why, the what, and the how covering critical elements seldom touched upon in these types of books such as leadership, culture, managing stakeholders, and so on. This is what makes it so useful and practical, along with the many case studies.

Another reason which makes it a really worthwhile read is that it is current and in sync, with the digital age we live in. We are all acutely aware of megatrends such as digitization and consumerization. THE STRATEGY JOURNEY takes it's starting point in these trends and the consumer. It weaves topics such as the digital economy, customer centricity, co-creation, and customer journeys into the broader theme of strategic transformation.

Companies across industries – from retail to financial services, and from manufacturing to the public sector – are facing needs to innovate across all those areas, and then bring that innovation to life across the enterprise in a transformation journey. The holistic approach taken in THE STRATEGY JOURNEY is particularly suitable for such endeavours.

Transformation, or change if you will, will be more important than ever in the 2020s. THE STRATEGY JOURNEY is a great asset for those who want to embark on, or work in, such transformation journeys. Reading it from start to finish, and then keeping it handy as a reference, will equip you with many of the things you will need on that journey as a leader, owner, or consultant.

**Victor Kotnik**
**Deloitte Consulting, Managing Partner Sweden**


In my role as a growth advisor, having helped transform many companies through service design and digital architecture innovation, from the largest of tech firms where I have driven 8-figure revenue returns to smaller SMEs who are only starting their digital transformation journeys, I would have previously loved to have had a reference like this book.  It provides an essential reference guide for any organization with a growth or transformation agenda.

THE STRATEGY JOURNEY is a comprehensive compendium of the frameworks, the processes and the templates behind strategy and its execution through the various lifecycles of a business' journey and growth. The focus on service design and especially digital services leveraging the power of data and AI technologies in a cloud and service-led ecosystem is the big step that many businesses need to take going forward.

The roadmaps in the book provide both the C-suite and practitioners of any-sized organization with methods to adapt how they have operated in the past to improve their performance and growth potential in today's and tomorrow's digital world.

**Peter Ikladious**
**Growth Advisor**
**Vice President Marketing at Safety Culture, Former Executive Director, Head of Product Management,**
**Head of Digital Transformation, Solution Sales Lead, Growth & User Engagement Lead at IBM (2014-2019)**

Over the years, we've worked with many customers and businesses who have tried to use different frameworks to help drive their business strategy through to execution. However, on many occasions, this has been hampered by a disconnect between the ambition, knowledge, and tools.

Rapid change and recent disruption have made this disconnect even more noticeable. Now and in the future, to thrive and even survive, it's imperative that organizations become operationally resilient by implementing an approach that can be adapted to meet the needs of a changing world.

In THE STRATEGY JOURNEY, Julie and Graham's approach takes individuals, functions, and whole organizations on a journey that not only includes the narrative, but also training and digital versions of the frameworks (for example digital target operating models and digital twins).

Based on years of experience and practical examples, THE STRATEGY JOURNEY helps to uncover and use organizational data and insights to align big strategic ideas with actions on the ground.

**Peter McNally**
**CEO BusinessOptix**


THE STRATEGY JOURNEY is written in a concise and easy to read manner. The graphics and design help you to capture the key messages. Digital transformation is a complex subject but the authors have summarized the topics into three easy to read sections and enable you to discover the WHY, WHAT and HOW in your business transformation needs. The various templates and canvases empower organization leaders and small and medium enterprise (SME) business owners to carry out their business transformation taking into consideration technology as an enabler, leadership, and organization culture in a structured manner. THE STRATEGY JOURNEY can be a handy business strategy manual and workbook.

**Michael S S Chow**
**President of The London Institute of Banking & Finance (Alumni Singapore)**
**Board Director/Council Member of UK Association of International Accountants**
**Advisor to Chung Hwa Medical Institution, RHT Intelligence Network PL and RHT Strategic Advisory PL**
**Member of the Panel of Judge for Brands for Goods Award**
**Ex Board Director of United Nations Association of Singapore**


THE STRATEGY JOURNEY offers a lot of value on two fronts, not often addressed in one cohesive story and discussed together.

- Having initiated and led operating model transformation programmes for FTSE100 clients and coached 100s of early stage start-ups, through their business growth journeys, I've seen how these journeys play out in a broad range of environments. THE STRATEGY JOURNEY is a must-have reference for anyone building or running an organization in the digital age.

- Being particularly passionate about the human dimensions of change and as the founder of MyKagami.com, a digital platform that empowers individuals to create and own their personal self-development journeys, I can also attest to the value brought by this book - from the ideas , frameworks and case studies within, for individuals embarking on their own transformational journeys.

**Yoram Percale**
**Founder MyKagami.com, Coach in Residence King's College Entrepreneur Institute**

Julie's insight, numerous examples, illustrations, and approach toward understanding the design and elaboration of customer-driven strategies are quick to understand. This book is a must if you're serious about improving the execution of your digital transformation.

**Daniel Lambert**
**VP Business Architecture at Benchmark Consulting, Venture Capitalist, CIO.com contributor**


When the CEO of Standard Bank Intl, developing, communicating and executing our strategy was a critical responsibility for me, Graham was the shining light in the strategy team. We both believed that cultivating and implementing an effective strategy was not based on a collection of abstract theories, but rather trying to determine what will matter and developing a clear, innovative plan to transform and achieve those goals.

In the words of John Templeton "It's impossible to produce superior performance unless you do something different."

This book is a practical guide to doing strategy differently: bringing to life techniques and examples, relevant in our digital world, on how "to do" strategy differently, purposefully and to continuously transform. It brings together the elements required to consider how a business should structure and deliver innovation-driven-transformation.
In a digital world where clients, colleagues and the community matter to be successful, the concept of co-creation is critical. Not getting better, not transforming and innovating is tantamount to failing – this book provides a recipe for how to apply a culture of continuous learning and deliver better results.

Both Graham and Julie have decades of practical experience; their research has its roots in the real world and the evidence of the book's effectiveness is sourced from the real world. This clearly isn't abstract theory.

I would consider reading this book as equivalent to 'an end-to-end MBA refresher' for senior executives, teaching them to think differently and providing a structured methodology to continuous-transformation from Strategy to Execution.

**Jenny Knott FCCA FMSI**
**Independent NED and Founder of FinTech Strategic Advisors**


Organizations need to remain relevant to their customers, investors and to society. Customers are well informed and their expectations have never been higher. Employees are demanding greater clarity, empowerment, and context to their work. Businesses need to adapt to meet all of these needs.

THE STRATEGY JOURNEY provides an easily accessible contextual framework and a set of practical methodologies for Business Owners, C-Level Executives, Managers, Coaches and Business Advisors which enable businesses to successfully navigate towards their strategic goals. It supports the critical foundations of both startups and larger organizations looking to re-calibrate and transform. Most importantly, it enables businesses to become more responsive, rather than reactive, to the fast changing world we live in.

The business world continues to evolve at great pace and COVID-19 has further highlighted the importance of "Enterprise-Wide Agility" and a culture of "Continuous Value Creation". Only the most adaptable firms will thrive, while others simply focus on surviving.

**Richard Bell**
**Executive Coach and Business Advisor**

An excellent, timely and practical book on business strategy for business practitioners and coaches.

I joined a round table session as Chairman of the Asian Entrepreneurs Exchange (AEX), a not for profit organization to business alliance of trust in the Asia region, to discuss the idea of the book and how it could help SMEs with their digital transformation journeys and I'm so glad I did.

It is therefore very gratifying for me and my AEX colleagues to learn that the book is ready for launch.

Excellent and timely because the book title says it all. It is not merely a book on business strategy in theory per se but rather a circular loop of strategy journey that includes business transformation; the one most critical challenge faced by companies, big, small and new startups, to be able to remain relevant and sustainable in the digital economy going forward, and on the immediate term, the rather severe post COVID19 challenges and market shift.

The book suggests THE STRATEGY JOURNEY as a framework to manage digital transformation in a structured way. It connects the dots, using data science, via roadmaps focused on helping businesses to thrive in the digital economy.

There are many good practical values for business coaches as well as practitioners, because it presents two very helpful frameworks - the Thinking Framework and the Problem Solving Framework. Not just thinking but also practical guides on doing as well.

The frameworks are relevant to all businesses, especially small businesses. All businesses must transform to leverage emerging technology to better serve the markets or customers. Otherwise, they will certainly lose their relevancy and competitiveness, perished by competition, or disrupted by a new business model.

To help readers better understand the frameworks and pathways of THE STRATEGY JOURNEY, the book provides numerous business examples, tips and tools.

This book is easy to read, and it is filled with thoughts provoking ideas and complete with guiding frameworks as well as real business examples.

A must read to walk THE STRATEGY JOURNEY in the digital economy!

**Teng Theng Dar, BBM**
**Chairman, Asia Entrepreneurs Exchange Ltd**
**Distinguished Advisor, School of Applied Science, Temasek Polytechnic**
**Singapore Non-Resident Ambassador to the Sultanate of Oman**

I must congratulate you (Julie and Graham) upon the concept and content - it's first class.

As a project/programme manager with 20 years plus experience perhaps not unsurprisingly I find myself often dealing with senior stakeholders when defining programmes and the underlying challenge is understanding what business benefits they are expecting to deliver by the intervention and how they link to business strategy. You would be surprised (or perhaps not) how many times they can not answer that question and you have to hand hold them on a journey to capture and define what the organization needs. Hence why I am subscribed to your book!

**Clive Smith**
**Senior Project Manager at UK Research & Innovation**

# Core Team

**Julie Choo**

Lead Author + Designer

**Dr Graham Christison**

Supervising Author

**Dana Adnan**

Illustrator

Sam Chia

Lauren Houghton

## Leadership & Mindset Content Team

Eric Leconte

Laura Winton

Oliver Christison

## Research & Support Team

# Welcome to the strategy journey

**As lead and supervising authors of this book, we wanted to tell you the story of this book and its strategy journey. Why did we create this book? What was its goal and the value that it provides? And how has it evolved from concept to its launch in the midst of the Coronivirus-COVID19 Pandemic, where businesses and jobs, operating models and supply chains are all facing unprecedented disruption.**

The strategy journey of this book has taken many transformations:

- It started as a suggestion and idea from a former colleague, boss and client of ours (Stuart McClymont) who wanted training support for this team of strategy & architecture consultants to serve his clients better and to help him grow his business from a small boutique consultancy, started with funding of £250,000, to a consultancy capable of taking in 25 to 100 million in revenue in just five years…

- We raised funds via a Kickstarter project in December 2017 to set out on the journey to write the book with a Framework built on all our career experiences that would help enterprises operate more effectively based on transforming their operating models…

- As we began researching and writing the book, our data-driven engineering, scientific and entrepreneur backgrounds led us to explore how we could use the Framework as a data science led resource and learning asset that could empower businesses big and small, for-profit and non-profit, to take a dot-joining approach to business and digital transformation, as it would appear the mighty Amazon has done. We have incorporated the three principles that every enterprise must operate with to achieve success in the digital economy … to be value-driven, customer co-created and network connected as they transform their organizations into the future …

- Finally, as businesses face ever increasing threats of disruption from the digital economy and the more recent turmoil caused by the Coronavirus-COVID19 Pandemic, we transformed **THE STRATEGY JOURNEY** into a guidebook that will support enterprises to join·the·dots, using data, via three practical and directed PATHS or roadmaps focused on helping them survive and thrive in the future. The book teaches practitioners of strategy, service designers, architects, and any one involved in the ongoing transformation of an enterprise to take a more holistic and end-to-end approach in how they conduct their businesses for the longer term, based on how customers and users think, act and behave, while still being able to incorporate strategically driven quick wins with the aid of data and digital technology.

This book has been divided into three sections to help you discover and investigate the WHY, WHAT and HOW of THE STRATEGY JOURNEY for the business or enterprise that you serve. It will empower you to apply digital transformation effectively and efficiently, and deliver more value-add, better and faster in your business, for your customers and clients and in your career.

As a book containing a PROBLEM-SOLVING Framework for businesses, the WHY section will challenge you to consider the problems that you face in your business and in your own role and career, before presenting different methods in the WHAT section, including the 5 Framework Models, that you can apply to help you solve those problems. In the HOW section, we provide detail on the three PATHS through the 5 Models which you can take to join·the·dots and bridge the gaps in your business between people, processes, data, systems and across different locations both physical and virtual. The three PATHS are supported by 5 data-driven tools in the form of 5 templated canvases that you can use to support your next and future strategy journeys. In line with the practical stance of the book, the MODEL canvases are fully worked through with detailed business examples included to help inspire you into action.

Always looking to help you join·the·dots,

*Julie Choo & Graham Christison*

# Contents of this book

This book is comprised of three sections supported by a framework with Five Models and numerous case studies designed and formulated to illustrate:

Why enterprises must transform better and faster with business agility along their strategy journey by leveraging the power of data to create value; or end up evaporating in the fast changing digital economy… characterized by disruption, rising customer expectations, and the need to sustainably adapt and continuously change – with operational resilience.

What is a business?
What is value in business?
What makes a business grow in value?
What is digital transformation?
What is co-creation, innovation and service design?
What operates and runs a business?
What architects the business?
What is optimal business agility?

**What**

What are the Five Models that form **THE STRATEGY JOURNEY** *Framework* to support the architecture of a business and business transformation in the digital economy.

How to successfully navigate from strategy-to-execution along the stages of **THE STRATEGY JOURNEY** end-to-end, to tackle specific business challenges. The journey will follow three guided-paths to achieve business transformation that delivers outcomes of value to customers, partners, and stakeholders in the digital business ecosystem. The goal is to reduce gaps in business transformation and capture opportunities through innovation of new services, while building business agility in the enterprise to empower its future transformation needs.

# THE **STRATEGYJOURNEY Framework**

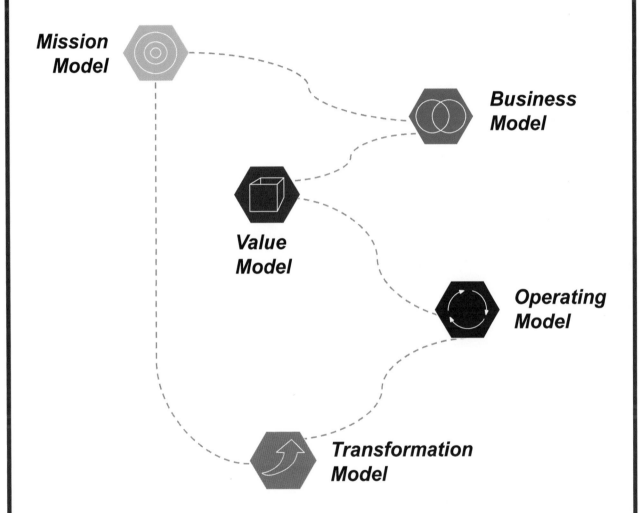

*Mission Model*

*Business Model*

*Value Model*

*Operating Model*

*Transformation Model*

The Five Models are structured into five **Strategy Journey Canvases** for design thinking and guided by three *Strategy Journey Paths* to provide a roadmap for strategy design and effective business transformation.

# Roadmap →

# WHY ⁇

# WHAT

# HOW

# Index of Terms

# References

Go to https://strategyjourney.com/book-references for a list of all additional references as indicated on relevant pages of the book and details of other co-creating contributors.

# Features

## Business Examples

## Tools

## Activities

## Tips

# *Why*

# Is this journey for you?

*(tick all that apply)*

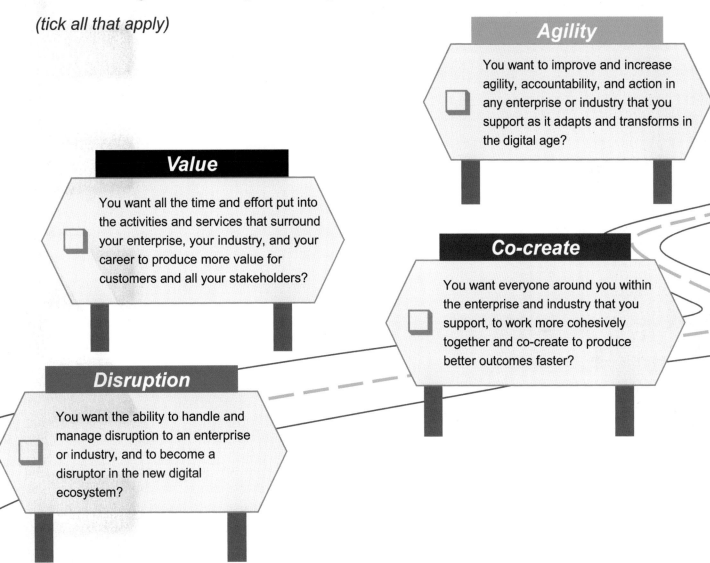

### Agility

☐ You want to improve and increase agility, accountability, and action in any enterprise or industry that you support as it adapts and transforms in the digital age?

### Value

☐ You want all the time and effort put into the activities and services that surround your enterprise, your industry, and your career to produce more value for customers and all your stakeholders?

### Co-create

☐ You want everyone around you within the enterprise and industry that you support, to work more cohesively together and co-create to produce better outcomes faster?

### Disruption

☐ You want the ability to handle and manage disruption to an enterprise or industry, and to become a disruptor in the new digital ecosystem?

*These are all typical challenges faced by enterprises, large and small.*

*In this book, we will show you how to change the game and overcome your roadblocks.*

# Who is this book for

*Are you a ...*

**CEO or COO**

**Entrepreneur or Intrapreneur**

**Board Member or Strategic Advisor**

**Shareholder or Investor**

... who wants resources and assets in the enterprise to produce a return on investment, build value in the business and a strong brand?

**Product Manager or Service Owner**

**Engineer or Scientist**

**Designer, Innovator or Inventor**

**CIO or Solutions Architect**

... who wants to design and create better products and services for customers, your organization, shareholders, and society?

*... who wants to achieve better outcomes faster*

**Project Manager**

**Change Consultant**

**Business, Process or Data Analyst**

**Enterprise Architect**

**Merger & Acquisition (M&A) Specialist**

**CTO or IT Manager**

... who wants to empower your enterprise with the capability, as well as agility, to transform and deliver better solutions that add value faster?

**Business Development Manager or Sales Specialist**

**Customer Experience Manager or User Experience Specialist**

**Operations Manager, Human Resource Manager or Finance Manager**

**Government or Industry Regulator**

... who wants to support the performance of the enterprise and deliver value-added services to customers while turning a profit?

*... this book will help you* **work together** *to achieve your outcomes.*

**Success lies in the journey**
**Not the destination.**

Ben Sweetland

# Why it's about the journey

*What is the real meaning of success?*

Business is a game full of challenges and obstacles that must be overcome in order to win.

In most cases, there is a race to the first finishing line or goal post for all those enterprises who have entered the competition. Before it starts again as the race continues into the next game. The journey from start-to-finish in each game has both risks and rewards for each enterprise as it navigates its way along the journey toward each target.

In the business game, success is not the destination. More often than not, it is not clear what that destination is, and the target can change at any time. This is especially true for start-ups, where uncertainty is high. It is also the reality for enterprises of all shapes and sizes in today's rapidly changing ecosystem driven by the digital economy. The ability to transform better and faster than the competition - an enterprise's *'business agility'* (p. 52) and operational resilience - has become the key difference between success and failure.

Upon reaching one target, the journey to achieve success simply starts again. Once a goal is achieved, lessons are learned ... before new goals are set for the next journey.

*Each time you overcome an obstacle, win a challenge, or achieve an outcome on your business journey ... that is success.*

# Five stages of THE STRATEGY JOURNEY

All enterprises, no matter their size, are continuously navigating through the Five Stages of **THE STRATEGY JOURNEY** as they tackle different challenges across their organization.

These Five Stages represent the business lifecycle, that is the journey from strategy to execution of every enterprise as it transforms to survive, thrive, and grow.

## Motivation & Leadership

Leaders must set the target mission, vision, and goals for the business along with values. This allows the appropriate strategies and tactics to be defined. It also rallies and motivates the team, by setting the organizational culture. This builds the brand that is needed to drive engagement from customers. It also drives agility, accountability, and action during strategy execution through an aligned organization.

## Business Design

With a clear vision and goals to focus on, ideas can be generated and problems prioritized. This allows the ideas to be tested for their viability as propositions with value for all stakeholders, including customers, staff, partners, and shareholders. The business must innovate new business models that enable its value propositions to be adopted by customers and produce profit.

## Value Design

For a business to grow and produce profit, it must have a strategic position in the ecosystem or value chain that it operates within. Value is created when the business can find the right balance between customer intimacy, product innovation, and operational efficiency across its value streams or processes and capabilities, all while tapping into the wider value ecosystem for sources of competitive advantage.

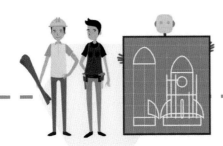

## Business Architecture

To support everyday functions as well as growth, a business must have highly agile capabilities or functions across its entire operating model. Its architecture has to support the most optimal use of people, process, data, technology resources, and funding, to allow remarkable services to be delivered in a way that can match the key performance indicators (KPIs), while enabling the business to scale.

## Business Transformation

No business will survive by being complacent with the status quo. Change and innovation are essential to stay in the game of business and get ahead. In order to deliver outcomes that are aligned with the strategies in the mission and vision, change must be managed as a portfolio of projects that are coherent across different business functions from front-to-back or end-to-end.

# 10 Transformation Challenges ...

While navigating **THE STRATEGY JOURNEY**, all enterprises are tackling their way through one or more of the following 10 universal business transformation challenges:

**1** Starting a business or launching a new product or service

**3** Developing customer relationships with sticky experiences

**5** Adapting to ecosystem changes to mitigate risks

**2** Creating a mindset or culture motivated by learning & change

**4** Growing through service extension or diversification

**6** Increase value by building business assets

# ... along THE STRATEGY JOURNEY

**7** Building agility to optimize capability efficiency & effectiveness

**9** Becoming more intelligent with data to drive innovation

**8** Optimizing transformation activities for ROI

**10** Leveraging local or global networks to improve operations

*... covered by the case study examples in this book.*

# Why Transformation is ...

*Change is constant and it is getting faster*

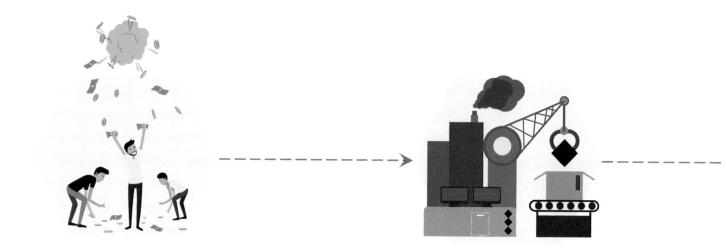

The world is full of instability ...

The Coronavirus health pandemic has caused massive disruption to lifestyles and livelihoods all over the world. Countries and regions have also been disrupted by:

- The Global Financial Crisis (GFC) where several financial institutions failed between 2007-2009
- Geopolitical factors e.g. US/China tension over trade
- The UK Brexit Referendum and subsequent impact on European trade and mobility
- The dot-com bubble bursting in early 2000s when several internal businesses failed impacting markets

Almost every decade, these events have caused uncertainty leading financial markets and economies to go through periods of turmoil.

The future is always uncertain ... and changing.

In the Industrial Revolution, we experienced the rise of machines that would automate and replace mechanical labor, and hence many jobs. Over roughly a century we adapted and created many new jobs.

We have now transitioned into the Digital Age, where the rise of information backed by automation is causing unprecedented changes to our society, our livelihoods, our jobs, our homes, our health, our food, and the way we think, act, and behave.

Early digital innovations such as the Internet and Smartphones have taken merely a decade or two to embed across two-thirds of the world.

# ... Getting Faster

*"The 33-year average tenure of companies ... in 1964 ... is forecasted to shrink to 12 years by 2027"*
_Innosight, 2018

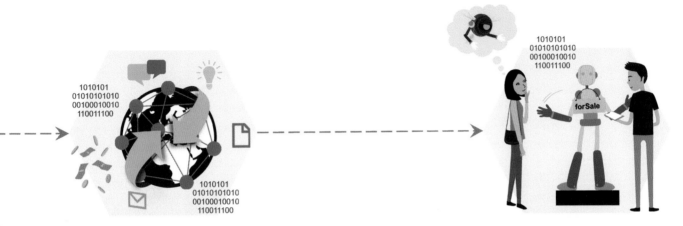

Digital innovations like the Public Cloud and Social Media have taken much less time to gain traction, with its ability to increase connectivity with improved speed and the promise of reduced costs for users.

Along with the Cloud, a decentralized ledger technology called Blockchain now provides a digital ecosystem that can fuel an exponential expansion of data exchange from anyone, almost anywhere. Blockchain supports a whole new set of digital or cryptocurrencies and crypto-assets that are being traded on digital exchanges that cannot technically be governed or regulated – in a new black economy.

We have moved beyond machines that replicate what we do, or replace what we don't want to do. We have created intelligent machines that can learn from what we do and think by themselves to do what we cannot do, as well as help us do things even better and faster.

Artificial Intelligence (AI) is now common place. We also have Internet of Things (IoT) devices that fill our homes or that we wear or carry.

With all this information at our fingertips, we, as consumers of goods and services, have also changed (raised) our expectations.

The Digital Economy is an *Expectation Economy*\* with customers who are (almost) impossible to please because of rising quality, positive impact, and the need for a personal experience. This expectation is only growing and getting higher and higher.

*\* The term Expectation Economy was introduced in Trend Driven Innovation (Wiley 2015) by the team from TrendWatchers.*

# Evolution of the industrial economy ...

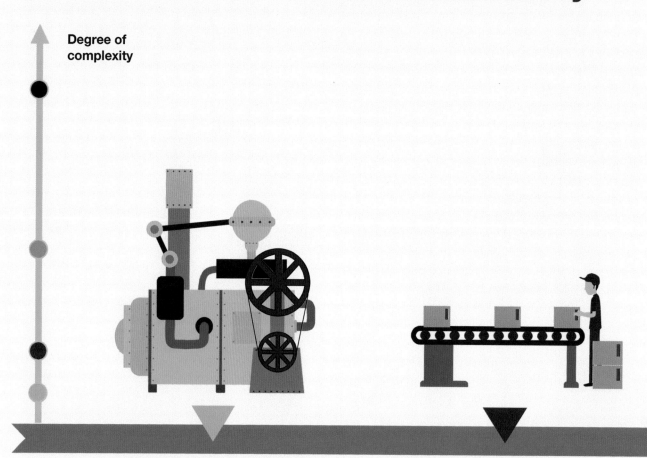

Degree of complexity

## First Industrial Revolution

Innovation using water and steam power led to mechanical production equipment that drove the first factories. First mechanical loom was invented in 1784.

## Second Industrial Revolution

Innovation using electrical energy enabled mass production, supported by division of labor. First conveyor belt was invented by Cincinnati slaughter house in 1870.

# ... and the digital economy

What Next?

## First Digital Revolution

## Second Digital Revolution

## Third Industrial Revolution

Innovation using electronics and information technology (IT) increased production via automation. First programmable logic controller (PLC) was invented by Modicon 084 in 1969.

## Fourth Industrial Revolution

Innovation using cloud technology, IoT and cyber-physical systems, all powered by big data, enables complex task automation, open information sharing, and early artificial intelligence.

*The Industrial Revolution is a short period in a 3000 plus year history of how businesses have evolved. Go to www.strategyjourney.com/tools to learn more about the history of business.*

# The Digital Revolution ...

*A summary of digital transformations that have changed society into a Digital Economy, and disrupted the way we think, act, and behave.*

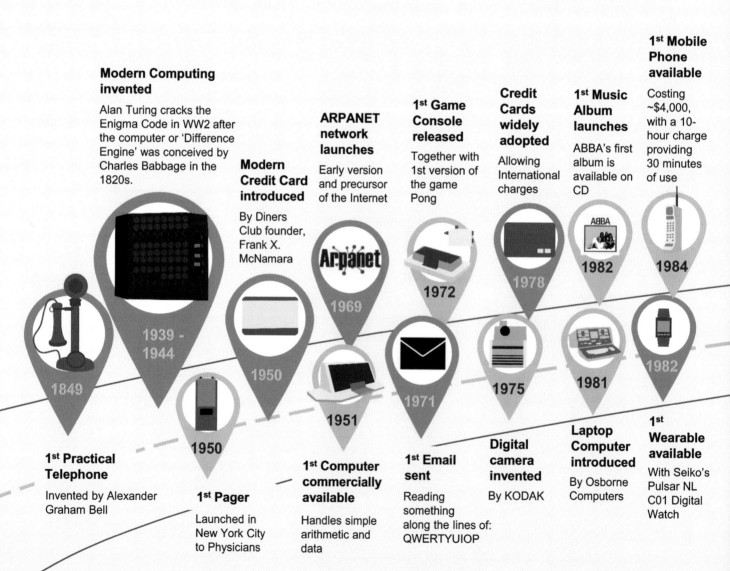

**Modern Computing invented**

Alan Turing cracks the Enigma Code in WW2 after the computer or 'Difference Engine' was conceived by Charles Babbage in the 1820s.

**ARPANET network launches**

Early version and precursor of the Internet

**1st Game Console released**

Together with 1st version of the game Pong

**Credit Cards widely adopted**

Allowing International charges

**1st Music Album launches**

ABBA's first album is available on CD

**1st Mobile Phone available**

Costing ~$4,000, with a 10-hour charge providing 30 minutes of use

**Modern Credit Card introduced**

By Diners Club founder, Frank X. McNamara

1939 - 1944

1969

1972

1978

1982

1984

1849

1950

1951

1971

1975

1981

1982

1950

**1st Practical Telephone**

Invented by Alexander Graham Bell

**1st Pager**

Launched in New York City to Physicians

**1st Computer commercially available**

Handles simple arithmetic and data

**1st Email sent**

Reading something along the lines of: QWERTYUIOP

**Digital camera invented**

By KODAK

**Laptop Computer introduced**

By Osborne Computers

**1st Wearable available**

With Seiko's Pulsar NL C01 Digital Watch

# A Brief History...

**Google tests self-driving cars**
Opening era of autonomous vehicles driven by AI

**1st VR¥ Headset available**
Consumers can buy Oculus Rift headset

**Amazon launches Echo & Alexa VA‡**
In US & UK

**Bitcoin launches**
Introducing digital currencies & blockchain

**Amazon launches 1st Online Bookstore**
Opening the world to online shopping & E-Commerce

**3D Printers introduced**
To consumers

**2016**

**Bluetooth available**
Technology introduced to the world

**Dial-Up Internet**
Available to consumers from home

**1st Social Media site**
Six degrees launches

**2009**

**Pokémon GO launch**
Brings AR□ to over 550 million users in its 1st 80 days

**World Wide Web invented**
By Sir Tim Berners-Lee whilst working at CERN

**iPhone ('07) & iPad ('10) launched**
Beginning of a new era for mobile computing

**2009**

**1995**

**1999**

**2007 - 2010**

**1989**

**1991**

**1994**

**1988**

**2003**

**2004**

**2005**

**1991**

**1994**

**1997**

**1999**

**2000**

**IoT* term coined**
At MIT Auto-ID Center by Kevin Ashton

**SasS** & Cloud Services born**
With launch of Salesforce

**Broadband available**
Becomes commercially available n the UK and globally

**Skype launches**
Bring VoIP◊ Telephony to the masses

**Facebook launches**
Changing how we interact via social media

**YouTube launches**
Garnering 40 million viewers on launch

**Digital camera released**
Offering storage for up to 10 photos

**1st Browser Software released**
For Public Use By CERN

**1st Smartphone available**
With calls, email and fax

*\* IoT stands for Internet of Things*

*\*\* SasS stands for Software as a Service*

*◊ VOIP stands for Voice over Internet Protocol*

*¥ VR stands for Virtual Reality*

*□ AR stands for Augmented Reality*

*‡ VA stands for Virtual Assistant*

## ... covered by some of the case study examples in this book.

# The service economy has expanded ...

*Changes in the Digital Economy have shifted customers ...*

A service economy, also known as the *tertiary sector*, is one that generates more value from services than the other sectors in the global economy. Primary sectors are where raw materials are produced (e.g. mining or agriculture) and the secondary sector, where products are manufacturing (e.g. automobile manufacturing). Advanced economies are locked in a long-term trend whereby services are becoming a greater percentage of economic output.

The Third Industrial Revolution (First Digital revolution) started in the 1950s from growth in electronics and computer automation. Customers changed their expectations from a focus on product quality towards the experiences provided by services, as efficiency gains in the manufacturing process, including savings in costs and time and an increase in product supply. As a result, many businesses began to introduce and grow new service-based business models to operate alongside their more traditional manufacturing businesses facilitating transformation of the global economy to a **service economy**\*.

---

### Example: How IBM business solutions provided increased value to customers

IBM's 'Business Solutions' business was formed in 2002, through an acquisition of the consulting arm of PricewaterhouseCoopers for $3.5billion. It enabled the company to maintain more consistent revenue streams compared to its manufacturing business, as demand for 'Business Solutions' services was much more price elastic than its hardware products. IBM benefited because customers were less sensitive and less likely to switch to substitutes from prices changes to services compared to goods such as hardware products. IBMs customers also benefited as they are able to 'buy complete solutions' to their problems rather than previously having to assess what product to buy, based on features versus limitations, and then having to make further modifications.

IBM delivered a higher level of value through the service model rather than just supplying a product and the customers gained a significantly higher benefit from having a solution from experts rather than a product that they had to procure, configure, and use to solve their problem themselves.

---

Many businesses that did not evolve and adapt their capabilities to embrace and leverage the service model during the third industrial revolution were disrupted. Examples include: Kodak, Xerox, Nokia, Blockbuster ...

*\* The service economy was coined by American economist, Victor R. Fuchs in 1968.*

# ... into information services

## ... towards the experiences provided by services

*"Like the revolutions that preceded it, the Fourth Industrial Revolution has the potential to raise global income levels and improve the quality of life for populations around the world."*

_**Klaus Schwab** (The Fourth Industrial Revolution, 2016)

### How will the Fourth Industrial Revolution affect business and the Service Economy?

We now sit firmly in the grip of the the Fourth Industrial Revolution (Second Digital Revolution) where new data-driven technologies with predictive capabilities such as AI, Blockchain and Cloud based services are driving unprecedented changes to how businesses can provide services to customers and what sorts of services are possible. This has transformed a customer's expectation of a company's services. There is emphasis on personalized customer experience and contextualized or tailored engagement. This means a business must focus more than ever on delivering a customer experience that differentiates it from the competition. The risk is not just about not getting a sale anymore ... It's about customers switching brand allegiance based on experience.

In an evolving digital economy, the capabilities of a business and its organization to design and innovate new and better services through digital transformation, that become adopted by customers, is the key in determining future success. Businesses must learn to adapt or be disrupted.

### Information Services

There has also been a shift into 'Information Services' (also referred to as 'data products') in the Second Digital Revolution. Cloud Technology has allowed 'Information Services' to be accessed virtually, and in many highly accessible digital formats, which has in some cases rendered the use of physical media channels redundant. e.g. reading newspapers online via an iPad.

Information Services is where data about customers, products, services, and business is created, harvested and sold as a service.

The global economy is increasingly digital as businesses are beginning to create and sell more information services. Traditional data service providers such as Bloomberg, Forrester and Gartner are having to enhance and expand their information services beyond data analytics and business intelligence. They have to compete with new data services such as those offered by Facebook and Google's advertising platforms that are more focused on customer behavioral data. Digital services can be created once and sold many times at no additional cost. They are delivered digitally to customers and have infinite inventory. Examples include: online courses, eBooks, graphic designs, templates, virtual workshops, scripts, spreadsheet and trackers, calculators, and software applications, including mobile apps and other SaaS applications.

# Big Data is driving changes ...

*Growth in the digital economy is increasingly driven by the power of data*

Data has always been a valuable asset for any enterprise due to its predictive capabilities that enable new opportunities to be captured through innovation, which lead to the delivery of new services to customers.  Advances in digital technologies including artificial intelligence (AI), blockchain, cloud technologies... have significantly increased the value of data and its role in business by enabling:

### Data to become big

Today, most people in the developed world spend the majority of their waking hours interacting with data through different digital platforms. According to Nielson*, in 2018 adults in the US spent more than 11 hours per day watching, reading, listening to or simply interacting with media data through different platforms, which is 32 minutes more than four years ago. Digital platforms are able to continuously capture more and more data on customers and users who are interacting with each other as well as with businesses to understand their behaviors. When any enterprise has accumulated a large volume of data that can be mined for information and used in machine learning projects and other advanced analytics applications, then it is said to have *big data*.

### Data to become more intelligent

The predictive accuracy** can be as high as 95 percent depending on the input data supplied and the *business use case*, the business application or scenario .This improved understanding of customer and user behaviors means that businesses with access to AI-based intelligence are able to improve the way they operate and transform, as well as how they serve customers to improve services. This also reduces the amount of waste produced by businesses who have the intel to be able to act on, as well as react to, specific business and customer problems and become much more productive and competitive overall.

### Data to become more useful

When *big data* is mined and machine learning is applied, the resulting advanced analytics can also provide predictions on what future *business use cases* are not only possible but also most likely to yield innovations that become adopted by customers and users. It is these future innovations, that is, the services and information services (p. 17) that are born from innovation that are the most valuable in the digital economy. The value increases if it is predicted that the future service can cause consumer behaviors to change and influence spending patterns. This value in the data is the reason why data that has been converted into information services (or data products) is bought and sold by companies, and why some companies can command valuations in the many millions and billions even when they have neither revenue or profit. For example, Facebook paid $19 billion for WhatsApp and $1 billion for Instagram, when neither had revenue or profits at the time of their acquisition. Cryptocurrencies, which are digital or virtual currencies that use cryptography for security and are used to acquire specific goods and services, are also being traded based on their predictive value.

*\* Nielsen Total Audience Report, 2018    \*\* Multiple sources. See references.*

# ... in consumer behavior

### Data's role in innovation

It is essential that businesses go beyond quantitative data and into qualitative data, that is, **'*thick data*'** that goes into the everyday emotional lives of their customers along with their customers' journey, to support business innovation efforts.  It is this *thick data* combined with technology applications, like artificial intelligence (AI), that can be used to find insights and predict future customer and user behaviors.

Only with sufficient and adequate data can an enterprise gain the appropriate insights for innovation and implement solutions through transformation, as well as introduce new **Business Models** that will deliver enough value to customers to attract them to innovation.

### Example: Amazon was born from two sets of data

Jeff Bezos was motivated to quit his job at a bank when he discovered a projected Internet adoption rate of 2300 percent per year. On further analysis of customer data with specific products and services, he identified books as being the most likely to achieve the highest adoption rates in an online marketplace. With these two sets of data, Bezos went about starting Amazon. Today, Amazon remains a customer-centric, data-driven organization, that is continuously obsessed with capturing data about customer and user behaviors through its omnichannel platform, that incorporates IoT devices including its Amazon Echo Home Speakers and Alexa Virtual Assistant app service.

### Ignore the business data at your peril

What are the consequences of looking at the wrong data or not being open to data?

A business that has lots of data, but not the right type of *thick data* and doesn't focus on the data to explore customer trends, will not be in business for too long in the digital age. The pace of change and the threat from disruption to business models through digital approaches has to be countered with *business Intelligence* that is backed by machine learning, that is *machine intelligence*, in order to keep innovating and stay relevant.

### Example: How Apple disrupted Nokia with data

There is no better example of good and bad use of business data than in the mobile handset market where Apple's entry into the market in 2007 brought about a business model change, which the market leading firms at the time neither saw nor were prepared for. The iPhone is a physical product but the business model behind it is a platform. The iPhone and its operating system were not just a pipeline, or a product, they were a gateway to that platform. This platform business model took Apple from no presence in the mobile phone market at launch, to a 92% share in 2015. Competitors, large- entrenched businesses such as Nokia, were sent into free fall because they didn't see the shift to a platform-based business model – they were not capturing the right data and connecting the right trends in technology and customer desires.

# Customer expectations are rising ...

Digital connectivity through big data has significantly increased customer accessibility to information and improved their knowledge ... **Knowledge** is POWER!

According to *Forrester*, 2018 see us five years into the "Age of the Customer," a 20-year business cycle where:

*"... power is shifting from businesses and institutions to end consumers ... as technology, information, and connectivity are combining to instill in people a belief that they can have what they want, when, where, and how they want it."*

The technological advances of the digital age led by the Cloud, Mobile, Social Media and Artificial Intelligence (AI) have provided customers with the knowledge, and the confidence or trust to change their behavior as they become more **'hyperadoptive'**. Hyperadoption* describes how customers are willing to switch to new products and services almost instantly, and even look for opportunities to switch, so as to be the first to try new innovations.

Those businesses and organizations both big and small that want to emerge triumphant in the digital economy will need to change the way they operate by placing the customer at the center of everything that they do, providing more value, better and faster, to customers.

If enterprises want to meet, let alone exceed, the new expectations of the customer in the Digital Era, they must transform their Operating Models. This includes their people, processes, data, or information systems, and this means becoming customer-obsessed at all levels.

*\* The concept of Hyperadoption was debuted by James McQuivey, Ph.D. Vice President and Principle Analyst at Forrester Research in his paper, Will People Really Do That? Marketers Must Get Ready For Hyperadoption Now (2015)*

# ... in the digital economy

*Immediacy*

Research from Salesforce.com, in the Second Edition of their report called ***State of the Connected Customer*** in 2018, indicates four new baseline characteristics for customer experience in the digital age: immediacy, personalization, consistency, and anticipation.

## 80% of consumers
report that ***immediate real-time responses to requests influence their loyalty*** to a given brand.

## Personalization

## 70%
of customers say ***connected processes—such*** as **seamless handoffs** or **contextualized engagement** based on earlier interactions—are very important to winning their business.

## Consistency

**75%** of consumers

expect **consistent experiences** across ***multiple channels*** (web, mobile, in-person, social)

With **73%** *likely to* **switch brands if they don't get it**

## Anticipation (as well as Predictive)

***By 2020***, 75% of business buyers expect companies that can **anticipate their needs and make relevant suggestions before they initiate contact**, while 73% expect that products they purchase will ***self-diagnose*** issues and automatically order replacement parts or service.

*\*\* Only a sample of key report statistics have been illustrated. See full report from Salesforce.com for remaining statistics.*

# Customers are shifting ...

*Disruption has become the expected norm ...*

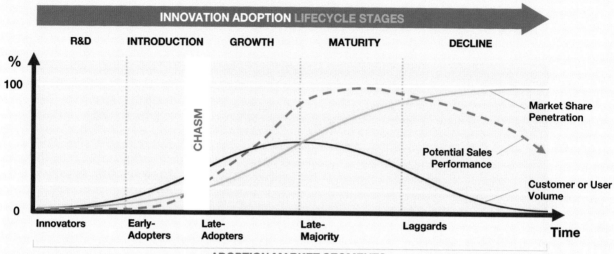

The Innovation Adoption Lifecycle was introduced in 1962 by Everett Rogers in his book, *Diffusion of Innovations.* Rogers proposed five customer segments in the adoption lifecycle: Innovators, Early-Adopters, Early-Majority, Late-Majority and Laggards. Successful innovations are adopted over time by each customer segment spread over a bell shaped curve, with products reaching the hands of its most cynical customers and users, the laggards, at the end of the lifecycle. A parallel S-curve indicates the adoption of the Innovation or Product itself, as its is introduced following initial research and development (R&D), before moving towards maturity and eventually decline. Some of the most widely known innovations to have reached the laggard market include the car, email, smartphones, and tablets.

Roger also illustrated how the customer journey stages align to the Innovation Adoption Lifecycle as they move from having awareness of the innovation to full adoption when the innovation is confirmed by customers and becomes a part of their behavior.

In 1991, Geoffrey A. Moore updated Roger's theory, with the introduction of a chasm as innovations move from adoption by Early-Adopters to the Early-Majority, in his highly acclaimed book, *Crossing the Chasm.* Innovations and hence many of the start-up businesses that are responsible for them, fail from not being able to cross this chasm.

With examples including Facebook, Tesla, and the Apple iPad, Moore also illustrates how products, in particular new technology products, are able to disrupt the market as they cross the chasm to mainstream customers.

In the digital economy, and as illustrated in this book, it is this change in customer behavior that is accelerating the rate of disruption. Disruption has become the new normal as customers have raised their expectations on the value that they can expect from goods and services and the businesses or organizations that provide them.

# ... the Innovation Adoption Lifecycle

## ... as customers expect more value in exchange for their time

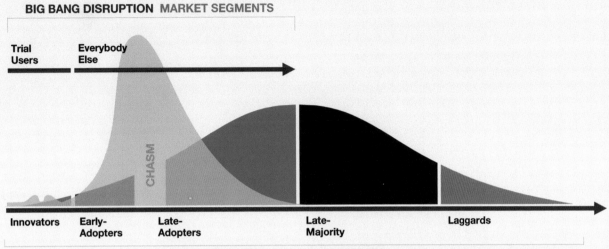

**BIG BANG DISRUPTION** MARKET SEGMENTS

Trial Users | Everybody Else

CHASM

Innovators | Early-Adopters | Late-Adopters | Late-Majority | Laggards

ADOPTION MARKET SEGMENTS

The behavioral change is one of *hyperadoption* towards better customer experiences as illustrated by research from both Forrester and Salesforce, but WHY customers are changing comes down to value.

In the digital age, as we have all come to lead increasingly busier and more stressful lives, where the information at our fingertips is not only overloading us but could also be fake news. The one thing we cannot change or get back is our time …. Time that could be spent on more valuable activities. It is our lack of time, that has changed how we, as consumers and customers of services, are really behaving. We expect innovations, including technology, to give us more time.

The new game or competition for businesses and the services that they offer is for the customer's time and why, what, where, how, when, and with whom customers would rather spend their time along with their customer journeys. Innovations that win the customer's time better and faster are able to cross the chasm better and faster too … and disrupt the market.

Overall, more and more customers have become Early-Adopters through their change in behavior. Through this, they have opened the door for the adoption of new and better innovations that provide more value, and are faster too.

This change in customer behavior has caused a shift in the bell-shaped curve of the Innovation Adoption Lifecycle to the left, allowing what Larry Downes and Paul Nunes call *Big Bang Disruption* in their 2013 Harvard Business Review paper.

When new *disruptive innovations* are the expected norm then mere incremental improvements, or what we call *continuous* or *sustaining innovations*, are simply not enough to command the customer's attention to cross the chasm in the Innovation Adoption Lifecycle. Companies that focus on these as their only source of transformation in the Digital age, are only asking to be disrupted by those who are leading the transformation efforts to find the new disruptive innovations of the future.

# Drivers and Consequences of ...

## Big Bang Disruption is WHY businesses must transform faster ...

As originally coined by Clayton Christenson:

*"**Disruptive Innovation** is ... a process by which a product or service takes root initially in simple applications at the bottom of a market and then relentlessly moves up market, eventually displacing established competitors."*

BUT *Big Bang Disruption*, where *"A new kind of innovator can wipe out incumbents in a flash"* as described by Larry Downes and Paul Nunes in 2003, illustrates how disruption itself has changed, as businesses big and small, and even entire industries, can be taken out completely by products and services from a non-competitor who may not even be part of the same industry at all – and unintentionally disrupt the market.

In this book, we aim to show how *Big Bang Disruption* is the cause and effect of faster transformation from *discontinuous* or *disruption innovation* that replaces the activities in the customer journey by capturing the customer's time.

We call this kind of innovation '**Co-created Innovation**'.

*Co-created Innovations* are created with customers and fulfill the customer's goals along their customer and user journeys. They become embedded in the customer's behavior through the trial process (p. 24), when the customer gets to experience and direct changes to the innovation as a user.

Since the telephone was invented by Bell, and computing conceived by Babbage extensive advancements in technology and highly connected digital transformation, which have fuelled the cloud-driven digital economy, are also empowering an explosion of *co-created innovation*.

# ... Big Bang Disruption

## ... through 'Co-created Innovations' along the customer journey

While most of today's business transformation efforts are still driven by the external influences described by the PESTLE model:

**P**OLITICAL
**E**CONOMIC
**S**OCIAL
**T**ECHNOLOGY
**L**EGAL
**E**NVIRONMENTAL

OR internal motivations that focus on one of Michael Treacy and Fred Wiersema's Three Value Disciplines:

**Product Leadership**

**Customer Intimacy**

**Operational Excellence**

## Business transformations that are capable of the Big Bang Disruption effect are:

**CUSTOMER CO-CREATED**

Co-created by customers, partners, and internal staff to fulfill customer goals along their customer and user journeys.

**VALUE-DRIVEN**

Capture and deliver multiple sources of value across all three Value Disciplines, plus more to all stakeholders.

**NETWORK CONNECTED**

Leverage network effects offered by Cloud Technology, Big Data and Social Media in the connected Digital Ecosystem.

# Big Bang Disruption examples ...

*Four Big Bang Disruptions that have become part of our everyday lives ...*

## Amazon, Online Marketplaces and Multi-Sided Platforms

It is difficult to know whether Jeff Bezos anticipated the evolution of today's digital marketplaces when he first launched Amazon in 1995 to sell books online, but today, we have moved beyond E-Commerce to marketplaces where we can exchange just about anything that is of value to anyone.

Customer co-creation has fuelled this explosion. Today's marketplaces have moved beyond just online supermarkets that sell groceries or other merchandise such as spare plumbing parts, or eBay-type auction sites. They have evolved into multi-sided platforms where business and consumers can interact in multiple ways, including business-to-consumer (B2B), business-to-business (B2B), business-to-business-to-consumer (B2B2C) and peer-to-peer (P2P).

There are multi-sided platforms for P2P Lending including Lending Club and Funding Circle, Freelancer networks such as Upwork, Travel Review websites such as Tripadvisor, and Music stores including Apple's iTunes, or the Android Market where you can buy mobile apps and games.

The Amazon Marketplace has expanded beyond selling books, into video and movies, household goods, clothes, and more. It acquired Whole Foods Market for $13.7billion in order to expand into groceries. This acquisition also made it the second most valuable company in the world prior to 2020 (behind only Apple), with a market capitalization exceeding $768 billion. Amazon has also launched its own App Marketplace for the Alexa Virtual Assistant supported by its Amazon Echo IoT gadgets.

## Skype, Internet Telephony, Video Conferencing and Augmented Reality

When a company's name starts to turn into a verb, it is clear that there has already been a movement. This is true of Skype, which launched the first Internet telephony service to everyday users for free across the world in 2003. Within its first three years, Skype had over 115 million customers, making it the fastest growing company during that time.

In 2006, Skype expanded its voice services to include video conferencing, fuelling an exponential growth in online connectivity services, as customers and businesses began to use video to communicate over the Internet, with the emergence of mobile devices, for just about every use case or purpose possible, with implications for every industry and saving organizations billions in expensive telephone, video, and travel costs as geographic constraints were removed.

This customer co-creation has paved the way for Live Webinars and Events that can be streamed to not 1000s or 100,000s, but millions of parallel customers across the world. It has spurred the rise in Augmented Reality (AR), with Pokémon GO, an AR based game, outperforming Facebook and Twitter in total number of concurrent downloads and users. The healthcare and biomedical industry currently leads the charge by launching AR services including virtual doctors supported by diagnostic tools that can be purchased at your local chemist, as well as conducting surgery with the aid of Smart Glasses, Robots, and Artificial Intelligence.

# ... in today's customer journeys

## ... *following customer co-creation*

### Facebook, Social Media Networks and Online Communities

Facebook was not the first social network to hit the market in 2004 ... pre-dated by Sixdegrees, Friendster, and more ... So how did Facebook become the market leader with in excess of 2.2 billion monthly active users as of the first quarter of 2018? The TOP 3 reasons include:

1. **Open API Platform**: Launched in 2007, the Facebook App Market allowed third-party developers to create apps for other users creating a network effect to make Facebook sticky, as customers and users started to co-create features together.

2. **Social sharing**: Facebook invented the "Like" button allowing its customer or users to personally voice their opinions with their vote on just about everything, including someone's daily activities, thoughts, success stories and failures, survey results, people's favorite reading list and music playlist, and more ... in an open forum ... again creating that sticky network affect.

3. **Community Groups**: Psychology has shown that human beings all want to belong to communities with common interests, and where they can get support and collaborate. Facebook Groups were revamped in 2010 to support collaboration or 'co-creation' between group members, and has become an integral tool for many small entrepreneurial businesses.

This model has been copied by Twitter, Tumblr, and Snapchat to grow and maintain their user numbers.

### Apple iPhone, Smartphones and Mobile Apps

2018 sees Internet users grow to over 4 billion surpassing half of the total world population of around 7.6 billion, and over 5 billion mobile phone users, with approximately half of those or 2.5 billion being smartphones.

This prolific growth started when the late Apple founder, Steve Jobs, launched what he called 'Magic' in 2007, in the form of the iPhone ... an all-in-one touchscreen device you can control with your fingers. The iPhone allowed you to carry your a phone, computer, and camera in your pocket while connecting you to the world.

Apple followed up quickly with the launch of the iOS App Market in the following year, while the Android App Market launched soon after to support competing smartphones from Google, Samsung, and the rest of the market.

Today, you can use your smartphone to do just about everything from taking professional quality photos, chatting with your friends via messenger apps such as Whatsapp, sharing your latest news or opinions via social media, paying for purchases with your digital wallet, reading books, listening to podcasts, watching TV on-demand, search for anything using Google, navigating from one location to another with GoogleMaps or Waze. There are billions of mobile apps available for downloading. Just suggest your idea and there are over 12 million mobile app developers as of 2018, waiting to co-create with you to turn your case into a reality.

# Why the rules keep changing ...

*Regulations need to be updated for the new digital economy ...*

With a digital ecosystem of constant change characterized by the ongoing innovation of:

- **New technologies** that serve to open up the world by increasing connectivity as well as accessibility to data and information.

- **New products and services** that are capable of big bang disruptions that can change people's behaviors.

- **New customer behaviors** that are increasingly virtual or operate across the virtual world through multiple channels.

... it is inevitable that today's government authorities are having to adjust their rules, and set new regulations in order to maintain a fair, safe, and sustainable ecosystem for everyone.

We have witnessed through the Global Financial Crisis (GFC) of 2008 and numerous corporate scandals in the last century, from Enron to Libor, how an imbalance towards financial gain within the culture of an enterprise, or even an industry, can lead to activities that are not in the interest of the general public and society globally.

These activities, caused by bad behaviors within some enterprises, often lead to disastrous events with major social and economic consequences, including the collapse of businesses and entire industries, unemployment, significant losses in the value of people's savings, homes, and other assets. ...

Since ancient civilization, governments have continuously introduced and changed regulations to maintain order, reduce the risk of harm, and to provide a fair and level playing field for its citizens and businesses who live and operate within their jurisdictions, bound by land, water, and air space in the physical world.

The digital economy has introduced a new dimension in the form of the virtual world that now operates alongside the physical world and with it new risks that need to be governed alongside new or updated rules to prevent a new set of bad behaviors.

As we witnessed through the Facebook and Cambridge Analytica scandal, those businesses that have successfully executed *Big Bang Disruptions* with access to exclusive personal data and information, which can be used to influence people's behaviors, have become so powerful that they can even influence government elections.

# ... and how to take advantage

## ... with new opportunities for change

The European Union's General Data Protection Regulation (GDPR) was mandated to prevent these sorts of situations along with many other potential risks, where people's personal data may be misused.

Since the launch of Bitcoin in 2009, the world has seen an explosion in the number of digital currencies, digital investment funds, and other crypto-assets, traded through digital exchanges operating 24/7 globally, and outside of normal rules and policies of any government in a virtual world.

This new economy of digital or crypto-assets has introduced a new wave of 'get rich quick' Ponzi schemes including PinCoin, Ifan and Prodeum ... that have been set up to scam investors of their hard earned savings. They are fooled into exchanging their existing currencies for these new digital and ungoverned assets.

The digital economy has also allowed most of the world's biggest companies including Apple, Amazon, Google, and Starbucks to operate as global and virtual companies that avoid paying taxes or with a significantly reduced tax burden. Many governments, EU nations in particular, have sought to claw back their tax income after many years of legal battles through fines.

While regulations may be seen as bureaucratic red tape with a heavy administrative burden due to all the process changes involved to comply with specific rules and the reporting of compliance to government bodies ... today they are becoming increasingly important to protect people and businesses from those who cheat the system and/or cause harm to others.

You can also choose to see regulation as an opportunity to play a new game. New regulations force transformation within enterprises and among competitors across the ecosystem which all face the costs to execute necessary changes. These changes present companies with the chance to build new advantages, if they are able to differentiate by providing newer, regulation compliant, Unique Selling Propositions (USPs) that are better than the competition and more desired by customers.

NEW IDEA

# Enterprises must Transform ...

## Build transformation capabilities ...

The Digital Revolution and the ease by which Big Bang Disruptions can occur and impact any enterprise, at any time, has created a new game and hence ecosystem in which all enterprises must operate in ... better and faster.

As they play this new game, enterprises are racing through the Five Stages of **THE STRATEGY JOURNEY** in order to transform better and faster, and to outpace both competitors and disrupters.

In a game, it is necessary to arm yourself and your team with the right tools and capabilities as well as develop strategies and tactics that will enable you to navigate stages quickly and safely to get to the finish line, that is, to achieve your goals. When the game is also a race, the objective is to beat the competition and to achieve those goals first.

This race to transform better and faster than competitors and disrupters to win is: *'Business Transformation'*.

*'Digital Transformation'* with *'Digital Strategy'* is the race to transform the enterprise using digital technologies to tackle or cause disruption, as the enterprise plays in the Digital Economy.

Enterprises that want to survive, outwit, and beat their competition, or lead in the new Digital Economy as disrupters, must learn how to navigate the Five Stages of their *strategy-to-execution journey* to transform and keep transforming better and faster.

To transform, and keep transforming better and faster, enterprises must build the right levels of agility, accountability, and action into their capabilities.

# ... or Evaporate

### ... to overcome the risk of failure

An enterprise without the capabilities to transform continuously is likely to fail – especially when change is constant in every activity that an enterprise performs.

Failure comes in many forms. It is not always a bad thing, or to be avoided in all circumstances.

If failure is managed and contained as part of prototyping that involves discovery and testing with customers or co-created, with the potential to gain information and hence improve from the lessons learnt, then it is a good thing.

Wasting resources in the form of time and money spent on activities that don't deliver any real outcomes to the enterprise, its customers or stakeholders, is failure.

Both the financial input to fund an activity as well as the time spent on an activity are costs. If spent inappropriately, the result is waste as well as lost opportunities, which we call an 'Opportunity Cost'.

An accumulation of this kind of bad failure, can lead to total failure when an enterprise enters into administration and then shuts down. The time it takes for a series of smaller bad failures to turn into a big catastrophe varies by the nature and size of each failure, and the size of the enterprise or its ability to handle failure. Some smaller businesses can simply evaporate.

The difference between success and failure is down to an enterprise's ability to navigate its strategy journeys to continuously transform with *agility, accountability, and action* ... and LEARN.

# A world of ᴧopportunities ~~failures~~

*Depending on your perspective, the world is full of failures or opportunities...*

## 92% of tech start ups fail

within 3 years

50% of new businesses make it past **5 years**

*\* Small Business Administration (SBA), a United States government agency that provides support to entrepreneurs and small businesses.*

A search on Google will provide you with many different start-up failure rates, including the famous '8 in 10 start-ups fail in the first 18 months' statistic. This figure was originally published in 2013 in Forbes and Bloomberg, and it soon went viral.

Other sources, including the Small Business Administration\*, have indicated that approximately half of new businesses make it past five years.

The problem with these statistics is they don't show what actual measures are used to represent failure or survival.

A study from UC Berkeley and Stanford called the Start-up Genome Report on Premature Scaling indicates that 92% of start-ups (high growth and tech venture backed) fail within three years.

Nevertheless, no one can question the fact that running a start-up and growing a small business is hard work.

This is especially true when research (p. 21) has indicated that it is becoming harder to satisfy rising customer expectations.

**70%** of **all change initiatives fail** to deliver on their *strategic objectives*

# $109M for every $1B
## is lost due to project failure

In the corporate world, larger enterprises also experience failure.

Many sources, including Harvard Business Review (hbr.org), IBM, PwC and McKinsey, indicate that 70 percent of change initiatives fail to achieve their objectives.

Even more alarming, the statistic from the Project Management Institute (PMI) Pulse 2014 Report on *The Cost of Low Performance* states that US$109M for every US$1B is lost due to project failure.

While there is considerable variation in measures of success or failure, for many people who live and breathe transformation in enterprises across both business and IT projects, the fact remains that failure or the threat of failure in all its different forms is part of life.

The question is … can we change this? Does human nature, with its default resistance to change, not sabotage the efforts to success? We avoid change because we are afraid to fail and we refuse to admit that failure even exists.

What does success or failure even mean when it is not clear how we should measure them? Can each failure we face also be seen as an opportunity, if we learn from it?

Is failure the key to success?

# Big failure examples ...

## How ignoring the digital customer journey busted Blockbuster

When Netflix first launched its mail order video business as a small start-up in 2004, Blockbuster was the market leader for video rentals, with a massive distribution network of 9,000 stores, 60,000 employees and $6 billion in revenue.

Over the next six years, Blockbuster continued to focus on growing and protecting its existing business model, as a retail store distributing movies and related merchandise, instead of transforming its operating model based on the emerging digital customer journey, with the content streaming and search services. It even tried to expand its store-driven approach by buying Circuit City for $1 billion in 2008, instead of purchasing Netflix for a mere $50 million while it had the chance.

As customers started to value the time and money saved from not having to trek to a physical store, including the late return fees which formed the bulk of Blockbuster's revenue, and a better online search and recommendations service aided by new digital technologies, they transitioned towards Netflix's digital services in droves. This disrupted the entire Blockbuster business model, leading it to file for bankruptcy in 2010.

*As the world transitions to electric cars, could Shell suffer a similar fate to Blockbuster? Will the Amazon Marketplace and other online retailers replace every other food and merchandise retailer, from supermarkets to convenience stores with brick and mortar buildings?*

## How operating model complacency led to Kodak's downfall

It was not under-investment that was the problem at Kodak, but an investment that turned out to be misguided. Since the company peaked in the 1980s, its management attempted to preserve its Unique Selling Proposition (USP) in the film and printing industry rather than adapt to the market and evolve its operating model.

Kodak's resistance to producing and selling digital cameras gave away its potential first mover advantage to Sony, who became a dominant force in selling high-end digital cameras to professional photographers, video makers, and bloggers, with its world class Zeiss lens and stabilization technology.

While rival Fujifilm leveraged its strengths in chemicals and film to diversify successfully into the cosmetics industry and even LCD screens, Kodak actually sold its pharmaceutical business in order to reinvest its resources in transformations that would help it grow and maintain its position as the dominant player in photo printing. This proved to be a crucial mistake as customer behavior shifted towards sharing digital photos online rather than printing them.

Kodak did attempt to compete in the digital market, with its cheap and inferior EasyShare Digital Cameras accompanied by its online EasyShare Gallery and Kiosks which focused on potential revenue from printing. However, it ultimately failed as this digital foray could not compete with the iPhone and other smartphones that allow customers to take free photos and to share them on free social media platforms.

# ... with lessons worth learning from

## How Sun Edison failed from growing too big too fast in too many directions

Through its entrepreneurial founder, Jigar Shah, SunEdison pioneered selling solar panel systems to businesses and homeowners. Its subscription service contained little or no upfront fees, while customers paid for the solar power over several decades at monthly rates typically cheaper than the local grid power. It was acquired by MEMC Electronic Materials in 2009, a semiconductor business who wanted to enter the Solar Energy market for $200 million.

Over the next seven years, MEMC Electronic Materials renamed itself as SunEdison and began to buy more renewable energy companies including a move into the Wind Power business in a $2.6 billion acquisition binge to become the biggest clean energy player in the world. This inorganic growth was funded by several billions in debt, and $1.5 billion in US government grant funding and subsidies.

There lies the problem: with sporadic inorganic growth of this size, fuelled by easy money which was artificially inflating the market, it proved to be unsustainable for SunEdison.

Along with a series of failed customer deliveries, which resulted in many expensive lawsuits (not including the investor lawsuits to block specific acquisitions), SunEdison's business model failed to generate the necessary sales revenue to help it service its debts. The company was also unable to transform its operating model by introducing the necessary efficiencies and cost cuts that would help it become a sustainable long-term business.

## How too much innovation almost killed Lego

The world's favorite toy company, Lego, actually survived a near catastrophic collapse, after accumulating more than $800 million in unpaid debt. The toymaker was losing nearly $1 million a day in 2004, before new 35 year old rookie CEO, Jorgen Vig Knudstorp took charge.

Lego's troubles started in the 1990s, after many years of success since Danish carpenter Ole Kirk Christiansen founded the company in the 1930s. The giant toy company began to over-diversify into too many trendy products and services, that were not directly aligned to its core mission and strategy. In addition, Lego's operating model, that is, its team and capabilities, were not at the right level of maturity and lacked the experience to grow and scale all these new business lines, which included watches, clothing, media, book publishing, and theme parks.

Lego tried to innovate across all of these very different ecosystems, which required very different capabilities from its core strength in innovating new toys around bricks for children. It lost its identity by going after unfamiliar customer segments, in unfamiliar industries, and suffered significant losses as it drained all of its resources in the wrong areas.

Since taking over, Knudstorp has transformed Lego's fortunes by undergoing operating model transformation that included building capabilities around Lego's central mission ... building toys ... in the right locations to maximize value and service design around its target customer ... children.

# SME and start-up failure examples ...

## How crowdfunded Sugru lost 90 percent of its value by underestimating the effort to scale

## How WebVan's pre-mature scaling led to its dot.com crash

Crowdfunding is a high risk for all investors. Fraud cases aside, the reality is that ideas are nothing without execution, and this is where most start-ups fail, as they attempt to scale their initial value propositions that have been validated by early adopters into real businesses that can turn a profit with mass market customers. Most crowdfunding campaigns come with a sufficient detail of growth projections, and the indicative costs to fund that growth. Yet, do any articulate the operating model transformation plans of the start-up covering HOW they will scale the business?

This detail into the operating model was certainly overlooked by all those Sugru investors who lost 90 percent of their equity investment, when UK parent company FormFormForm Ltd (FFF) announced that it would sell out to German adhesive manufacturing giant Tesa for just £7.6 million, £25.4 million less than what was crowdfunded to help Sugru grow via the Crowdcube platform.

As a moldable adhesive, Sugru was actually a great product, and liked by customers, with many practical applications. Its massive devaluation had nothing to do with the product and was more a case of mismanagement from not understanding the costs required to properly scale the operating model of the business to support growth targets.
In the last round of funding, Sugru's business plan lacked many details particularly around the company's operating costs, burn rate, and funding position including details about any loans and inherent risks, which should have provided the warning signs for investors of troubled times ahead.

**WebVan** was an online grocery store that launched in 1999 in the San Francisco Bay area with ambitions to serve the entire United States market with a large product variety, supported by highly automated technological infrastructure.

Valued as high as $1.2 billion by investors, the start-up filed for bankruptcy after only two years of operating in 2001, from running out of money.

From the beginning, WebVan was spending its venture capital funds like a big corporate to set up its very expensive infrastructure in multiple regions across the country, while it still needed to operate like a bootstrapped start-up to test and prove that its business model and the logistics of its operating model were workable within just the San Francisco Bay area. Management's determination to expand and scale, before the company was ready, led to logistic problems and a daily expense or burn rate of $1.8 million compared to average sales of $489,000. WebVan spent almost $1 billion on expensive high-tech warehouses and refrigerated vans across the country, as well as $400 million a year in labor, hiring 10,000 people during its three years of operating.

At a time when Internet adoption was still low and most customers were still early adopters of shopping online, this kind of pre-mature scaling and spending was simply unsustainable, as the expected mass market customers were not yet ready for the kind of service that WebVan wanted to offer. This data was actually available but ignored by WebVan's over-ambitious executives.

# ... with lessons worth learning from

## How Tutorspree shutdown from having one strategy and no game plan

**Tutorspree** was a Y-Combinator start-up that showed a lot of promise, securing $1.8 million in funding in 2011 to help it grow. In its early days, the double sided platform or marketplace successfully converted all of its customers from SEO traffic. The platform had all the functionality needed to support its customers, that is parents searching for the right tutors for their children using an Airbnb like review system.

When Tutorspree shut down in 2013, the company was able to return money to its investors, and wasn't actually in any financial trouble. So why did the founders close shop?

Being a former Wall Street worker, Tutorspree's founder Aaron Harris, was actually very good with data as well as finances, and spent a lot of time looking through all the data, trying different approaches to marketing the service including many Pay Per Click services from Facebook to Google Adwords alongside his well-tuned SEO strategy, which for a time was bringing in all of Tutorspree's sales revenue at little to no cost. This led Tutorspree to a transactional business model that was focused on sales through customer acquisition, made worse by using just one channel, SEO, rather than building sustainable long-term relationships with customers by adding value along the customer and user journey. When Google changed its SEO algorithm, Tutorspree suffered an immediate 80% drop in customer volume and sales. There was no other game plan for building sustainable revenue. The founders came to the realization that they had built a brokerage business with neither sales revenue nor the branding to warrant any equity value.

## How Everpix overengineered and burnt itself to death

**Everpix** was a online photo app that automatically sorted, organized, and stored photos with a clean and intuitive user interface, driven by an AI algorithm. It was actually a great product that managed to build a loyal following of 55,000 users, at a time when online photo apps were starting to attract users by the millions.

Launched in 2009 by 34 year old French co-founder Pierre-Oliver Latour, who at the time had a solid tech entrepreneur record having sold his first company, PixelShox Studio, a motion graphics software, to Apple, Everpix quickly amassed $2.3 million in funding by 2012. The app prototype was a popular finalist at TechCrunch Disrupt, and both Facebook and Dropbox tried to acquire it, but were turned away by Everpix's founders.

Just one year after its early success, Everpix was broke, having spent all of its funds on product engineering the perfect app. A look at Everpix's Profit and Loss (P&L) statement tells a story of mass overspending on the wrong things, with little effort put into marketing the product to customers ... thus delivering a dismal subscription revenue of just $254,060, from fewer than 19,000 signups. The leadership team spent almost $570,000 on consulting and legal fees, over $1.4 million on personnel, salaries and payroll costs, $130,000 on office expenses and other operating costs totaled $361,000. A clear case of not building out other capabilities like sales and distribution along the value chain and into an operating model of the business to support an end-to-end service.

# A world of <sup>wasted</sup> opportunities

*Enterprises are not utilizing resources efficiently to deliver ROI on their digital transformation investments, and to build sustainable organizations*

Digital Transformation investment in 2018

## $1.3 trillion

*with spending is expected to double to*

## $2.1 trillion by 2021

*Source: International Data Corporation (IDC)*

## Improving Efficiency is the
*TOP DRIVER* of Transformation but

# 42% of Top US Executives
believe it is the **most missed investment**

*Source: Wipro Digital May 2017
Digital Transformation ROI Survey*

In every enterprise undergoing transformation, big or small, there is always at least one person who feels that they lack the resources required to make their transformation project successful.

Yes, some early stage start-ups and micro-businesses with high set-up and running costs can truly claim a lack of funding, and hence the inability to hire the right people or purchase the tools and equipment necessary to help them build and grow their businesses …

BUT when we review all the transformation budgets of organizations, especially digital transformation spending, the numbers show that budgets are getting bigger. This includes budgets for greenfield projects, innovation and growth, also called *discretionary funding*, as well as the budgets reserved for changes associated with maintenance, compliance, and other mandatory changes required to keep the business running, our *non-discretionary funding*.

According to IDC, spending on Digital Transformation is expected to double from $1.3 trillion in 2018 to $2.1 trillion by 2021. *So transformation is getting more expensive.*

*Or are most organizations just bad at utilizing their resources, wasting both time and money?* A report from Wipro Digital of over 400 executives in the US in 2017, illustrates that it is both. Poor utilization and inefficiency increases costs, which is often passed on to customers to maintain profitability.

Let's not forget there are also opportunity costs, which is the cost in time and money or value that could have been captured and delivered if utilization was able to provide good yield or returns, as well as growth in the business.

Source: The Sustainability Imperative Report 2015 , Nielson

## 73% of **Millennials** are willing to pay more for ***Sustainable Products***

Source: Digital Helix Book & Forbes

# 84 percent
## of **Digital Transformations fail**

Research from the Digital Helix Book in collaboration with Forbes on over 1000 business indicates a lot of wasted resources and wasted opportunities, with 84% of all digital transformations failing.

How can enterprises build more sustainable organizations ... capable of surviving the onslaught of faster changes, big bang disruptions and continuous transformations that come with being a part of the Digital Economy?

The answer lies in what really constitutes a *Resource*. It is more than just time and money.

In today's Digital Economy, changing customer behavior, particularly from Millennials, who have now become our primary consumers with over $2.5 billion in spending power, is indicating that enterprises must act more responsibly across People, Planet, and Profit, also known as the Triple Bottom Line (3BL) of Corporate Sustainability* and become BCorps$^\phi$. In fact, 66% of consumers and 73% of Millennials are willing to pay more for sustainable products, according to the Nielson Report, an online survey of 30,000 consumers in over 60 countries in 2015, which is also proved with actual data gathered from over 1300+ brands.

Along with profit from both past performance and future projections, which drives the availability of financial resources, it has become increasingly important for enterprises to invest in their people and planet resources, if they are to capture the attention and wallets of consumers in the future and grow their organizations.

If you want to grow anything, then you need to plant the seed, provide the necessary support to allow that seed to grow, and then you can reap the rewards of the harvest. This is just as true botany and biology, as it is in business.

So, if you want your business to grow and flourish to produce the goods and services that provide a return on investment (ROI), then you need to identify the right people. Support your people in learning and developing their talent by providing them the right capabilities, tools, and working conditions to do the best that they can. Invest in improving all the inputs and outputs that form your ecosystem, including processes, data, systems, raw materials and the suppliers that you source from or work with.  This is everything that forms your enterprise's entire end-to-end value chain - your 'end-to-end operating model'.

*\* Introduced by John Elkington in 1994 and in his 1997 book, 'Cannibals with Forks: The Triple Bottom Line of 21st Century Business'.*

*$\phi$ B Corps are for-profit companies certified by the non-profit B Lab to meet rigorous standards of social and environmental performance, accountability, and transparency*

# Faster transformation creates ...

## *More complexity is making it harder to deliver and add value ...*

Unfortunately, one of the by-products of faster transformation is added complexity.

In the bid to transform better and faster across one or more of the *10 Business Transformation Challenges* (p. 9-10), organizations can inadvertently introduce more complexity while they speed through the five stages of **THE STRATEGY JOURNEY**.

As we will show in the WHAT section when we describe the architecture of a business, enterprises are complex when you break down their many layers.

So additional complexity, resulting from processes and data added during transformation, that are not required and performed by technology systems or by people who are also not necessary, can actually create debt for the enterprise—especially if it is not managed properly, there is no value added, and nothing is done to reduce or eliminate the waste that is being created.

## *How do you ensure the added complexity from transformation is justified from the value added?*

# ... more complexity in organizations

## ... amongst a minefield of disconnected projects

The process of managing the transformation journey is actually a minefield littered with many disconnected projects, made worse by faster transformation.

In most cases, these disconnected projects are:

- **Tactical**: they are reactions to problems that have surfaced in the organization and do not address the root cause of specific problems buried among complex processes and/or caused by missing data;

AND

- **Siloed**: they tackle just one of the Five Stages of **THE STRATEGY JOURNEY** and do not join up as part of the end-to-end strategy-to-execution journey;

By being both tactical and siloed, they are unlikely to be properly aligned to the underlying long-term strategy of the enterprise. This fragmentation of disconnected projects is a major contributor to why 70% of initiatives fail to deliver on their strategic objectives (p. 34).

## How to manage your way through the minefield of transformation complexity to deliver strategic value?

# Why organizations really fail

## Failure is the result of poor 'transformation culture'

With the added complexity and minefield of disconnected projects caused by transformation, it is easy to put blame on these six common symptoms as the reasons for failure.

**Common symptoms of failure in business ventures**

Numerous management frameworks have been developed to help organizations find solutions to these problems, but we are still nowhere with a real solution.

The problems keep persisting in enterprises both big and small … WHY is that?

The fact is, we have been treating the symptoms rather than working on a cure for the root cause of the problem.

The root cause is poor '**transformation culture**'.

When an enterprise's culture is dominated by a fear of failure, rather than an openness to learn, and by individuals who seek to be heroes rather than working in a coordinated team that wins together through a central mission or goals, then the result is poor **agility**, **accountability** and **action**.

One thing that's important to clear up is that poor *transformation culture* doesn't mean that there is no risk taking in an enterprise. The fact is, every action taken on every activity in business and in running an enterprise is a potential risk of failure, especially in a highly volatile and fast-changing ecosystem such as our Digital Economy.

Many organizations big and small with poor *transformation culture* are spending millions or billions (and collectively, trillions) on transformation. They are just transforming the wrong things, with the wrong actions, resulting in very slow change and little, if any, valuable outcomes.

To succeed in transformation, an enterprise must foster a **culture of learning**, backed by a common language to support coordinated and focused execution effort, while working to eliminating the behaviors that reflect a poor *transformation culture*.

# Characteristics of Poor Transformation Culture

## *to be eradicated in an enterprise ...*

Don't know
how to
convince others
to support and
help

Don't speak
up when
they think
something is
wrong, and just
conform

Don't validate
or test ideas
properly with
customers or
stakeholders

Don't listen to
other people
so unwilling
to change and
learn

Don't see or
understand the
real value so
why bother to
try at all

Don't know
what to do but
not willing to
get help from
those that do

## *to be replaced with a culture of learning ...*

*Supported by a common language that fosters cohesion between the enterprise, its staff and customers – 'Co-created Innovation'.*

# Gaining competitive advantage by ...

## Co-creating services along the customer journey ...

Customer experience has become the top transformation priority for many organizations and their board executives (eg. CEO, CIO …)

# 72%
of businesses say that improving the customer experience is their top priority

*Source: A Customer-Obsessed Operating Model Demands A Close Partnership With Your CIO (Forrester Research 2017)*

BUT... research from multiple sources including IBM, Forrester and Accenture, illustrates that there is still a disconnect between what executives in businesses think customers want and the customer's view, especially when it comes to the digital customer journey and the customer's time.

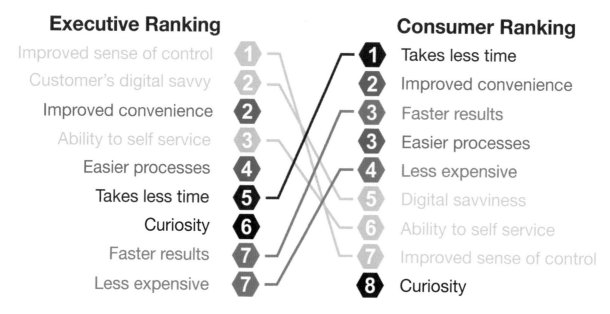

**Executive Ranking**

| | |
|---|---|
| Improved sense of control | ① |
| Customer's digital savvy | ② |
| Improved convenience | ② |
| Ability to self service | ③ |
| Easier processes | ④ |
| Takes less time | ⑤ |
| Curiosity | ⑥ |
| Faster results | ⑦ |
| Less expensive | ⑦ |

**Consumer Ranking**

| | |
|---|---|
| ① | Takes less time |
| ② | Improved convenience |
| ③ | Faster results |
| ③ | Easier processes |
| ④ | Less expensive |
| ⑤ | Digital savviness |
| ⑥ | Ability to self service |
| ⑦ | Improved sense of control |
| ⑧ | Curiosity |

*Source: Executive vs Customer ranking of factors driving willingness to try digital customer experiences (IBM 2017)*

# ... servicing customer journeys better

## ... enables organizations to capture more opportunities

Only

# 7 percent
*of brands are exceeding customer expectations*

*Source: Expectations Vs. Experience: The Good, The Bad, The Opportunity (Accenture & Forrester 2016)*

With only seven percent of brands exceeding customer expectations, there are many more opportunities for organizations to design remarkable services that can capture the customer's time and gain competitive advantages.

Organizations have the opportunity to save on the high cost of customer switching as a result of poor service, which is estimated at $1.6 trillion in the US alone, with businesses losing $62 billion a year.

The benefits that come from improved customer satisfaction and loyalty are well worth the effort with 'Customer-centric' organizations being 38% more likely to report greater profitability than their competitors according to the Harvey Nash, KPMG CIO Survey 2018.

In fact, statistical evidence from KPMG Nunwood's 2018 Customer Experience Excellence Survey of 54,233 consumers and 1400 brands in 14 countries, illustrates that aggregate revenue from the Top 50 brands in Australia, France, Italy, UK and US was 54% greater than the Bottom 50 brands, while EBITDA growth was 202% greater.

In the US
### *Cost of customer switching*
due to poor service is

# $1.6 trillion

*Source: Accenture Global Consumer Pulse Survey 2016*

## With businesses losing
## $62 billion a year
due to poor customer service

*Source: New Voice Media Report 2015*

**'Customer-centric' organizations** are

# 38% more likely to report
## greater profitability than their competitors.

*Source: Harvey Nash, KPMG CIO Survey 2018*

*In this book, we show you how to co-create services with customers along their customer and user journeys to capture and deliver more value ...*

# Digital Transformation Trends ...

## Where are the new opportunities for 'Co-created Innovation'?

Amongst all of the failure, instability and uncertainty in today's digital economy, with rising customer expectations, is a multitude of new and untapped opportunities ...

Co-creation is all about the customer and finding out what he or she needs and wants ... so it makes sense for opportunities to be among Aristotle's* *Pillars of a Good Life*:

### Health

The massive advances in the innovation of modern medicine have resulted in people living longer, but society has also introduced new stresses that challenge our wellbeing ... both mind and body. As a result, a new and extended ecosystem of industries is required to support our ongoing vitality over a much longer period of time.

**Industries impacted**: Medicine and Healthcare, Pharmaceuticals, Beauty and Cosmetics, Sport and Fitness, Food, Recreation, Tourism, Human Resources, Public sector and Government, Insurance, Technology including Electronics, IoT Wearables and more ...

### Wealth

Wealth comes in many forms and is not necessarily limited to financial wealth. While money is the main driver for employment, people pursue wealth in order to have the freedom to do whatever they want, whenever they want, and to buy anything they want. Our time and what we choose to do with it is the real driver of our actions—from our jobs to our purchases—and society is beginning to change the way we value our time as well as what constitutes wealth. This change in our values and value systems has implications for the sorts of activities we choose to take part in within a finite amount of time, driving significant changes in almost every industry in our ecosystem.

**Industries impacted**: Financial Services including Banking and Insurance, Employment, Public sector and Government, Legal, NGO & Non-Profit, Retail, Food, Recreation, Tourism, Technology including Fintech, Blockchain, and more ...

*\* Aristotle (384-322 BCE) was a Greek Philosopher and Scientist who explored and wrote about the Theory of Human Nature including the Pursuit of Happiness, as well as physics, metaphysics, psychology, theatre, music, logic, rhetoric, linguistics, politics, government, ethics, biology and more... His work has influenced much of today's society and culture including politics and religion.*

# ... And Opportunities

*You just need to spot them and start your Strategy Journey Path ...*

### Knowledge

Our propensity to learn and grow is the very essence of evolution. Digital advances have enabled almost anyone, anywhere, access to significantly more information, anytime, and have changed the value of information. Data has become a currency in its own right. This has changed what, how, where, and when we need to learn and keep learning in order to grow and to keep up with the rate of change, as well as the choices we need to make around learning. There are also new challenges around information quality and integrity.

**Industries impacted**: Education & Research, Employment and Human Resources, Public sector and Government, Media, all forms of Technology including Machine or Artificial Intelligence (AI), Information Management or Big Data, Information Security, Materials Engineering or 3D Printing, Virtual and Augmented Reality, Gaming, and more.

### Connectivity

Aristotle referred to a person's need to feel connected with friends, family, and their environment in the pursuit of happiness and this basic human need hasn't gone away. Advances in digital technology have just provided us with many new and accessible ways in which to connect with everyone and everything else in a greater ecosystem. This is changing our behavior, how we as customers consume goods and services, and how we function as a society with a set of new social challenges to be governed or managed.

**Industries impacted**: Public sector and Government, Legal, NGO & Non-Profit, Media, Telecommunications, Transport and Automotive, Logistics and Distribution, Energy, Environment and Sustainability, Technology including Cloud Computing, Big Data, Software Engineering, IoT gadgets, Cyber Security and more.

*The case study examples in this book will explore opportunities for transformation through co-creation, based on these four pillars ...*

# Why success is planned

*WINs are sponsored, focused, coordinated ... and planned*

Many battles have been lost from not having a cohesive strategy, or game plan, where teams are focused on achieving a common mission with interrelated goals and lead by a champion.

This lack of central focus and strategy allows individuals to resort to random and uncoordinated tactics in the hopes of a lucky break.

In the same way, failure is likely for a transforming enterprise working to battle rivals in the digital ecosystem if its transformation projects are disconnected, with no leader to coordinate and focus execution effort around a central game plan. In this circumstance the door is then left open for the scope creep and for ingress of random ideas.

Let's be clear about this ...

We are not saying you should not prototype and test ideas. In the innovation lifecycle, an openness to new ideas, supported by prototyping, is essential to ensure the best use of resources while increasing the chances of discovering that silver bullet to victory.

We are not saying your projects should follow plans that are so rigid that any new information with the ability to change the course of the journey, no matter how relevant, should simply be ignored because changes are simply not allowed ... and the project must stay on course to deliver on time and on budget.

It is easy for project coordinators to move toward one of these extremes. Unfortunately, in both extreme cases,  the net result is a lack of *business agility* which leaves the project, the wider enterprise, and its existing business model, open to disruption.

Almost all plans are challenged by rivals and broken over time. This is part of the game of business: Planning for victory by creating game plans that are practiced, deployed, executed when needed, and adapted to the situation. This different to creating a plan on paper that doesn't get executed properly (or at all).

What's important is a central mission, supported by a common language or framework, along with a process or methodology and tools to align and coordinate the execution effort .

*You won't find it difficult to prove that battles, campaigns, and even wars have been won or lost primarily because of logistics.*

**General Dwight. D. Eisenhower**

# Joining the dots ...

*Benefits of transforming ...*

Strategy designs are hypotheses which amount to nothing without the right execution. Both the design and execution plan are equally challenging to get right in today's fast changing Digital Economy.

With the added complexity from faster transformation and the minefield of disconnected projects that need to be executed in order to deliver any value, it is essential to have a joined-up approach through the strategy-to-execution journey.

What if the wrong strategy is designed and then executed? Or the right strategy is poorly executed?

Both cases lead to undesirable outcomes and unfavorable or even disastrous consequences. They also waste valuable resources, if poor or insufficient data is collected, leading to further opportunity loss when no lessons can be learned from the failed projects.

This was how Lego, Blockbuster, Kodak and especially SunEdison failed in their Big Bang approaches to transformation as they navigated through their strategy journeys.

This kind of *Big Bang Transformation* approach is highly risky, because the enterprise is transforming and using valuable resources in most cases too fast, leaving little scope for course correction or new opportunities to be discovered along the journey.

Faster transformation is necessary to cope with the onslaught from disruption by the Digital Economy, however an enterprise can transform itself to death, by speeding up its path to self-destruction, if it takes a Big Bang approach to transformation.

Faster transformation is not the same as agile transformation, which is to build *business agility* in order to transform both better and faster.

# ... to build Business Agility

## ... *with an agile approach*

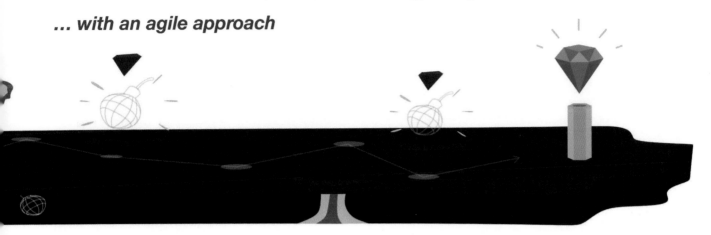

**Business agility** is about joining the dots along the Five Stages of **THE STRATEGY JOURNEY** in order to navigate through them better and faster ... before starting again on the next journey.

The benefits of building *business agility* include:

- *More time to learn, adapt, and improve* using smaller projects that allow strategies to be tried and tested, as part of the strategy execution process;

- *Better outcomes and hence more value added* as the gaps between disconnected projects are reduced with a joined up and aligned end-to-end strategy that can capture both quick wins and deliver on strategic objectives; and

- *Better and faster solutions* as co-creation increases the perceived value of solutions and embeds them into the customers and user journey at the same time, leading to faster adoption.

The net effect is a transformed *culture of learning* that can accelerate exponentially and become embedded within the DNA of the entire organization.

Unlike Blockbuster and Kodak, which both failed because of complacency and hence the inability to identify and execute the right strategies on time, or SunEdison who thought it was possible to buy a new business model at an inflated price without having to make any changes to improve the business model and operating model, Lego actually had a strong and mature innovation-driven culture and operating model. Perhaps this is why it was able to change once it was able to focus its efforts on the right strategies through *business agility*.

Innovation is great, but if you're innovating randomly as Lego did, without an end-to-end strategy to guide efforts and take people down the right paths, then the consequences can be disastrous. Lego attempted a Big Bang approach to transformation, putting significant resources into diversification and new products that weren't adopted beyond the initial trial period. Unfortunately, Lego wasn't conducting a trial; it diverted all its resources to these new initiatives.

Lego was able to turn things around after it almost ran out of cash in 2003, by introducing the necessary structure to transform its Operating Model to one led by *business agility* that includes better directed innovation.

# Building business agility with ...

*Invest in building an effective business transformation capability*

To build and sustain its *business agility*, an enterprise needs to assess, architect, action, account and accelerate how it operates continuously better and faster. These five business activities which form an enterprise's 'business transformation capability', need investment in time and resources, including the upskilling of staff to manage and perform the activities, if the business is to have *business agility* and all its benefits (p. 52) for the long-term.

## Assess

## Architect

## Action

The enterprise's ability to assess its current state of operation and its performance relative to competitors and comparable peers in the marketplace, while predicting its own trajectory based on understanding impacts and influencers from its surrounding business ecosystem.

The enterprise's ability to architect the foundations and paths by which it will continue to operate and change to enable growth and sustain its existence. This involves understanding exist operational efficiencies and costs, versus the requirements to support deliver of current and future services to customers, and where best to invest funds for business transformation.

The enterprise's ability to perform and make relevant changes to how it operates including its effective deployment and user of resources, while maintaining speed to market as well as quality of service. This involves managing capacity, productivity, quality control, security, risks for business as usual as well as during business transformation.

# ... strategic quick wins

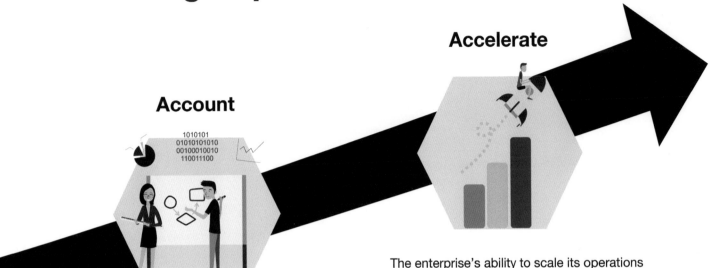

**Account**

**Accelerate**

The enterprise's ability to measure and predict the performance of current and future business activities including business transformation efforts based on the data that it has about customers and transactions, and its utilization of resources.

The enterprise's ability to scale its operations including its capabilities, activities and resources up or down with appropriate speed and time, based on different transformation challenges. This includes threats that could disrupt the business, as well as new service innovation opportunities that if capitalized would support future growth.

Where an enterprise does not have this long-term *business agility*, because it is a start-up with limited resources to invest, or a large corporation with too many people and older systems to support and change, what can it do to 'change the game'? Long-term *business agility* can be difficult to achieve, when decisions have to be made between short term gains that could cause pains in the long term, versus making sacrifices in the short-term for longer term benefits.

What it the right balance between achieving long-term *business agility* versus investing in quick wins?

An enterprise needs to assess for quick wins that are strategically aligned, that it can action quickly, to help it accelerate. As it conducts this assessment, and through this strategic alignment, it is architecting and accounting for each quick win. This is how to build *business agility* through 'strategic quick wins'.

*This approach to building 'business agility' is what we recommend as you go through this book and begin to explore, try, use and apply the tools and techniques presented in* **THE STRATEGY JOURNEY** *Framework.*

# Leverage Best Practices ...

Enterprises today face continual challenges and often have to solve a number of problems simultaneously. Survival and future success come down to their ability to transform better and faster in the rapidly changing Digital Economy.

Business transformation has become complex and difficult, and all enterprises are susceptible to Big Bang Disruption. To survive and thrive, an enterprise must embrace business agility and avoid a Big Bang Transformation approach that drains resources while it is focused on the wrong strategies and activities, and hinders it from adapting to new opportunities.

Transforming with a *business agility* approach works best when you have a framework to follow too.

It is beneficial to use frameworks that have been tested through a process of iteration within real enterprises, as this is how they become best practices.

There are many best practice frameworks and models to help solve specific challenges along the end-to-end strategy journey .... so which ones do you use?

In this book, we have done the hard work for you and curated what we believe are the best practice frameworks and models that you can use along the Five Stages of **THE STRATEGY JOURNEY** as you embark on transforming your business in the digital age. We also cover HOW to use these best practices with our Five Model *Framework* of **THE STRATEGY JOURNEY**.

# ... to solve specific problems

### Best Practice Frameworks* to leverage along
## THE STRATEGY JOURNEY

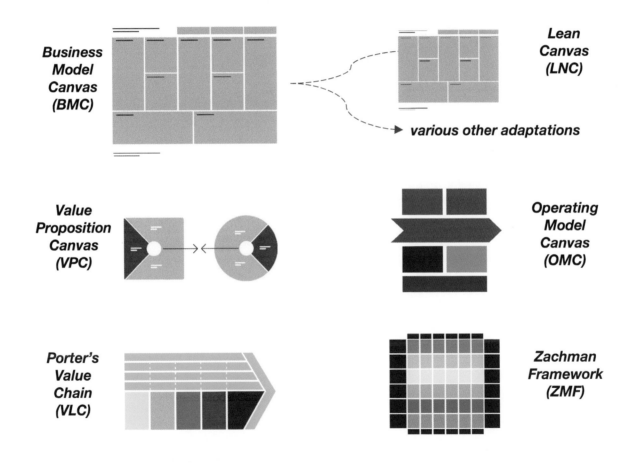

**Business Model Canvas (BMC)**

**Lean Canvas (LNC)**

*various other adaptations*

**Value Proposition Canvas (VPC)**

**Operating Model Canvas (OMC)**

**Porter's Value Chain (VLC)**

**Zachman Framework (ZMF)**

*\* These six frameworks are referenced in more detail within THE STRATEGY JOURNEY Framework and in this book. Other frameworks may also be mentioned, referenced and adapted.*

Trademark notices
Business Model Canvas is a registered trademark of Strategyzer AG

# Three Guided-Paths ...

*To navigate through* **THE STRATEGY JOURNEY** *end-to-end ...*

While practitioners in the Management Consulting industry sometimes use the terms *'framework'* and *'methodology'* interchangeably, they are not the same. They provide two distinct functions, and when used together, they can improve the business agility of your enterprise.

A *'Framework'* guides you through the WHAT, and provides a common language to align different activities and teams during business transformation.

*Frameworks* however, don't cover the HOW part, including:

- HOW to define the strategies and actions to perform using the *Framework*;

- HOW to execute the strategies and actions defined with the *Framework* to deliver the desired outcomes; and

- HOW to leverage different *Frameworks* to help you solve specific problems within an end-to-end journey, and join them up to complete the end-to-end journey from *strategy-to-execution*.

This HOW is where a *methodology* comes in.

A *'Methodology'* deals with the HOW, and provides the process to execute strategies and deliver transformation changes.

In this book, we will introduce ...
**THE STRATEGY JOURNEY** *Framework*

WHAT is it? WHAT is in it?

We also provide 'guided-paths' on HOW to use **THE STRATEGY JOURNEY** *Framework*.

Three guided paths have been designed to address the three major areas that most impact enterprises in our fast changing Digital Economy:

- Business Model disruption
- Servicing new customer journeys
- Sustainable transformation

Joining the dots between all three paths to bridge the gaps between strategy and execution end-to-end is how you build, improve, and achieve *business agility*.

# ... to go end-to-end faster

## Assess which guided-path to start with ...

All enterprises navigate through the *Five Stages of* **THE STRATEGY JOURNEY** differently based on their existing *business agility* and the specific challenges that they are facing at any point in time. This means that they can have different *points of departure* or *starting points.* This is why enterprises should commence each end-to-end strategy journey with the guided-path that fits the problem they want to solve. The three paths do not need to be taken sequentially and it may only make sense for new start-ups to navigate through the three paths in sequence from concept to implementation.

**Three *Strategy Journey Paths* to guide your enterprise on its end-to-end journey using THE STRATEGY JOURNEY *Framework***

*Join the dots end-to-end to achieve 'business agility'*

**Business Design for Disruption**

How to address the threat of disruption to the Business Model, and make appropriate decisions on what strategies and tactics to undertake in the next phase(s) of the business.

**Transforming Operating Models with Service Design**

How to design new services that deliver value according to customer and user journeys, and develop the new value stream and capabilities required in the Operating Model.

**Managing the Transformation Journey**

How to deliver changes in your Operating Model using co-creation, and instill a 'culture of learning' while improving operational efficiency and resources across geographies.

*Which guided-path and 'roadmap' should your enterprise commence with?*
*Assess our enterprise or project with the FREE*
**THE STRATEGY JOURNEY Analyzer *to find out ...***

https://strategyjourney.com/analyzer-tool

# Winning the game by ...

## How to use this book ...

1010101
01010101010
00100010010
110011100

Every business challenge, big or small, goes through a journey, which we have framed using the five stages of **THE STRATEGY JOURNEY**.

In the rest of this book, we will show you WHAT **THE STRATEGY JOURNEY** *Framework* is, and its component models and tools, that you can use to help your enterprise navigate through its strategy journeys.

We will also show you HOW to navigate through your journey using the guided *Strategy Journey Paths*, and join the dots to help you build, improve and achieve business agility in your business.

So, besides reading the rest of this book, which provides you with a reference guide of tools including five **Strategy Journey Canvases** and techniques that you can dip into whenever you need to ...

Is there a PROCESS to follow?

The process to use this book enables you to build your *business agility* ...

## 1 ASSESS your business

Conduct a current state review of your enterprise, including what happens if you do nothing, what goals and objectives you want to achieve, and what transformation journeys you may need to embark on.

You can use **THE STRATEGY JOURNEY** Analyzer to assess what *Strategy Journey Path* to take, based on your role and the challenges faced by the enterprise that you are serving.

## 2 ARCHITECT your business

Select the appropriate *Strategy Journey Path* to help you solve your priority challenges and follow the guided steps including which tools to use on the path ...

To re-shape your business,
To design new services,
To optimize your transformation journey (All in the HOW section).

## 3 ACTION your strategies, tactics and roadmaps

Begin to execute the actions within the strategies, tactics and roadmaps that come from each *Strategy Journey Path*. Iterate and improve each hypothesis by co-creating with customers, users, partners and stakeholders, until the right actions are adopted and become embedded, while collecting data as you execute in order to support continuous learning.

# ... blending science and art

## ... To transform your business in the digital age

**4 ACCOUNT for your business performance**

Measure and review performance to determine future scenarios, using data collected from all activities including customer and user's journeys and internal processes.

Make decisions about what data to validate and the new strategies and tactics to start, stop, or change in your ongoing co-creation process with customers, users, partners and stakeholders. Update your transformation roadmap and communications to improve transparency and alignment.

**5 ACCELERATE your business growth ... ... improve business sustainability**

Determine what capabilities can be repeated or re-used, and prioritize which ones to scale based on how they support business transformation, and add value ... to help you grow and become more sustainable.

Identify any assets and resources that need to be maintained, stored, and enhanced. Invest in building up these assets and resources including people, processes, data and systems, across your entire operating model, as part of the co-creation and transformation process.

**THE STRATEGY JOURNEY** *Framework*, the **Strategy Journey Paths**, along with all the illustrative cases studies in this book, have been designed to provide you and your enterprise with a science to transform better and faster ... giving it the best chance of success in the fast changing ecosystem ... that is our Digital Economy.

But don't forget, one big thing ...

Science is great but only when it works after you invest in the effort to explore, try, use, and embed each hypothesis to make it a proven standard. Even Artificial Intelligence (AI) has its limits, and the significantly faster machine-learning process still requires decision making from a brilliant mind to accept the risks and take action.

Like in any game or sport, such as football or soccer, you can design strategies and build a team to follow processes with a lot of practice in order to deliver the best possible result, but that highly determined and motivated striker must take a risk, and take his or her shot, to produce that stroke of brilliance that will make the difference to change the game and win the game. It is the same in the game of running a business.

In this book, we cover HOW you can use both hearts and minds through a *culture of learning* to ensure the science of strategy is open to the art of possibility ... to help you capture all those opportunities for your business and career.

*What*

# What's in ... THE STRATEGY JOURNEY

**THE STRATEGY JOURNEY** describes the five stages of the business lifecycle, as an enterprise moves from design to execution of its strategies, tactics, and business activities, transforming itself to continually deliver value to customers and all its stakeholders.

*To be able to successfully navigate the* **Five Stages of THE STRATEGY JOURNEY**, *we need to understand the components that make a business what it is, drive its very existence and shape its evolution.*

What is a **business?**

What constitutes **value** and what is **growth** in business?

What **motivates** business **customers** into action?

What is **business strategy** and **business transformation?**

What is the **digital economy?**

What is a **value proposition** and **innovation in business?**

What are the new **digital business models** of the future?

What **data-driven** techniques enable **digital transformation?**

What is **service innovation** and **co-creation?**

What **customers** and **stakeholders** work with and in businesses?

What **value models** yield business advantages?

What **transformation strategies** sustain and grow a business?

What **capabilities** transform the **Operating Model?**

What **runs and transforms** the business?

What is a **culture of learning** and **business architecture?**

What does it take to operate at **optimal business agility?**

*Together, these components form the underlying architecture that supports the ...*
**Five Models of THE STRATEGY JOURNEY** *Framework.*

# Problem solving with ...

**THE STRATEGY JOURNEY** *Framework* is a problem solving toolkit, comprised of five models that can be used as blueprints to guide a business through its strategy journeys (p. 7-8). It provides the means to develop the strategies, tactics, and roadmaps needed to tackle *business transformation* challenges (p. 9-10), and enable a business to transform into the digital age with agility, accountability, and action to deliver value growth (p.69-72) to customers and stakeholders (p. 121-122).

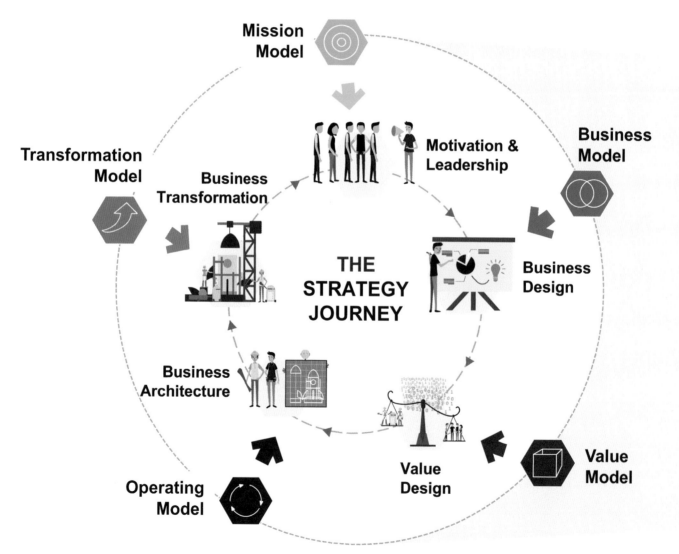

# THE **STRATEGY JOURNEY** *Framework*

The **Five Models of THE STRATEGY JOURNEY** *Framework* provide a standardized end-to-end foundation supporting *business strategy* (p. 79) formulation and transformation path definition. Each of the five models align to the **Five Stages of THE STRATEGY JOURNEY.** They address the transformation challenges of a business in the wider business ecosystem, that is the global digital economy (p. 95).

**Mission Model**  The **'Mission Model'** describes the core purpose of an enterprise providing laser focus on the target *mission* that it seeks to achieve, while enabling the business to pull followers toward its future *vision*.

**Business Model**  The **'Business Model'** describes what constitutes and drives a business, giving it the means to make profit as well as growing the value of the business itself. It encompasses customers, *value propositions,* and details of what makes the business grow.

**Value Model**  The **'Value Model'** describes what constitutes value for an enterprise or a customer, encompassing where the value is created, the exchange of value between different stakeholders, and most importantly, how to find new opportunities to create value in the wider global business ecosystem.

**Operating Model**  The **'Operating Model'** describes HOW the business runs to support the design, build, testing, and delivery of its *value propositions*. Comprising processes, data, technology systems, people and governance of the business's capabilities to operate at a cost to achieve business outcomes.

**Transformation Model**  The **'Transformation Model'** describes the effort in time, resources, costs and the governance of the roadmap associated with the transformation journey of an enterprise, as it executes changes to its capabilities and improves its business agility, for continued value delivery and growth.

# What is a business

A **'business'** is an organization or enterprising entity which engages in commercial, industrial, or professional activities in order to capture value from, and produce or deliver value for, its customers and other stakeholders including shareholders and staff (p. 121-122).

A business exists to serve different customers by providing them with value. Without customers to adopt the value propositions (p. 97-98) that it is offering, there is no business.

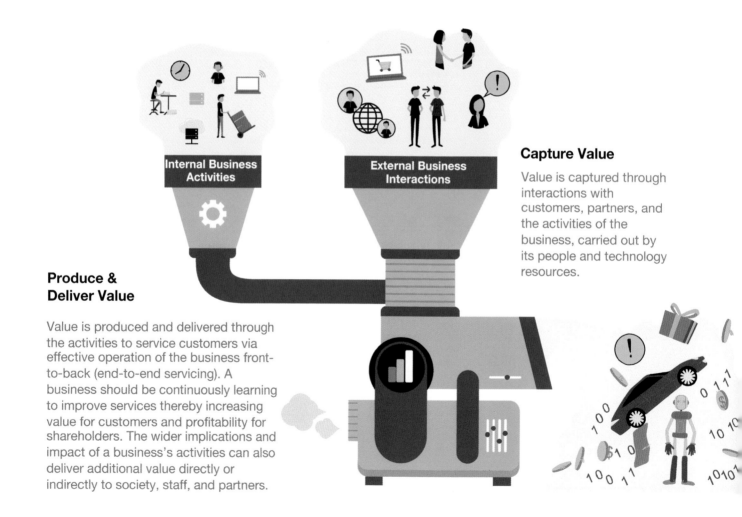

**Internal Business Activities**

**External Business Interactions**

**Capture Value**

Value is captured through interactions with customers, partners, and the activities of the business, carried out by its people and technology resources.

**Produce & Deliver Value**

Value is produced and delivered through the activities to service customers via effective operation of the business front-to-back (end-to-end servicing). A business should be continuously learning to improve services thereby increasing value for customers and profitability for shareholders. The wider implications and impact of a business's activities can also deliver additional value directly or indirectly to society, staff, and partners.

Businesses can be for-profit or non-profit.

A 'for-profit' business exists to add value via the exchange of services, which may include physical products for income or revenue at a cost, thereby generating a profit. We will discuss throughout this book, why all businesses are service oriented (p.17).

A 'non-profit' business exists to fulfill a charitable mission or social cause. It functions as any business should: to add value through its services to stakeholders. The difference is that it does not make a profit. Income and revenue is used or invested differently. The value that is delivered produces different outcomes that are aligned to the charitable mission and social causes.

The business communities and economic bodies from around the world have come to define three different types of businesses:

- **Small Businesses:** including start-ups in their early stages of development

- **Scale-ups:** high growth businesses typically medium in size

- **Corporates:** incumbents that are larger with multiple business lines and many business functions working together.

These three business types provide an indication of the relative sizes of businesses, their funding and resourcing needs, and the strategies and tactics they require to operate effectively in the marketplace.

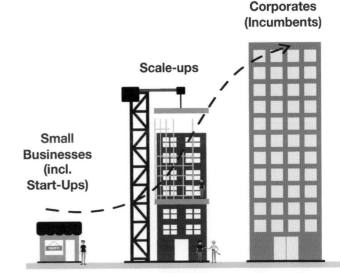

Most businesses start out small with very limited funding and resources, and then grow overtime by scaling up through their strategies and tactics into large incumbent corporate organizations or their 'non-profit' equivalents, including government institutions.

# What constitutes value in business ...

**'Value'** means different things to different people, especially customers and the stakeholders (p. 121-122) in the organization that support a business. When discussing what value is, the 'context' is key.

*By operating as a business, an organization captures and produces four types of value:*

### Business Value

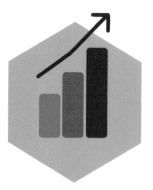

Business Value describes what strategic growth has been achieved by a business that would benefit shareholders and staff.

It includes:
- Profit growth (p.141)
- Asset growth (p. 149)
- Share price growth

NB: Non-profit organizations can have business value because they have assets.

### Social Value

Social Value describes the contribution to society from a business. It covers the value and culture of a business and its governance of behaviors and attitudes, which can have an influence and hence an impact on society.

Examples of social value include:
- Honesty
- Support
- Learning
- Care

Many government institutions and non-government organizations (NGOs) take on this responsibility to provide social services that will deliver different forms of social value to people and the environment that surrounds them.

'For-profit' organizations tend to be more focused on Financial Value and Business Value, while 'non-profit' organizations are focused on Social Value. All businesses should be focused on Customer Value, especially to attract the customer's attention, onboard them, and to build loyalty as customers adopt their solutions.

## Financial Value

Financial Value is what something is worth to a buyer or purchaser. Financial value is often also referred to as commercial value when an object or thing is a product or service that is sold or provided by a business or organization to a customer or user, and a transaction is involved.

Financial value encompasses both cost and quality.
Value = cost + quality

Financial value is thus usually measured through revenue or income from sales, or projected sales.

## Customer Value

Customer Value describes what customers are really paying for when it decides to buy and use the products and/or services provided by a business. It is the value as perceived by the customer relative to their expectations, and thus it also sets future expectations.

It comprises solutions that provide outcomes and experiences.
Solution(s) = outcome(s) + experience(s)

Examples of the outcomes and experiences expected or perceived by customers and users include peace of mind, time saved, excitement, and pleasure.

# What is growth in business ...

Every business has a purpose, as described by its *mission* and *vision*. Growth is an outcome of success in achieving the purpose.

**'Business Growth'** is the result of growing the value that the business captures and delivers through its activities. These activities support the interaction of external stakeholders (including customers) and internal resources.

Growth is not limited to 'for-profit' organizations, as 'non-profit' businesses must also keep growing the value that they produce for stakeholders to justify their existence.

See pages 115-116 to learn the different methods, the 'service innovation' techniques, by which a business can achieve growth or sustain itself to stay relevant to customers.

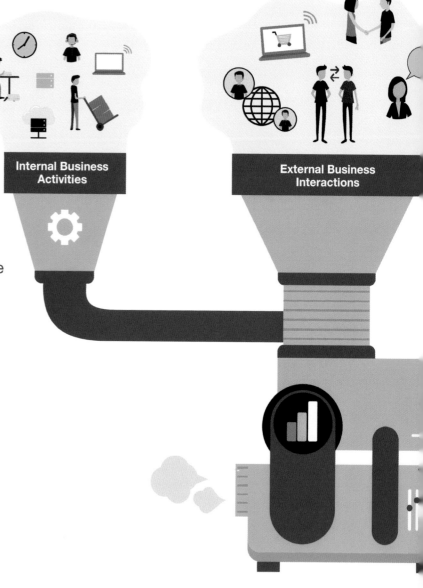

Internal Business Activities

External Business Interactions

The drivers of value that describe WHAT areas or disciplines a business needs to focus on in order to grow, to capture, and to deliver more value for customers and stakeholders, fall into six 'value measures':

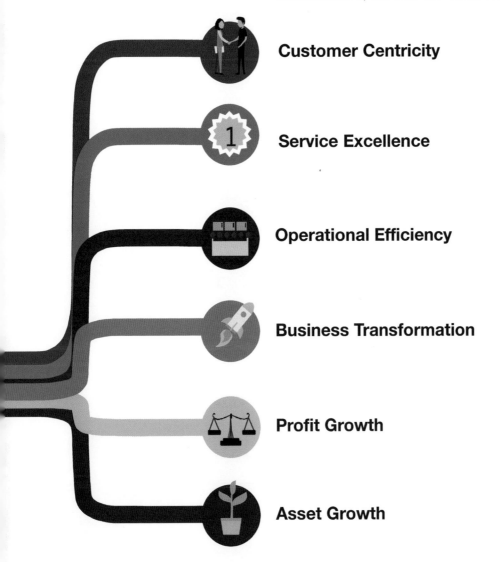

**Customer Centricity**

**Service Excellence**

**Operational Efficiency**

**Business Transformation**

**Profit Growth**

**Asset Growth**

# Six drivers of value to grow a business

Traditional methods of measuring value and business growth, which direct the different areas in an enterprise to focus businesses activities, include:

- **Value Discipline Model***
  comprised of three value disciplines (p. 26): Customer Intimacy, Product Leadership, Operational Excellence;

- Assets and liabilities in the **Balance Sheet**;

- Financial performance as described by income and costs in the **Profit and Loss (P&L) Statement** of a business;

These measurements focus on business activities in specific functional areas of an enterprise and need to be extended to included the necessary considerations of the digital economy (p. 95).

*\* Treacy and Wiersema introduced the Three Value Disciplines in their Harvard Business Paper 'Customer Intimacy and Other Value Disciplines' in 1993*

## Customer Centricity

What are the key customer experience journeys that the business will focus on to drive customer awareness, satisfaction and advocacy?

## Service Excellence

What standards and quality will your services include or provide to customers and users? How are they differentiated from competitors with a unique position? What makes them market leaders?

**Value**

## Operational Efficiency

How will you leverage your operational *resources* and assets like people, processes, data, and systems, or work with partners within the wider business ecosystem to maximize capacity and productivity?

## Asset Growth

Does your business have any assets, both tangible and intangible, including Intellectual Property (IP)? How will you be growing assets in order to increase your business's future growth potential and valuation?

The digital economy has changed how the assets of a business are valued, to include the potential of an asset to produce value, as well as the value that it holds based on the market forces of supply and demand in the future. The *business agility* (p. 51-54) of an enterprise to execute and realize *business transformation* changes, is also a value measure that drives business growth.

## Profit Growth

What are the financial targets and how will you achieve them? How will you increase sales or sell high value services without disproportionally increasing costs to build growth in profit sustainably?

**Measures**

## Business Transformation

How can your business change and innovate new solutions to get them to market quickly? How will you change the organization to make it more agile and innovative?

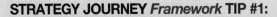

**STRATEGY JOURNEY** *Framework* **TIP #1:**

These six 'value measures' should be used to describe the goals and objectives of the business. Strategies and tactics are formulated and executed using them to enable the business to grow – in its **Mission Model**.

# What motivates a business

A business must be motivated to grow. Motivation is driven by leadership and culture.

'**Leadership**' is required to set the right direction to bring about the necessary business activities that will deliver the value that leads to growth. Leaders set targets and provide strategies and guidance to direct actions in an organization.

'**Culture**' encapsulates the beliefs and behavior in a business and this drives or incentivizes the organization. It motivates the people who work within it into action to deliver what its leaders have set as the path to follow. Culture shapes how the business activities are performed.

It is no coincidence that the most profitable companies also have the strongest brands, which are reflected through their culture. After all, as so cleverly said by Tony Hsieh, CEO of Zappos:

> *"Brand and culture are two sides of the same coin."*

However, a business doesn't instantly have a brand, culture, and is not instantly profitable. These all need to be built. New business start-ups start very small. To grow and to succeed, they must build brand, culture, and profit as quickly as possible through being agile and efficient both internally and externally within the marketplace or ecosystem by which they operate. They have to navigate a growth path avoiding overspending beyond their means as sustainability is paramount to success.

Well established modern businesses like Amazon, Apple, Google, and Facebook, and older longer established businesses, such as General Electric, and even big banks like Goldman Sachs, HSBC and Citibank all have brands, culture, and profits – some good and some not so good at different times. No matter their current standing in society today, the brand, culture, and profit of these established businesses have been built over time.

Brand, culture and profit are all outcomes born from the success and failure of strategies applied by the leaders of a business over several years, and in some cases decades. There are outcomes that have come to fruition from achieving many collective business wins as the business navigated through each business lifecycle or strategy journey.

Behind the scenes, what really focuses the efforts of the business to achieve wins in brand, culture, and profit is the 'context' - the *mission* and *vision* by which the business will operate.

A well-defined *mission* and *vision* is what unifies and drives the entire business organization to produce the value desired by customers and stakeholders.

*Mission* and *vision* are connected by purpose. The purpose of the business is to fulfill its *mission* by realizing its *vision* of WHAT to do and achieve in the future. This '**purpose**' is demonstrated by the organization's values and the values of its stakeholders.

Apple's enormous profits in the 100s of billions of dollars (which would enable it to purchase several established global banks or even a small country) whilst impressive, is not the sole motivator for Apple's senior executives and staff, nor what draws or pulls the company's loyal fans. Its founder, Steve Job's original Mission Statement in 1980 is what drew everyone in and continues to motivate Apple today:

*"To make a contribution to the world by making tools for the mind that advance humankind."*

Strong *Motivation and Leadership* pulls customers to follow a business and to buy its *value propositions* (p. 97-98). It also steers and motivates the teams of people in the organization behind the business, and attracts new talent.

**STRATEGY JOURNEY *Framework* TIP #2:**

Improve a business **Mission Model** by reviewing and updating the Mission and Vision Statements and the 'values' of your enterprise using the guidance on pages 75-78. This will ensure they are meaningful and capable of creating a 'pulling' effect as well as directing how staff and stakeholders should behave when representing the organization.

# How To Pinpoint The Target Mission And Vision

Whether your business is a startup or a large Fortune 500 conglomerate, it is necessary to ensure that your target strategy, as defined by the *mission* and *vision,* can be easily communicated. It must also be motivating and actionable by all stakeholders as your business navigates through the challenges along **THE STRATEGY JOURNEY** stages.

*We provide the following guidance to pinpoint the target mission and vision for your business:*

## A Good Mission Statement

**Does your business have a Mission Statement that you and others in your organization at all levels feel passionate about?**

*Mission* is an essential part of telling your big-picture brand story to the world. *Mission*, along with the *vision*, and values of a business are what pulls its customers to follow it and to buy its products and services. It also steers and motivates the team, attracting new talent along the way. The Mission Statement must describe why your business exists and what it does that will make a difference.

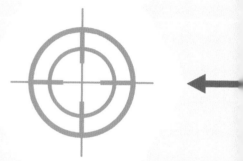

Three key characteristics that distinguish a good Mission Statement from a bad one are:

### Relevance
The most important feature of the Mission Statement is to be relevant to the customer. It must mean something to the customer so that they want to engage with your business and trade with it.

### Simple yet focused
The Mission Statement needs to be short, sharp, and focused. It must provide a very clear and simple message to be effective at drawing followers, including customers, and keeping them loyal. If your message is confusing in any way, or tries to describe all things to all people, customers will probably find it difficult to relate and be drawn to something else instead.

### Unique
A very good test for your Mission Statement is to throw it at the 'So What?' question. The Mission Statement should stand out in some unique way, and through its uniqueness, it will show how your business is differentiated.

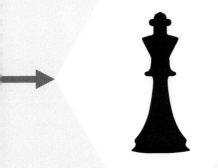

# A Good Vision Statement

**Does your business have a Vision Statement that you and other stakeholders at all levels across your organization believe in and strongly align to?**

A good Vision Statement at its most basic must describe to your followers and workers, what your business intends to achieve in the future. It should be written in an accessible manner to the business workforce, your prospective customers, and any partners involved in product innovation or servicing of customers.

Three key characteristics that distinguish a good Vision Statement from a bad one are:

### Inspiring
With a strong or killer Vision Statement, your business has the opportunity to inspire and hence pull both customers and team members along your strategy journey and towards your *vision*.

### Aspirational
The Vision Statement should be aspirational, rather than a target that can be easily reached. Many leaders are afraid that their *vision* is unrealistic but that is the point of the *vision*. It is not something you want to achieve too easily. A good horizon for the *vision* is five to ten years or more.

### Specific
To have an impact and to be taken seriously, your Vision Statement must not be vague. It needs to be measurable to state the intent of the business to achieve something tangible. However, that tangible achievement should be a rather big or bold target.

# Aligning Organizational Values With Stakeholders

The 'values' of a business are the behaviors of the organization and its people, as it goes about its business of producing value. WHAT constitutes value in business from the viewpoint of the different customers and stakeholders (p.121-122) of the business was outlined previously on p. 71-72.

*We provide the following guidance to help you communicate and align the **'values'** of your business to stakeholders:*

## Organizational Values

### Does your business represent its values through its actions and how it operates to produce value for stakeholders?

Values should describe behaviors that represent the culture of the organization that sits behind a business. Good values that attract and influence are demonstrated through the actions of people, especially its leaders. When leaders strongly display good values, this can have a positive effect on an organization, as staff and stakeholders will follow and align themselves to those values. Equally, a display of compromised values by a leader provides the excuse for misbehavior by staff and other stakeholders.

Three key characteristics that distinguish good and strong Value Statements from bad ones are:

### Coherent
Each Value Statement should be consistent with, as well as supportive to, the purpose of the organization (as described through the *mission* and *vision*). It should neither contradict other values nor their actions.

### Actionable
A Value Statement should clearly outline how the organization and its people will carry out and deliver on the value that is to be demonstrated. It should be a clear statement of how the organization will act and behave with customers and all its stakeholders.

### Measurable
A very good test for your Value Statement is whether it indicates the measures by which the organization and the people who are responsible for demonstrating and delivering the value will be held accountable for their actions.

## Stakeholder Values

**Do your customers, staff, partners, and other stakeholders in society share and even champion your organization's values to encourage more followers?**

Successful businesses can attract and influence those stakeholders who share their values. Stakeholders, and especially customers, can provide testimonials of the value that you have brought them, but an even more powerful promotion of your business comes when these individuals start to share your values, including the value that your business provides to others.

Before you decide if and how to work with different stakeholders, it is useful to assess their 'mindsets' (p. 113) and if there is an alignment between their values and the organization's values. With this data and information, you can influencer and embed expected behaviors through the following methods:

**PARTNERS**    Embed expected behaviors into a partnership agreement or contracts, and even earlier if possible via a Request For Proposal (RFP) or a Service Brief.

**CUSTOMERS**    Embed expected behaviors into service agreements, terms of use for websites, or into specific interactions during the sales, onboarding, and delivery of the fulfillment processes.

**STAFF**    Embed expected behaviors as tests both directly and indirectly during the hiring process, or as part of ongoing staff training and coaching.

*Go to strategyjourney.com/tools for a list of recommended assessment tools you can use to measure your mindset style to understand how you think, act and behave. Use these tools to assist you in performing specific tasks and/or to evaluate your staff before placing them on projects.*

# What is business strategy

A **'Business Strategy'** is a process or steps taken in the attempt to win in the 'game of business'. Depending on the size and complexity of a business, it is a 'journey' of steps to transform the business, to solve problems, and to produce outcomes that add value for customers and the other stakeholders involved in the business.

In any game or competition, from a simple family board game, such as Monopoly, to a team game like soccer, tennis, basketball or golf, it takes several rounds, involving an overall *mission*, and many strategies and tactics to score numerous incremental wins that ultimately accumulate into a big win.

When you consider why a business exists, what is does, and how it needs to perform in competition amongst other players in the business ecosystem - you realize it is playing a 'game'.

In a business, an overall *mission* drives direction, and specific strategies are tried and tested along with tactical steps taken to steer a path toward the goals and objectives of the *mission*. This *mission* is also aligned to an overall long-term *vision* that the business seeks to achieve in the future.

Some games have become businesses, football, soccer, and basketball, being clear examples, wherein the *business strategy* is dependent upon a good 'game' strategy.

*You were born to win, but to be a winner, you must plan to win, prepare to win, and expect to win.*

**Zig Ziglar**

# What is business transformation

A successful business does not stand still. There is a constant need to change, upgrade, and migrate the *value propositions* (p. 97-100) offered to stakeholders, as well as making efficiency improvements, up skilling, and scaling how the business operates - its **Operating Model** - to adapt and evolve a business from its 'current state' towards a 'target state'. In a business ecosystem of constant change, businesses must either transform or they will be disrupted and evaporate.

**'Business transformation'** is the act of changing a business from how it operates in the 'current state', through a 'transition state', and towards a more desirable 'target state' in order to deliver existing or new value-added outcomes to stakeholders, better and faster.

A business navigates the **Five Stages of THE STRATEGY JOURNEY,** traversing the business lifecycle (p. 7-8), to sustain itself and grow. As it does, it is applying its *business strategy* (p. 79) to continuously operate delivering value to stakeholders and executing *business transformation.*

**Current State**

**Target State**

**Transition States**

Unfortunately, while the intention of *business strategy* is to add value for stakeholders, the outcome of *business transformation* when the strategy is executed isn't always positive. Instead of adding value, *business transformation* can also produce nil or negative outcomes. There is no guarantee of success.

Ongoing and sustainable *business transformation* is the only way forward to grow, tackle disruption, and for a business to have the chance of causing its own 'big bang disruption' (p. 25-28) in the digital economy (p. 95).

# Components of a business strategy

To set the direction for an enterprise's strategy journey, its leaders should create a '**strategic blueprint**', which we call the '**Mission Model**', to describe the core purpose of the business. The **Mission Model** provides a laser focus on the target *mission* that a business wants to achieve and enable it to pull followers (customers, investors) and staff towards its future *vision*.

The '**blueprint**' of a **Mission Model** should capture all of the goals and objectives that drive the business forward over a period of time. This blueprint directs WHAT strategies and tactics to deploy through different *game plans* to solve the business's problems, achieve specific targets, and grow the value produced by the business along the **Five Stages of THE STRATEGY JOURNEY**.

## Blueprint

The '**Blueprint**' is a map that presents the different paths including goals and objectives to fulfill the business *mission* and enable the *vision* to be realized.

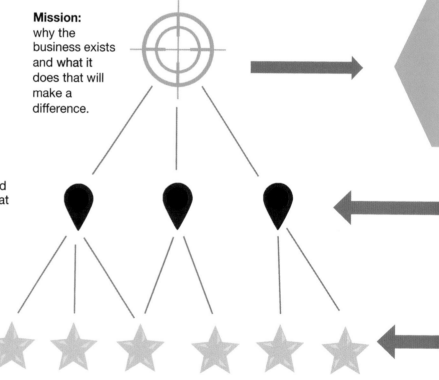

**Mission:** why the business exists and what it does that will make a difference.

**Goals:** the measurable milestones to be achieved by *business strategies* that contribute to realize the *mission* and *vision*.

**Objectives:** the measurable outcomes including Key Performance Indicators (KPIs) of projects and actions that the business needs to take to deliver value and achieve its goals.

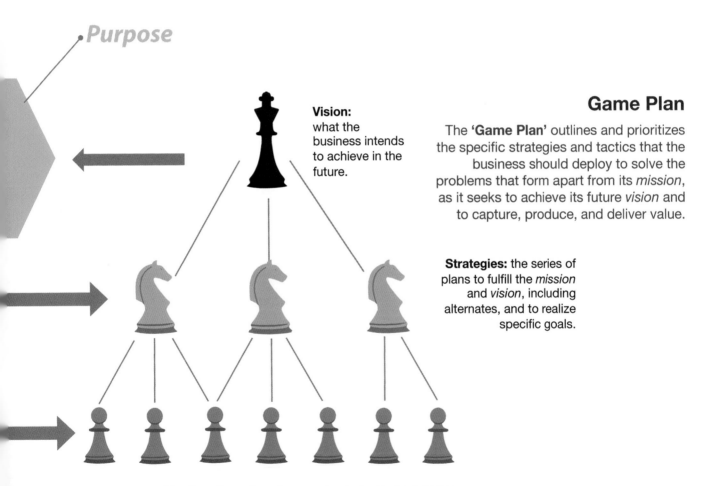

*Purpose*

**Vision:** what the business intends to achieve in the future.

# Game Plan

The **'Game Plan'** outlines and prioritizes the specific strategies and tactics that the business should deploy to solve the problems that form apart from its *mission*, as it seeks to achieve its future *vision* and to capture, produce, and deliver value.

**Strategies:** the series of plans to fulfill the *mission* and *vision*, including alternates, and to realize specific goals.

**Tactics:** the actions to execute strategic plans and to achieve the business objectives.

# Identifying Paths And Determining Goals

In any game including the 'game of business', targets can be achieved in multiple ways through different paths. The paths are comprised of activities that join up to enable the business to achieve its target and depending on the circumstances surrounding a business from its ecosystem, there are different ways to sequence business activities and the milestones that it needs to achieve along each path.

The multiple paths to the target can also be achieved in parallel by multiple teams, and if aligned or balanced to deliver multiple sources of value, they can create a cumulative effect to create an even bigger win for the business.

# Defining business goals that 'join the dots'

**Are all of your business's goals clearly defined through milestones that are achievable by your teams?**

**Are your business's goals aligned to organizational values and do they support delivering multiple forms of value?**

'Goals' describe WHAT milestones the organization behind a business needs to deliver over a period of time. They are set by a business, to enable it to address its priority problems. The priority on which goals to achieve should be based on any internally or externally influenced gaps, that enable the business to capture new opportunities, mitigate threats, whilst building on the organization's strengths and overcoming its weaknesses.

Goals should also work together to enable the business to achieve its overall *mission*, *vision*, and organizational values sustainably, by empowering the business to deliver multiple forms of value. When defining the **Mission Model** of a business goals should be defined across the 'six value measures' or drivers of value (p. 71-72). The 'Mission Model Blueprint' canvas, described in detail in the HOW chapter, provides a template to support the production of a viable business *mission* and *vision*.

Three key characteristics that distinguish a well-defined goal from a poorly-defined one are:

## Strategic alignment

The most important feature of a goal is that it must align to the purpose and values of the business. This ensures it is relevant to stakeholders, including customers, shareholders, staff, partners, and followers, and sets out to support the strategy.

## Set milestones

A goal should not be endless or it is simply not achievable. It is necessary to timebound a goal to ensure that it describes a milestone that can be achieved when the organization behind the business takes appropriate actions.

## Tangible

A goal should indicate what cumulative value will be delivered when its milestone is achieved. This cumulative value should be tangible so that the milestone can be broken down into value-added outcomes that can be achieved through the application of strategies and tactics that are delivered through business activities.

# Defining Value With S.M.A.R.T. Objectives

There are many reasons for failure in business, but more often than not, failure occurs because the organization is executing strategies and tactics that miss the mark. Business activities including business transformation activities are not delivering the desired value-added outcomes to stakeholders because they are not defined within the business objectives by which strategies and tactics are formed.

## Defining business objectives that add value

**Do your business objectives indicate what value-added outcomes will be achieved by the successful execution of business initiatives?**

**Are your business transformation initiatives delivering the same valued-added outcomes to stakeholders as projected?**

An **'objective'** or **'business objective'** describes WHAT value-added outcomes a business needs to produce or deliver to its stakeholders via the execution of business transformation activities.

Clear objectives that are **S.M.A.R.T.** enable teams within the organization to formulate the best possible strategies and tactics for execution in different business initiatives across the organization.

A well-defined and effective business objective is not only **S.M.A.R.T.** but also supports the achievement of multiple business goals, while delivering value across the different 'value measures' or drivers of value (p. 71-72).

Business objectives form the final layer of detail in the **Mission Model** of a business to empower *business transformation* initiatives and their strategies and tactics that get executed through different *game plans* and *game plays*. **S.M.A.R.T.** objectives act as levers and provide direction for key performance indicators to be set within the strategies and tactics of different business initiatives where actions are taken to transform the business.

A *S.M.A.R.T.* business objective is:

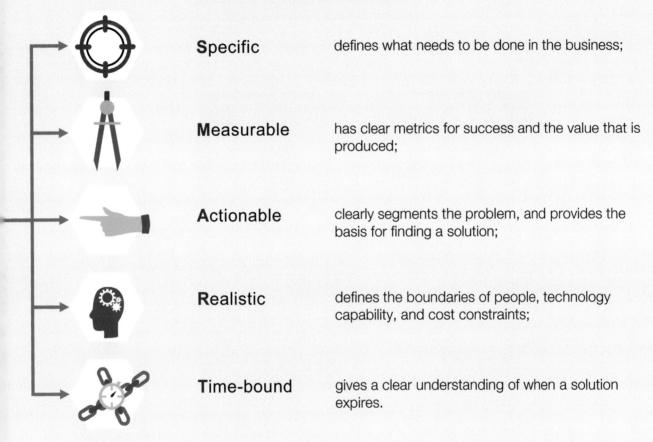

**S**pecific — defines what needs to be done in the business;

**M**easurable — has clear metrics for success and the value that is produced;

**A**ctionable — clearly segments the problem, and provides the basis for finding a solution;

**R**ealistic — defines the boundaries of people, technology capability, and cost constraints;

**T**ime-bound — gives a clear understanding of when a solution expires.

A '**Key Performance Indicator**' (KPI) is a target measure that is set to direct WHAT performance levels are to be achieved including WHAT value should be produced or delivered by a specific set of business activities in an organization. KPIs measure the success of business initiatives and their strategies and tactics, to help the costs associated with *business transformation* (p. 81-82) activities to provide a Return On Investment (ROI).

**STRATEGY JOURNEY *Framework* TIP #4:**
Make sure the strategic objectives that you set in the Mission Model Blueprint are S.M.A.R.T.

# Weighing priorities, pain points & risks

No matter the size of a business, there is always only a finite amount of funding to pay for the resources required to help it address and overcome its business challenges. The most successful businesses are able to prioritize the right problems or pain points to address through business strategies and tactics.

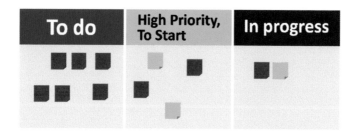

All businesses and the organizations that support them exist to solve stakeholder problems and provide solutions that will deliver outcomes that add value.

The most successful businesses in the world solve a lot of problems for their customers and users. For example, Apple provides devices for us to communicate with our loved ones, save us time, give us important reminders, make memories and then share them, monitor our wellbeing, and more. Amazon provides a platform for us to consult with or seek advice on things we want to buy, buy them from the comfort of our homes, and deliver our purchases to us at convenient times that suit our schedules and lifestyles. It also provides a platform for hosting web services that enable businesses and users to store our data and digital assets, and another platform for devices to answer our questions on the latest news and weather forecast, and much more …

A problem can be both good or bad. The term **'Pain Point'** is used to describe the painful or troubling outcome that has manifested from a problem as experienced by a stakeholder. You can also see every problem despite its pain points, as an opportunity to add value through the solutions, that is the value-added outcomes provided by a business.

On pages 9-10, we outlined *Ten Business Transformation Challenges*, forming the problems that are universal to every business as it navigates along its strategy journeys to grow the value that it delivers to stakeholders. With so many problems to solve, a business can quickly drain its limited resources on the wrong things or too many projects at once. This can leave it with nothing left in the tank, or worse debt, as was the case for Lego (p. 36), in an effort to carry on the ongoing challenges that come as part of a business's participation in the digital economy.

Good business strategy is based on good 'Prioritization'. A business's ability to prioritize is key to its ability to execute its strategies and tactics to achieve its goals and objectives. Good prioritization comes from good decision making by enterprise's leaders. Good decisions help to set the direction of business transformation, while ensure the best use of resources which are limited, no matter the size of the enterprise.

We have seen how companies large and small, as illustrated by the examples on pages 35-38 with relatively large sums of investment funding can still fail when they make the wrong decisions and take the wrong actions to transform their businesses.

An organization may have plenty of funds to attack specific problems, but those funds may still not be enough, depending on the scale of the problem, including its severity, and urgency, which are influenced by its risks.

'Risks' are the negative outcomes that result from not addressing the problem.

In making decisions, leaders must understand the severity and urgency of risks to help prioritize which problems warrant immediate or further action. Risks also need to be weighed in both pros and cons, as well as considering the resources and funds available that will support the business to take specific business transformation actions.

Leaders must have the data and evidence to help them prioritize the key business activities and business transformation activities by which funds are allocated, while less important pain points are held back on a backlog for future consideration.

It is important to consider and weigh different priorities, pain points and risk, when considering what goals and objectives form an enterprise's Mission Blueprint.

**STRATEGY JOURNEY *Framework* Activity #2:**

Gather a list of the enterprise's existing business problems describing the 'pain points' that manifest from them, and the risks that eventuate if they are not dealt with, including the severity and urgency of the problem. When you have completed this list, determine the TOP 3-5 problems to prioritize as reflected in the Mission Model Blueprint, and track their progress using a Kanban board. Move the remaining problems into a backlog list.

# Identifying The Gaps To Address With Business Strategy

In order to formulate the *game plan* that has the potential to solve a problem, it is necessary to analyze the gaps by which to attack and address with specific strategies and tactics.

Gaps exist everywhere in a business, and change continuously, based on the relative strengths and weaknesses within the business, as well as the opportunities and threats that come from its external business ecosystem.

Undertaking transformation without proper direction through strategy and planning can have disastrous consequences as illustrated by the case studies of Blockbuster, Kodak, Sugru, Webvan and other examples from the WHY section of this book (p. 35-38).

Effective strategy and planning requires a business to conduct a gap analysis of the relative strengths and weaknesses of its internal resources and **Operating Model**, as well as the opportunities and threats posed by the external business ecosystem by which the business operates against its priority problems and pain points.

The best method for conducting the gap analysis is the SWOT Analysis technique*. SWOT Analysis helps you to identify the underlying issues affecting your business that form the root cause of its problems and pain points.

A limitation of SWOT Analysis, as with all design thinking techniques, is the subjective nature of its output, which is only as good as the data or information that you have used as input, including the people who are involved in the strategy design process. This is why we recommend using the SWOT Analysis along with other tools in **THE STRATEGY JOURNEY** *Framework* for defining *business strategy*.

*\* The SWOT Analysis Technique is credited to Albert Humphrey from his research project at Stanford University in the 1960s and 1970s on top companies.*

# Questions to consider to help you identify problem gaps in your business:

## STRENGTHS

- What are our assets? What is our strongest asset?
- How is my business different from competitors?
- What unique resources do we have access to?
- Do we have a sustainable competitive advantage?
- What is our unique selling proposition?
- Does my business have any exclusive relationships with suppliers or distributors?
- Where do our sales and marketing teams excel?
- What skills do our employees have that our competitors' employees don't have?
- Can we easily get additional capital, if we need it?
- Do we have a strong customer base?
- What things do our customers say we do very well?

## WEAKNESSES

- In what areas do we need to improve?
- What expertise do I lack?
- In what areas are our competitors better than we are?
- Is there one customer carrying our entire company?
- How much debt does my company have?
- What complaints do we regularly get from customers?
- What objections do we most often hear from potential customers?
- Do we have any technology or equipment that needs to be updated?
- Are we understaffed and in what functions?
- Do we have any cash flow problems?
- Are our profit margins lower than our competitors'?

## OPPORTUNITIES

- What trends might positively affect our industry?
- Is there talent available that we could hire?
- Is there a need in the industry that we're not meeting, but could?
- Can we package our products/services differently and set a higher price?
- Do our competitors have any weaknesses that we could take advantage of?
- Is our target market changing in a way that could help us?
- Is there a niche market that we're not currently targeting?
- Do our customers ever ask for something that we don't offer, but could offer?
- Could we steal our competitors' customers by offering something they don't?

## THREATS

- Is there anyone who's not currently a direct competitor, but could become one soon?
- Are my employees happy and supported, or could they easily be poached?
- What happens if a manufacturer or supplier runs out of materials we need?
- What if a natural disaster strikes?
- Is our website secure, or do we run the risk of being hacked?
- Are our competitors planning on expanding or offering new products soon?
- Is our target marketing shrinking?

**INTERNAL INFLUENCERS**

**EXTERNAL INFLUENCERS**

*Source: Adapted from '39 Questions' in the Workful Blog at https://blog.workful.com/39-swot-questions/*

*Go to strategyjourney.com/tools for more information, examples and reference materials on the SWOT Analysis technique.*

# Ecosystem Influencers Impacting Business Strategy

No business exists in isolation. Any factors that can influence and impact the performance of a business directly or indirectly must be taken into consideration when forming business strategies.

Every business is surrounded by an ecosystem that can influence how it should operate in the present and in the future. How the business already operates internally may not necessary be able to handle the changes ahead, with its own influence on how the business reacts and adapts to change.

The best way to review the external influencers that impact a business and its organizational performance is via the well known strategic management framework known as PEST* analysis, which comes in many forms and variations.

PEST stands for: Political, Economic, Social and Technology. A popular variation extends the PEST analysis to include Environmental and Legal factors, also known as the PESTEL (or PESTLE) Model.

When conducting this method it is important to back your identified impacts with evidence through data, that is 'Market Data', on the performance on economies, the spending patterns of consumers, their social and mobility needs, and the trends from

the introduction or embedding of new technology, laws, as well as environmental impacts.

As well as external influencers, it is also important to consider the internal influencers from inside the business, that is, how it currently operates its people, process, data, and technology resources in different locations. Internal problems and pain points can make execution of specific strategies and tactics difficult or even out of reach for a business and hence, direct WHAT it seeks to achieve.

**STRATEGY JOURNEY *Framework* Activity #3:**

Complete the SWOT and PESTEL analysis for your enterprise. For each identified item indicate which component resources they impact in the enterprise's Operating Model: people, process, data, systems or technology, and location (p.179).

*\* The PEST analysis method is believed to have been invented by Harvard Professor, Francis Aguilar, who introduced a scanning tool called ETPS in his 1967 book, "Scanning the Business Environment".*

## ECONOMIC

how and to what degree consumers and businesses are able to transact, through the exchange of goods and services dictating their supply and demand

Influencer examples: business lifecycle, economic growth, interest rates, exchange rates, inflation, disposable income, distribution of incomes, labor supply and costs, business funding availability ...

## SOCIAL

how and to what degree the population (or the general public) think, act, and behave, including population growth, age distribution, health consciousness, career attitudes ...

Influencer examples: population growth, age distribution, health consciousness, education and social mobility, employment patterns and career attitudes, lifestyle trends, socio-cultural changes, press attitudes, public opinion, social taboos ...

## POLITICAL

how and to what degree a government intervenes in the economy to change how businesses operate and how consumers behave

Influencer examples: Government type and stability, Freedom of press, bureaucracy and corruption levels, regulation and de-regulation trends, tax policy, employment laws, trade and tariff controls ...

## LEGAL

how and to what degree the specific laws in a jurisdiction bound by land, sea, air space, and virtual space dictate what behaviors and actions are or are not permitted by a business or consumer

Influencer examples: health and safety, equal opportunities, advertising standards, consumer rights and laws, product labeling, product safety ...

## TECHNOLOGY

how and to what degree new technological advancements have changed the way goods and services are produced, distributed, and communicated or marketed to customers and users

Influencer examples: Research and Development (R&D) activity, emerging technologies, cost of connectivity infrastructure, communications costs, speed of connectivity services, increased remote working, impact of technology changes ...

## ENVIRONMENTAL

how and to what degree environmental resources are impacted by the actions of a business during the production and consumption of its goods and services, and how it should operate

Influencer examples: air quality, water quality, transportation and parking, pollution discharge, waste management, land use, coastal resources ...

*Go to www.strategyjourney.com/tools for more information, examples and reference materials on the PEST Analysis technique and the PESTEL (or PESTLE) Model.*

# What is the digital economy

Today, all businesses operate in a wider and faster business environment or business ecosystem. *We have referred to the digital economy throughout this book, so what is it?*

The Fourth Industrial Revolution, which is also the Second Digital Revolution (p. 13-14), has shifted all the economies by country around the world into a global ecosystem that is much more interconnected and accessible through the power of data and information. In this global ecosystem, consumers and customers, are sharing their knowledge through digital technology, resulting in very high customer expectations and an even more competitive environment where disruption has become the norm (p. 21-24).

This global digital business ecosystem is the **Digital Economy**. It is comprised of all activities across the world or globally, that involve an exchange of data or information, through any interaction or transaction between people and businesses.

## An Open Digital Economy

Every business or enterprise, big or small, is comprised of its internal environment or business operations managed through its **Operating Model**, while surrounded by an external environment or business ecosystem, which has two layers:

- **Micro-economic Environment:** comprised of the immediate industry specific environment of customers, competitors, partners, and government authorities or regulators ... that can influence how the business or enterprise operates

- **Macro-economic Environment:** comprised of the wider global environment of customers, competitors, partners and government authorities, and regulators ... that can influence how the business or enterprise operates

The accelerated rate of change in the digital economy, that is the global digital business ecosystem and the macro-economic environment, is forcing every business or enterprise to operate differently ... better and faster ... and to transform continuously or risk becoming irrelevant from disruption.

In the global digital economy, the barriers to trade and geographic boundaries, which during the industrial economy, helped some companies to grow while hindering others from market entry/penetration are either diminished or no longer exist. The competitive advantage strategies of previous Industrial Revolutions need to be replaced by new strategies or approaches fit for a digital economy.  These approaches are connected through data and are much more open to new opportunities and innovation.

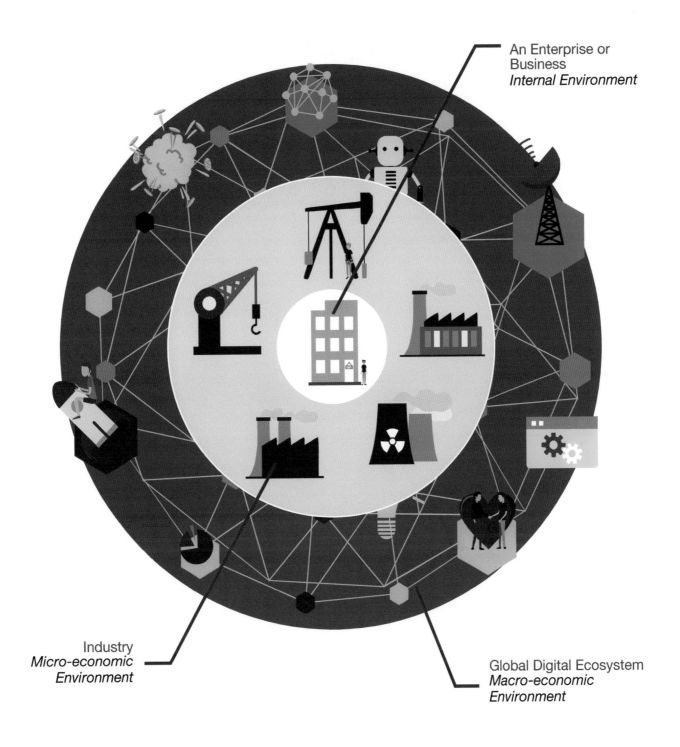

An Enterprise or
Business
*Internal Environment*

Industry
*Micro-economic
Environment*

Global Digital Ecosystem
*Macro-economic
Environment*

# What are value propositions

In business, we often use the term 'product' or 'service' to describe a *value proposition*. But customers don't actually buy products or services, and many businesses have spent millions on marketing product and service flops to customers. Customers buy and pay for an **outcome** from a product purchase or service engagement that presents them with value. Without value aligned to the customer's needs and expectations, in relation to their customer problem (p. 119), a product or service will neither be purchased nor consumed.

A **'Value Proposition'** is a physical and/or experiential vehicle (a container), that holds and delivers a set of value-added outcomes and experiences in the solution that is provided to the customer. The terms 'product' or 'service' are used to describe this container of outcomes and experiences, the solution. As well as customer value, a valuation proposition also provides the other forms of value: financial value, business value or social value (p. 71-72) to the other stakeholders of a business; depending on the composition of the *value proposition*.

## Product

The term 'product' is often used to describe a *value proposition* when the container and all the customer value that is delivered is experienced through a physical object, such as a car (e.g.. a Toyota Prius or a Ferrari).

## Service

When the value that is delivered and received by the customer is mostly experiential, such as riding in a car or taxi (e.g.. an Uber or other type of ride), the *value proposition* is described as a 'service'.

Businesses interact with their customers and deliver value to them through their *value propositions*. Their *value propositions* must provide enough value-added outcomes and experiences to convince a customer to part with their time and/or their money to pay for the product or service on offer, or both.

A payment provided by a customer in exchange for a *value proposition* from a business creates a 'transaction' between the business and customer. When this payment is financial in value, represented by some form of currency (or money), then it becomes a source of 'income' for the business, which is also called 'revenue'. When a business has collected a lot of 'revenue', which is greater than the 'expenses' it has incurred to generate *value propositions* for customers, then it has produced a 'profit'. **'Profit'** contributes to increase business value, which matters most to shareholders, who have invested their own money in a share of the business.

A payment does not, however, have to be financial, although most businesses typically only provide *value propositions* in return for financial value. A payment may come in the form a testimonial or attestation of the value that has been received, or through a change in environmental conditions. When the *value proposition* has provided value-added

outcomes and experiences that are social in nature, where the customer is a user of the *value proposition,* there is no financial or monetary exchange for the outcomes and experiences.

Within any organization, value is also captured, produced and exchanged between the different teams of resources that operate different functions or provide different services. So, there are also internal *value propositions* that support internal customers and users within the business. These internal *value propositions* are also known as *value streams* (p. 154) and form part of the organization's **Operating Model** to support its **Business Models.**

The internal customers and users who form the *internal stakeholders* (p. 106) of the business can impact a business's ability to deliver and achieve its desired goals and objectives within the organization's **Mission Model**. They influence the business activities through the actions that they perform, the level of accountability that they take, and their agility to adapt and implement changes when required.

How these internal stakeholders think, act, and behave in operating the business, defines the organization's culture. It is a major motivator of the business's actions devised to deliver results. Good culture means the best results possible results: more value.

# Successful value propositions ...

*Value propositions* are only successful if and when they become adopted by customers and/or users at the start of the *Growth* stage of the **Innovation Adoption Lifecycle** having cross the 'chasm' (p. 23). Up to this point, failure is always a possibility, regardless of whether the **Business Model** has been able to reach a break even point or not.

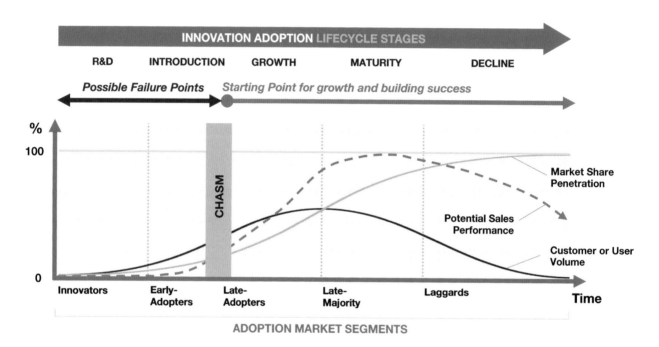

### GOOD versus GREAT value propositions

A good *value proposition* resolves the customer's pains and provides them with gains as they navigate through their *customer journey* (p. 161-166). Good *value propositions* solve the *customer problem* in a way that meets and even exceeds their expectations. This is what makes the *value proposition* as well as brand of the service provider 'sticky', further creating brand loyalty and advocacy.

Great *value propositions* have the ability to gain stickiness with customers to create a big bang disruption effect (p. 25-26), by replacing what customers and/or users do with their time and form a part of their natural and daily behaviors. We illustrated how the technology giants of today, such as Amazon, Skype (now owned by Microsoft), Facebook, and Apple, who were once start-ups, have successfully managed to create their big-bang disruption effects on p. 27-28.

# ... solve customer problems and stick

## Deriving sticky value propositions

An essential and common practice when designing *value propositions* is to profile the customer (p. 125), by creating a *customer avatar* that describes the *customer persona* – how the customer behaves. This enables product and service designers as well as marketers to develop compelling *value propositions* that attract the right customers and users into adoption, through purchases and ongoing usage that creates stickiness.

Data and information about the customer, in terms of how they think, act, and behave, provides valuable input into the process to derive a sticky *value proposition*. However, in order for the **Business Model** to be viable, it is necessary to validate WHAT is the customer problem and that a problem actually exists. The problem must also be substantial enough to warrant further investment in *service innovation* (p. 115), to develop a *value proposition* that will be adopted by enough customers along their customer journeys.

The odds of success increase when gamification techniques are applied through the creation of a *game plan* (p. 84) that considers the appropriate options to give the **Business Model** the best chances of success. The *game plan* should incorporate competitor analysis and consider the wider business ecosystem where the game is played between customers and different enterprises. It is important to trial or test a *game plan* to determine how it will work and if changes are required. Co-creation (p. 117) between different stakeholders including customers, users, and employees or staff, can simulate the conditions of play to enable a *value proposition* to be refined. This practice should occur until it meets the needs of customers and users along their customer and/or user journeys.

**STRATEGY JOURNEY** *Framework* **TIP #5:**

If you have a big problem that you need to solve, come up with a *Game Plan* first based on the right 'context' (p102), before taking action. Take 1-2 hours to consider a few different 2 or 3 options and weigh each option with a list of pros and cons including consideration of existing pain points and risks (p. 89-90), before identifying the ideal solution.

# Building Context To Scope Problems

There would be no reason for businesses to exist if we didn't have problems for them to solve. Before building or transforming a business so that it can produce and deliver a *value proposition* (p. 97) for customers and users, it is necessary to define the problem, as part of a **'game plan'**. This requires an understanding of the inner workings of the problem so as to create a solution that can provide the value-added outcomes. Context is key.

## Understanding the problem context

**Does a problem even exist? What are the circumstances and facts surrounding the event where and when the problem occurred?**

**'Context'** is the set of circumstances and facts surrounding an event or situation; it describes the characteristics of the problem and its root causes, to provide a proposed solution with a focal point.

Market research about customers and users, including data insights acquired from third parties, is often used to gather as much information as possible to understand a problem, if one even exists.

Only with context, is it then possible to make the necessary decisions around how to formulate and execute the appropriate strategies and tactics that will deliver the transformation, and provide new or improved *value propositions* with the desired outcomes to customers, that meet their expectations.

The best way to start gathering the information to set the context of a problem is to ask the Five Ws, which has been used extensively in research, journalism, and across almost every industry*. A popular sixth question expands into HOW the problem occurs.

*\* First introduced in the poem from Rudyard Kipling's "The Elephant's Child"*

**W**ho
Who is involved?
Who is affected?
Who will benefit?
Who could be harmed?

**W**hat
What happens or has happened?
What does it involve?
What is it similar to or different from?
What might be affected or impacted, and needs to change?

**W**here
Where does/did/will/should it take place?
Does it matter where it takes place?
What is the effect or outcome by location?

**W**hen
When does/did/will/should it take place?
Does the timing of when it happens matter?
How often does it occur and when?
What is the effect or outcome, when it happens?

**W**hy
Why does it matter?
Why is it important to whoever is involved/affected/benefits/harmed?

**H**ow
How does it work/function/perform/change? What is its speed?
How did it come to be or manifest?
How are those involved affected or impacted?
How serious or severe are its effects? How big is it?

When these questions are asked and answered, the information gathered provides the necessary context that will help to define the problem. In turn this allows a scope to be drawn up for solution proposals to be crafted and designed through a *business strategy* where *game plans* are formulated.

# Competitor Analysis with the game plan

No game plan is complete without a valid competitor analysis of existing rivals as well as potential rivals. Successful transformation comes from learning faster than competitors and learning about what they are doing, so you can beat them in the game.

Understanding what competitors and non-competitors are up to, and hypothesizing their strategic plays and *game plans* can go a long way to helping an enterprise identify potential gaps and hence opportunities which may be missed otherwise. It also helps to determine their unique position to alter the game and win.

In addition, this is how to identify the the risks involved in specific strategic plays that may have deterred rivals from specific activities and actions. These risks should form as inputs to the **Business Model**, and as part of the *Business Design for Disruption* path (see HOW section) in **THE STRATEGY JOURNEY** methodology, where the effort and costs to deliver a Return On Investment (ROI) are analyzed and considered to determine what constitutes as a viable **Business Model** with the potential for growth.

## Competitor

Any enterprise, that is involved in similar business activities and racing to produce and deliver an alternate *value proposition* (p. 97) that may be better and faster to the same customers and/or users.
*e.g. Ebay versus Amazon, Google versus Yahoo.*

## Non-competitor

An enterprise operating in a different industry or *value ecosystem* (p. 156), that is racing to produce and deliver a *value proposition* that indirectly provides a viable alternative to the same customers and/or users.
*e.g. Banks versus Apple, Amazon, Facebook ...*

*The Only Sustainable
Competitive Advantage
Is An Organization's Ability
To Learn Faster Than
The Competition.*

- Peter M. Senqe

# EXAMPLE: How Grab really beat Uber in South-East Asia

Grab may have started as taxi app just like Uber but it beat Uber at its own 'game of business' in Singapore and other South-East Asian countries. In 2018, Grab acquired and took over control of Uber's assets and operations in Cambodia, Indonesia, Malaysia, Myanmar, the Philippines, Singapore, Thailand and Vietnam, including UberEats, which the company plans to leverage to expand its own food delivery service, branded as GrabEats.

Obtaining significant investment capital through Venture Capital (VC) funds has helped Grab to grow, but that is not HOW it really kicked Uber (equally or even better funded) out of the South-East Asian Market.

For the South-East Asian Market, Grab had the better *game plan*. It was able to win the market by truly understanding the customer problem and matching its service offerings to the right customers.

*In this case study example\*, we have analyzed the Game Plan used by Grab including what it understood about the problems faced by South East Asian Customers that Uber didn't, compared to Uber's Game Plan.*

Easy access to book or hail taxis at affordable prices via phone line including mobile app or queuing at a rank. Shortage of taxis during peak times. Cash only system with limited credit card facilities on taxis.

*Uber failed* to see that the existing taxi services were abundant and peak times shortages were accepted as normal. Customers wanted to reduce wait times during congestion and existing surcharges have not improved this problem. Low percentage of customers had access to credit cards because of their aversion to owning debt. The cost to own private cars and vehicle ownership is very high relative to personal and household incomes.

Efficient, convenient and better ways to get around, pay for things and connect with family and friends, faster and where possible safer too. No easy way to do all of this quickly from one source.

*Grab understood* that customers were frustrated with not having enough cash around to pay for things including taxis and other emergency situations. This created the inconvenience of having to go to a cash machine as well as safety concerns from petty theft. Low access to credit cards by most consumers is cultural and based on preference to using cash versus acquiring credit card debt.

*Produced based on analysis conducted by Stratability Academy from public information

**Uber thought** that lots of increasingly mobile savvy customers across the region would want the convenience of being able to hail taxis and pay for their rides through credit facilities (same as in San Francisco). Surcharges should allow customer to pay a premium for better and faster service.

**Uber copied and dropped** its existing **Business Model** and **Operating Model** into South East Asian countries with little change except to match local currencies, pricing, and language differences.

**Grab saw** how customers could potentially buy or pay for things, including different forms of transport such as taxis, bikes, and scooters, as well as food delivery, more easily, faster and with the safety of not having to carry lots of cash around. It could also help customers to own the vehicles more easily in order to increase the volume and hence availability of ride-services.

**Grab offered new digitally enabled mobile solutions** that solved the customers problems related to connectivity, convenience, safety, and payments or transactions through:

- GrabTaxi
- GrabBike
- GrabPay
- GrabEats

Unlike Uber who remains a taxi or transport and delivery service, Grab is a Fintech connectivity service.

106

# Orchestrating wins with game plays

In any game, including the 'game of business', you win when you apply and successfully execute the right *game plan* at the right time, based on the circumstances of the problem you are attacking i.e. its context. You must play the game to learn how best to play and when to deploy your strategic *game plays* containing the tactics that lead to small wins, as well as accumulating the ultimate big win.

In a football or soccer match, a team that walks onto the pitch without:

- a *game plan* formed from studying the opponents
- a specific style of play aligned to the game plan
- players with the right skills to play the game
- practicing play as a team
- fit players ready to play to play

will inevitably struggle to score, let alone win the game or last a season to win a championship.

It doesn't matter if a team has one or a few of the most talented players, capable of individual displays of brilliance, although having such assets will certainly help. If that team hasn't done their homework by planning and practicing what they want to achieve as a team, play-by-play and game-by-game they will not progress. Different *game plans* comprised of different strategies and tactics are required to attack the different opponents or cater for different operating conditions.

Without these they will not be able to achieve their *mission* and *vision* and deliver the *value proposition* to the fans (customers) as expected. Operating without a plan or without practice brings low team moral, making the team more susceptible to mishap losses. These in turn lead to a loss of momentum, and loss of the positive mindset that is required to achieve a big win, such as the Premier League, World Championships or an Olympic Medal.

The same rules of play apply to any business. Success comes from having prepared suitable *game plans* (p. 84), and having the agility supported by a strong team to deploy them, on the playground through the right *game play*.

**STRATEGY JOURNEY *Framework* TIP #6:**
Create a list of next steps to achieve your ideal solution in your 'Game Plan' – this is your 'gameplay' that lists all your tactics.

**_Strategy without tactics is the slowest route to victory. Tactics without strategy is the noise before defeat._**

**- SUN TZU**

# What is innovation in business

*Innovation* is a simple concept. It is the creation of something new. Perhaps this is why it is such a widely-used term these days when so much of what we are doing in the digital age is new to us.

Unfortunately, the term *Innovation* has also become a loaded buzzword when we talk about entrepreneurship and new ideas in the digital age. Innovative ideas proliferate around us. Often these ideas aren't new at all. They are old ideas, repackaged to look new again. They are pure marketing. So, is marketing 'innovation', or is there more to it?

## Two distinct but interlinked definitions of 'Innovation' in business:

The practice of *business innovation* as a process including the innovation of a new *value proposition* and new **Business Models**, is an essential ongoing activity that every business must operate in as it navigates **THE STRATEGY JOURNEY** stages and business lifecycle, if it is to avoid and/or survive disruption.

*Innovation* itself isn't a *business strategy* (p. 79). Instead, the act of *innovation*, is a tactic and a *business transformation* technique, that can deliver a valuable outcome, in the form of a *value proposition*, and in doing so it supports the execution and fulfilment of a *business strategy*.

### Business Innovation

**'Innovation'** is a process and behavior, which when practiced by the people working inside a business, leads to 'out of the box' thinking, that results in the creation of new and disruptive *value propositions* that are supported by the right **Business Models** for customers and users.

In practice, this involves solving business problems in a completely different or revolutionary way. It is the source of new opportunities and has the power to create new markets full of customers and users.

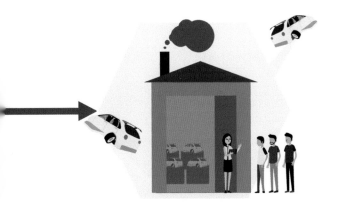

## Disruptive Value Proposition

An **'Innovation'** is a new *value proposition* (p. 87-88) that yields a remarkable result for its customers and users, and disrupts a marketplace because of its unique differences that are captured and delivered through the right **Business Model**.

In practice, this means that the business has created a *Unique Selling Proposition* (USP) that attracts a market full of customers and users. Marketing plays a big part in educating customers and users to become aware of, try, buy, and use the new *value proposition*.

A truly successful *innovation* must be able to add significantly more value for one or more customers or stakeholders of a business, so much so that the *innovation* becomes adopted and demand reaches a Growth stage (p. 99). When no value is added, then there is no *innovation*, even if an innovative process was used to try to create a new innovative solution. As we highlighted on p. 39-40, when transformations including *innovation* attempts, don't add any value or lessons learned, then they lead to a waste in time and resources.

# What are the new Business Models

The **'Business Model'** describes what constitutes and drives a business giving it the means to make profit as well as growing the value of the business itself. It encompasses customers, *value propositions* and details of how the business grows. It is a *business strategy* (p. 79) that determines how a business delivers the value-added outcomes and experiences of its value propositions to different customers and stakeholders. In order to compete amongst other players in the 'game of business', every business seeks to operate with at least one or more **Business Models**.

## Business Model Canvas*

| Key Partners | Key Activities | Value Propositions | Customer Relationships | Customer Segments |
|---|---|---|---|---|
| | **Key Resources** | | **Channels** | |
| **Cost Structures** | | | **Revenue Streams** | |

*Introduced in 2004 by Alexander Osterwalder and Yves Pigneur, and published in their 2010 book, Business Model Generation (WILEY) Business Model Canvas is a Registered Trademark of Strategyzer AG (www.strategyzer.com).*

The *Business Model Canvas** is one of the best *business design* tools, using nine building blocks to help you derive the right **Business Model** for an enterprise. It encouraging you to experiment as well as co-create *value propositions* with trial users who could become loyal customers.

**STRATEGY JOURNEY *Framework* Activity #4:**

Document your current and/or propose **Business Model** for your enterprise using the *Business Model Canvas*. Identify what gaps exist and proposed transformations required. If you don't have an existing Business Model, document a close competitor that you want to emulate and improve upon.

*An online tutorial on how to complete the Business Model Canvas is available on strategyjourney.com/tools.*

# ... driving the digital economy

## Business Models driving the global digital economy

*Business Transformation* (p. 81) and *innovation* (p. 109) spurred by rising customer expectations (p. 21) from the Fourth Industrial Revolution or Second Digital Revolution (p. 13-16) has seen the emergence and growth of new **Digital Business Models** – that are service and information services based (p. 17), driving much of the economic activity and value creation in today's digital economy.

Traditional Business Models, which have operated with a pipeline based *value chain* (p. 155), need to evolve to become more digital. They must operate using digital solutions as well as offering digital services. Business Models should look to leverage existing platforms, become digital platforms or evolve to multisided digital platforms to support different types of customers (p. 121-122) with multiple transaction models (p. 129), if they are to survive in the rapidly evolving digital ecosystem. Businesses should extend their *business transformation* activities in order to innovate new **Digital Business Models** that can compete in the digital economy. They need to incorporate *digital transformation* approaches (p. 113), that leverage the power of networks (p. 133), *customer co-creation* via multiple channels, and even develop their own omnichannel marketplaces that operate as *value ecosystems* (p. 128).

## Evolution of the Digital Business Model

 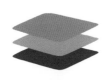 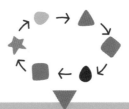

### Pipelines

Products and services are offered using a pipeline, following a traditional *value chain* (p. 155, 181-182) where they are designed, manufactured, marketed, and sold to customers, and an ongoing relationship is supported through servicing.

*e.g. All manufacturers, consumer goods companies, food retailers including cafes and restaurants...*

### Platforms

Multiple parties of customers and users, including consumers, producers, and providers are brought together and served through a marketplace, which acts as a platform. Parties are charged different fees for interacting and transacting through the marketplace, which acts as broker of services.

*e.g. Online streaming, search and social media services such as Netflix, Twitch, YouTube, Google, Facebook, Twitter...*

### Omnichannel Marketplaces

An ecosystem of integrated services with ongoing subscription charges provided to customers and users, using multiple channels that are supported through a platform, to ensure they enjoy a cohesive and seamless experience, as part of their customer journeys and user journeys.

*e.g. Amazon Marketplace, Disney, VIP.com, Topshop, Timberland, Virgin, Sephora, Crate & Barrel...*

# Using digital transformation to ...

Using the latest applicable digital technologies to support business activities, and as part of *business transformation* (p. 81) can help a business to tackle disruption better and faster. This *digital transformation* can lead to new *value propositions* that are potentially *disruptive innovations* (p. 23) with the ability to create a competitive advantage.

However, application of new technology through use of the latest tools, including platforms and omnichannels, alone does not guarantee an effective **Business Model** that will thrive in the digital economy with the desired mass adoption by customers – which is what makes an *innovation* successful (p. 89). As demonstrated by businesses such as Everpix, Webvan, and Tutorspree (p. 37), many new *innovation* attempts have failed from not being able to develop **Business Models** that will stick with customers or inability to scale their **Operating Models.**

In order for companies to innovate truly *disruptive innovations* that deliver the desired value to customers and stakeholders through meeting and exceeding their expectations, effective *digital transformation* approaches as demonstrated by Apple, Amazon, Facebook and Skype, through their 'big bang disruptions' (p. 25) that have changed the way we think, act, and behave, and dominate today's customer and user journeys are required.

**'Digital Transformation'** is an application of *business transformation*, where a company's business activities are data-driven by being *customer co-created, value driven* and *network connected. The data-driven enterprise* is enabled by digital technology, as it innovates and transforms how it operates continuously, to capture, produce and deliver more value-added outcomes and experiences to customers and stakeholders.

**STRATEGY JOURNEY** *Framework* **Activity #5:**

Take the **Digital Business Blueprint Challenge**, a short course including a templated workbook to develop a Digital Business Model following the **Strategy Journey methodology.** Available exclusively through the **Strategy Journey Accelerator** program: https://strategyjourney.com/accelerator

# ... innovate and transform the business

## Three data-driven approaches to Effective Digital Transformation

The business applies *'service innovation' with human centered design* techniques (p. 115) through all business activities, to constantly engage and co-create with external customers, in order to deliver valued-added outcomes and experiences to them. Data and information about customers, users and other stakeholders is collected along their customer and user journeys, to support *business transformation* activities including *innovation* of new and improved *value propositions*. The business uses digital technologies to foster and build a long-term relationship along the customer and user journey, as it engages with the customer or user through its *value propositions*.

### Customer Co-created

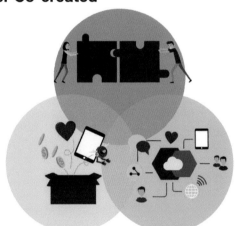

### Value Driven

There is a culture to serve, with application of *gamification* techniques using data that encourage learning and teamwork focused on producing and delivering more value to customers and stakeholders end-to-end, across the entire enterprise. *Business strategy* and *business transformation* activities are agile, accountable and actionable to ensure valued-added outcomes can be produced, across multiple 'value measures' (p. 71-72). *Resources* including usage of digital technologies are deployed based on what value can be captured, produced and delivered to deliver quick wins that support speed to market, while also improving the business's long term *business agility* (p. 51-54).

### Network Connected

The business takes a wider view of the business ecosystem, that is its *value ecosystem* (p. 154), that surrounds the organization and its ability to connect and work with different stakeholder groups. These include customers, users, partners, and regulators with new or different relationships, to support its *business strategy*, execution *capabilities*, and *business transformation* activities. It is constantly changing how it leverages and even partners with digitally-enabled networks (p. 133). It also activates more channels, using the latest digital technologies to support its connectivity and its own *value chain* or supply chain, across all of its business activities.

# Designing Business Models ...

The shift in demand towards customer experiences that leverage digital technology to solve customer problems along their customer journeys (p. 45) as evidenced through rising customer expectations (p. 21), means that companies must adapt and shift their *innovation* and *business transformation* practices. They need to incorporate *human-centered design\** approaches focused on servicing the journeys of customers and adopt the practice of **'service innovation'**. The purpose of 'service innovation' is to design, develop, and deliver the most competitive *value propositions* (p. 97) and **Business Models** including **Digital Business Models** (p. 111) that are most likely to be adopted by customers.

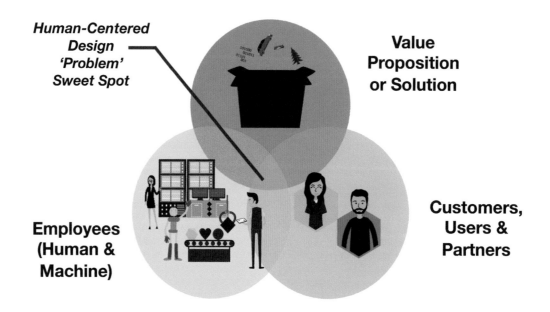

**Human-Centered Design 'Problem' Sweet Spot**

**Value Proposition or Solution**

**Employees (Human & Machine)**

**Customers, Users & Partners**

**'Human-Centered design' (HCD)** is focused on problem-solving and specifically involves the human perspective in all steps of the problem solving process in order to develop solutions to problems for customers and users.

In practice, it includes participant involvement or co-creation with customers, while developing processes and systems in technology to support innovation. It is how customers and employees, both human and machines, and the *value proposition,* co-exist to solve a problem and create a solution together.

*\* Coined by Horst Rittel, championed by Nobel Prize laureate Herbert Simon, expanded by Mike Cooley who termed "Human-Centered Technology" in his book Human-centred Systems in 1989, and now part of ISO 9241-210:2019.*

# ... through service innovation

## Service Innovation in THE STRATEGY JOURNEY *Framework*

As a problem-solving framework, the **Five Models of THE STRATEGY JOURNEY** *Framework* (p. 63-64) apply *human-centered design* by guiding practitioners to conduct:

### Customer Modeling to direct innovation

'**Customer Modeling**' (p. 125) an in-depth study of customers and users in how they think, act, and behave based on a specific context. It involves collecting many forms of quantitative and qualitative data and information at different levels of detail or granularity, collected over time and in different situations to help understand the *mindsets* of customers. Consequently, this will support predictions on how they are likely to behave and change behaviors, which drives their needs and wants. The data collected is used to drive *Service Design* and innovate the best **Business Model** that will mostly likely be adopted by customers.

### Service Design to derive *value-driven* customer experiences that stick

'**Service Design**' is the process of *value modeling* to create and enhance new *value propositions* in order to solve the customer's and/or user's problems along their customer and user journeys (p. 119). It involves modeling different *value-driven* experiences with customers and users delivered to them through services that span their journeys end-to-end. This is in order to create short, medium, and long-term stickiness effects based on how expectations are met, not met, or exceeded, relative to alternate experiences from competitors and non-competitors.

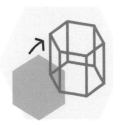

### Transformation Design to realize solutions and deliver outcomes

'**Transformation Design**' is the of process identifying, defining, and implementing changes in the business across its **Operating Model**, that is all activities that its resources and employees conduct to deliver services fulfilling customer outcomes. The Transformation Design delivers the new services that encompass the business's new *value propositions* and **Business Models**. It involves adapting and improving processes and data, as well as how employees, systems and technology across geographies, maximize all the different forms of value (p. 71-72) created or produced by the organization.

'**Service Innovation**' is the practice and application of these three innovation activities combined through following the ***Strategy Journey Paths*** (see HOW section) supported by data science.

# What is co-creation

There is no way of knowing if a newly designed **Business Model** will work without testing it. The experience of almost every business large or small, including entrepreneurs, is that they never get it quite right at the first launch of a new product or service. Most initial launches really need to be seen as a test by which to learn from. The rapidly changing digital economy also means that many **Business Models** will need to change, by adapting and evolving much more quickly, or they will be disrupted (p. 25).

Continuous testing through *co-creation* with customers and users is key to survival and future **Business Model** success.

There is no getting around the fact that *value propositions* have to be tested with customers, users, and partners to see if they are fit for purpose. It is necessary to gather as much information as possible and learn from customers and users by understanding how they will think, act, and behave around a product or service - as well as the operating of the internal business itself and its employees.

It is also important to validate if there is a market or *target customer segment* (p. 127) for a *value proposition*, and what are its characteristics, in order to work out how to price a *value proposition* to make a **Business Model** viable through 'profit' (p. 97). The cost to execute a **Business Model** must be tested and refined or optimized as a business needs to have enough working capital to keep running. Moreover, further investments are constantly required to fund minor updates and upgrades as well as bigger *business transformation* activities.

'**Co-creation**' is comprised of all the activities to design and test *value propositions* and **Business Models** on an ongoing basis with customers, users, and partners, as well as employees supported by technology. It is implemented through *service innovation* (p. 115).

## Six Data-Driven 'Co-creation' Techniques

The following six techniques can be applied during *Service Innovation* where data and information are gathered and tested. Techniques have been listed based on the level of active involvement or interaction with different customers and users, as well as the effort and costs involved in execution … starting from simple surveys to full co-creation where an innovation is embedded into the customer or user behavior during the customer or user journey (p. 119).

 **Market Surveys**

Prospective and existing customers are asked or enticed to answer a list of questions in relation to how they are likely to think, act, and behave with respect to the product and/or service, either online, over the phone, face-to-face or via other channels. This includes getting feedback from customers.

 **Focus Groups**

Prospective and existing customers are invited into a closed environment where they are monitored and measured based on how they think, act, and behave with respect to the product and/or service, through simulated customer or user journeys.

 **Hackathons**

Different customer groups, as well as any potential third-party partners, are invited into a closed environment or event where they are asked to participate in the innovation process to solve a problem over one or a few days. They compete to win a large prize or reward.

 **MVP Prototyping**

A Minimum Viable Proposition (MVP) is co-created through prototyping with customers, users and partners, over a defined period and with a capped budget to work out all the details from resources, costs, and pricing, until the right *value proposition* and **Business Model** that works are discovered.

 **Pilot Testing**

The *value proposition* and **Business Model** (with at least a completed or finished MVP) is live tested through a soft launch with a smaller market (e.g. a single location) that initial research has deemed to provide a good sample for potential results. Learnings from this test are used to adjust, fix, and fine tune the solution, before a bigger launch.

 **Co-created Innovation**

While serving an existing customer or user journey, the business learns, during the process of producing and capturing value, what changes customers and users need, want, and are willing to pay for, and adapts and transforms its business activities according including adding new features and services that can influence how customers think, act, and behave. The aim is to deliver a value-added customer or user experience that keeps the customer or user wanting more.

*Increasing customer and/or user involvement, interaction and costs*

118

# What problems and experiences …

A business would cease to exist if it had no customers. Its purpose, as defined by its *mission* and *vision*, is to capture, produce, and deliver many different forms of value (p. 71-72) to different types of customers both external to the business (p. 121) as well as internal customers - the organization's stakeholders (p. 122).

What customers value most are the outcomes and experiences in the solutions provided by a business and its *value propositions*. This is what constitutes *Customer Value* (p. 68) and solves their problems and meets, or even exceeds, their expectations. It is these outcomes and experiences contained within an organization's end-to-end service solutions that entice customers to make an exchange in value through transactions that may include payment (p. 97). The objective of sales and marketing efforts is to convince customers to make this exchange with an enticing *value proposition* that is accompanied by a matching **Business Model**.

In order to determine WHAT solutions will have the outcomes and experiences that customers desire, it is necessary to study customers by collecting as much data about how they think, act, and behave as possible, especially along their journeys to pin point what is the context and root cause of their problems, that is their **'customer problem'.**

Examples of a customer problem include:

- *Buying a house*
- *Going on holiday*
- *Saving for retirement*
- *Improving fitness and health*

The **'customer journey'** is the sequence of events and activities that the customer goes through on their own journey to solve a problem and achieve a certain outcome – their end *goal*.

The journey to reach the customer's end goal is characterized by different challenges and obstacles with varying degrees of importance and urgency along the way. These cause a set of concerns that need to be addressed in order for the customer to feel satisfied that their end-goal is achieved. The *value proposition* and the service that delivers it must be able to provide a

# ... do customers have and want

solution that resolves all of these concerns, with many experiences that meet the customer's expectations. This is what makes the customer satisfied with the valued outcomes that have been delivered and received along their journey to solve their problem.

The **'Customer Experience'** (CX) is how the customer feels about a business and its brand, when they are interacting with it via its *value propositions* (products and services).

It is when expectations are met, and even exceeded, that the customer begins to feel a pull to repeat certain behaviors in order to gain the same or similar experiences and even look forward to new experiences from the same solution provider.

This is how a business creates **'stickiness effects'** with the customer over time, in the short, medium, and long-term.

Increase customer stickiness over time creates 'brand loyalty' which is what encourages the customer to make more and more future purchases. This is how a business maximizes **'Customer Lifetime Value' (CLV)** - the predicted total net profit to be gain from the future relationship with a customer.

**STRATEGY JOURNEY** *Framework* **Activity #6:**

List and review your existing and/or proposed *value propositions* (products and services) to identify the little customer pain points resolved and the main or big customer problem that the business is involved in solving – what is the end goal of the customer.

# What customers and stakeholders ...

Every business co-creates with and serves many different types of customers through the different forms of value that it seeks to capture, produce and deliver (p. 67,68,71,72).

We have summarized the different types of customers who interact with and in a business into the following categories of external customers and internal customers or stakeholders.

## Three 'External Customer' types who interact with a business:

**Buyers**

'**Buyers**' are the individuals, or businesses (both *for-profit* and *not-for-profit* organizations) who buy or pay for *value propositions*. They make the decision to exchange payment for the value provided by the *value proposition*, that creates the buyer-seller transaction (p. 129). In a *business-to-business (B2B)* transaction, there may be many individuals involved in the buying process, including the ultimate decision maker that approves the payment, while there are other influencers who are involved in the buying process, including users.

Buyers may, but do not necessarily have to be the consumers or users of the *value proposition*. When an individual is both the buyer and consumer, there are two experiential journeys: the customer or buyer journey and the user journey that interconnects to inform the individuals total or combined experience.

**Users**

'**Users**' are the individuals who consume and use the *value proposition*. A user may be the buyer, or they are just an influencer of the buying decision by another individual because they will experience the solution provided.

When the user is not the buyer, and does not know the payment value or price of the *value proposition*, the user experience through the user journey, becomes the means by which a business can create a relationship and any *stickiness effect* that will lead to repeat use and exchanges of value. User expectations also differ from customer expectations as the way that a user perceives what constitutes value, including any sense of entitlement will be different to that of a paying customer. Examples include: children who consume and use products and services paid for by their parents, citizens who consume public services paid for by the government or indirectly through paying taxes, and sales staff who use different tools or software applications to support their sales relationships with customers. The apps are purchased or licensed by the CTO or other technology stakeholder.

**Partners**

'**Partners**' are other organizations that influencer and support a business, in how it runs itself and transforms, to produce and deliver *value propositions* for different customers and stakeholders.

There are many ways for a business to interact with its partners that are either bound by a legal agreement, a government regulation, or less formally where there is no agreement. Partners can come in many forms and are often named by their role or the function that they perform in the chain of business activities. These activities are part of the *value chain* (p. 153-156) that are required to produce and deliver the *value proposition*. Partners can be 'suppliers' of equipment, 'vendors' of complementary or supporting services, or 'governors' who provide clarity on rules of engagement including: manufacturers, distributors, agents, resellers, consultants, regulators, governing bodies, information and content providers. They should all form a part of a co-creation relationship (p. 117).

# ... work with and in businesses

## Five 'Stakeholder' or 'Business Role' categories who support a business:

**'Stakeholders'** are individuals who play a role in supporting the organization of a business in how it functions to capture, produce, or deliver value.

### C-Suite, Senior Executives & Board of Directors

These stakeholders are responsible for making decisions about the strategy of the entire business, its brand, and how and where it should grow from new or existing value propositions. Board directors and senior management review the competitive landscape and the problems faced by the business, and define the scope with which the organization will undertake its business transformation activities over a period of time, in order to achieve the specific targeted valued-added outcomes. They set the targets and the *mission* of the business.

### Business Management

Business managers are responsible for making decisions in relation to specific *value propositions* and how the business will operate to deliver value to customers, while increasing the revenue and profit from the value proposition, e.g. service owners and product managers. They define and manage the **Business Model** to deliver the customer and user journeys, while meeting targets set by senior executives as well as receiving support from other roles in change management, engineering & technology, and sales & operations.

### Change Management

Change management stakeholders are responsible for process design, architecture, as well as managing and delivering *business transformation* (p. 81), to support the business to change from its current state of operating to its target state **Operating Model**. They manage the governance process for the organization using a strategic transformation plan and roadmap to enable changes to be orchestrated and executed with a good level of *business agility*. This supports speed to market, while ensuring the changes and outcomes from transformation activities are aligned to strategy set by senior executives, and the **Business Model** as defined by Business Management.

### Engineering & Technology

Led by engineering and supported by technology including various tools, it is where the *value propositions*, that is, the products and services are physically designed, built, produced and even delivered especially for digital products and services, in different locations, to appropriate target customer segments (p. 127). They also deliver technology or IT services to other parts of the organization, including management of physical infrastructure including assets (p. 149-150) required to produce and deliver the *value propositions*.

### Sales, Operations & Servicing

Where the value is delivered to customers and to the organization in the form of output and outcomes. These roles are the doers who put the strategies and innovations from the organization, supported by technology where possible into action via their interactions with customers and users. They are also responsible for the physical transactions that serve the balance sheet, where the 'profit' or 'loss' is made, through sales and for managing the customer relationship over the long-term to deliver the organization's financial growth targets such as CLV (p. 119).

# What motivates and drives customers ...

In our fast changing digital economy, an organization's ability to transform and differentiate itself, is increasingly dependent on the level of customer and stakeholder (p. 121-122) participation and contribution to *continuous transformation* and *co-creation* activities (p. 117-118). Measuring and influencing *mindsets* can help a business to increase and improve engagement, which will impact the performance of its *service innovations* in the **Innovation of Adoption Lifecycle** by customers, as well as staff performance in the organization across all innovation, transformation and business-as-usual activities.

## The Make-Up Of A Person's Mindset

A **'mindset'** is a set of beliefs, assumptions, methods, and ideas held by an individual, that drive how they think, act and behave.

The *mindset* of a person, that is, WHAT drives their visible behaviors, is comprised of two more invisible inner layers: Core Values and Thinking Patterns.

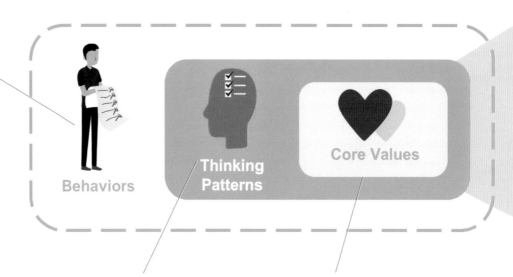

The visible and measurable choices and actions taken by an individual in the activities and tasks that they perform (in both work and life)

**Behaviors**

**Thinking Patterns**

**Core Values**

The beliefs and thoughts that shape an individual's habits, and hence influence behavioral choices. An individual will vary in their 'mindset style' with relative tendencies across Four Thinking Patterns*, as an Analyzer, Explorer, Stabilizer and Relator. Their mindset style is influenced by prior experiences which can set certain expectations.

An individual's personal values that form his or her inner beliefs and thoughts. Values rarely change. They can be described using Aristotle's Four Pillars of a Good Life (p. 47-48).

# ... into action

Understanding the deep seated drivers beneath the *mindsets* of customers and stakeholders, is how a business can better manage the complex interplay of people and tasks, and get the best out of its customers and staff, in the digital ecosystem through data-driven *service innovation* design. With insights into the *mindsets* of the people in and surrounding the organization, and what roles they are meant to play, an enterprise will have the intel by which to act where needed and motivate the behaviors that will enable its activities and its service innovations to succeed. It can encourage people's choices in how they think, act and behave in their roles and jobs … especially disruptive thinking that supports innovation where appropriate, that leads to exceptional performance levels.

## Four Thinking Patterns* that shape behaviors to define our 'mindset style'

| | | |
|---|---|---|
| **Analyzer** |  | The **"Analyzer"** is described as someone who is logical, factual and data driven when processing information so that he/she can make rational and reasoning decisions. **They ask the question: what's the evidence supporting this issue?** |
| **Explorer** |  | The **"Explorer"** is described as someone who is open minded and has a "big picture" view when he/she reflects on the information. He/she will explore all possibilities and can be creative when coming up with solutions. **They ask the question: How can we challenge the status quo?** |
| **Stabilizer** |  | The **S tabilie r"** is described as someone who can organize complex facts and information so that he/she can plan actions in a structured, systematic and controlled manner. **They ask the question: How can we make this happen?** |
| **Relator** |  | The **R elator"** is described as someone who puts emphasis in recognizing the emotions and feelings of other people so that he/she can connect with them when making decisions or taking actions. **They ask the question: How do we involve all members of the team, to get the best outcomes?** |

*Adapted from the iceberg theory (sometimes known as the "theory of omission") and the whole brain thinking from Herrmann Brain Dominance Instrument® (HBDI®) to aligned with data-driven techniques applied through **THE STRATEG JOURNEY** Framework*

# Modeling customers to service ...

Modeling the customer is all about understanding who they are and what problems they have, in order to predict what they might do through data. The objective of **'Customer Modeling'** is to narrow down the data and information that describes exactly how a target segment of customers will think, act, and behave, so that a matching service offering – comprised of the *value proposition* and **Business Model** – with the highest likelihood of mass customer adoption (p. 89), can be designed and implemented by an enterprise.

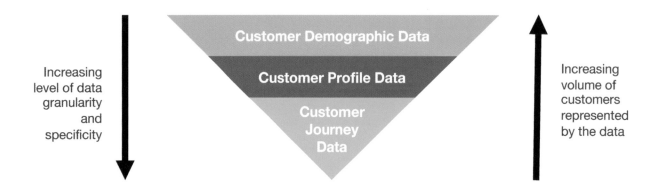

The process of **'Customer Modeling'** involves the study of three levels of detail from the data associated with a customer in order to drill down to more granular or specific data and information about the target customer segment to get to the heart of their problems.

**'Customer Segmentation'** is the exercise to group customers based on common attributes in order to target them with sales and marketing tactics to facilitate adoption of a *value proposition*. It explores two types of customer data: *Customer Demographic Data* and *Customer Profile Data*, to identify a target customer segment and its behavioral economics. This is where the general behaviors of target customers that define their **'customer persona'** are gathered into a *customer avatar* through profiling (p. 127). The data and information about the *customer persona*, documented in a **'customer avatar'** is used mostly by organizations to support sales and marketing efforts, including the pricing strategies (p. 139) that form part of the **Business Model**.

**Customer Modeling** extends the *customer segmentation* process into the specifics of how customers think, act, and behave in relation to the problems they face in their day-to-day lives, by capturing *Customer Journey Data* to support the design of solutions, outcomes, and experiences that form a target customer service.

# ... their customer journeys

**Customer Demographic Data** has the lowest level of specificity to the customer, but it is representative of the greatest volume of customers. Demographic data is quantitative and relates to a customer's overall circumstances in life (e.g. age, social grouping, financial worth and spending patterns). It allows customers to be segmented into larger groups, where a **Business Model** can be established. When used alone, this data is most suited to the design of social and public sector or government services, as well as utility-based services where the goal is to provide fair and equal *value propositions* to large groups of many customers or citizens.

*Analysis applied to demographic data can be used to establish a viable Business Model. It is also used to establish the transaction model for the value proposition (p. 129)*

**Customer Profile Data** makes up the customer persona. There is a mix of quantitative and qualitative data that describes the general behaviors of a particular customer segment (e.g. shopping, investment, holiday preferences/ habits). This data can be used to identify how to co-create *value propositions* with a customer segment, and is most useful for developing marketing and sales strategies to entice customers into a purchase and repeat purchases.

*Analysis of profile related data is useful for marketing purposes in order to target specific value propositions.*

**Customer Journey Data** describes the thoughts, emotions, and actions of the customer as they undertake their journey to achieve their end goal, that is, the customer experience of using different *value propositions* or services if hey exist o solve their big problem. The data is more granular as it is behavioral but also experiential, that is, ***thick\**** in nature and specific to a customer problem.

*The qualitative nature of experiential data is used to define the value generated to the customer.*

As the data delves into the customer problem, it can be analyzed to identify the outcomes and experiences that customers want within their solutions along their customer journeys (p. 119) that would also meet their expectations – in the Service Design process (p.116).

*\* **Thick data** is comprised of qualitative informative materials, tools or techniques that help organizations gather granular, specific knowledge about their target audience – defined by Brandwatch in 2014*

Today, a lot of *Customer Journey Data* can be found on online platforms especially within marketplaces and on social media networks, where customers give away their data freely when they share or engage in different activities as part of their regular transactions and in their daily lives through posts, reviews, tweets, and likes. Learn more about the different types of networks on p. 133.

# Deriving customer segments ...

The probability of innovating a winning *value proposition* starts with identifying the *target customer segment*, where a viable **Business Model** can be established because there is the potential to recoup the cost of *innovation* and to grow the business through profit growth (p. 141) and asset growth (p. 149).

**Business Model** viability of the target customer should be validated alongside the developing of the *customer avatar*, where the details of the *customer persona* are identified while profiling the customer, to understand how to market and sell to them (p. 127).

### Validate Business Model viability

This involves analyzing *Customer Demographic Data* to isolate the most attractive *target customer segment* by:

- **Market Size** - volume of customers
- **Wallet Size** - customer spending power
- **Market Reach** - are there any location-specific restrictions?
- **Transaction Model** - the transaction types accessible to customers

### Derive the Customer Persona

This involves creating a *customer avatar* that profiles customers' lifestyles, by capturing the profiling details that form their *customer persona, that is:*

- **WHO** they are
- **WHAT** they do in their free time
- **HOW** they feel or behave in their free time
- **WITH WHOM** do they associate or engage
- **WHERE** they tend to spend their free time
- **WHEN** is that free time

**STRATEGY JOURNEY** *Framework* **TIP #7:**

Analyze the viability of your current and proposed Business Models based on the market size, wallet size, market reach and transaction model, using the guidance on pages 129-132.

# ... and their customer personas

## Six Attributes to derive the Customer Persona

These six attributes or common characteristics that describe a *customer persona* should be considered when creating a *customer avatar*:

 **WHO** — Who is the customer/user based on their personal information such as age group, sex, social economic background, income and wealth profile, religion and/or ethnic background, etc. This is based on *Customer Demographic Data.*

 **WHAT** — What are the journeys that the customer/user has today or what are they planning for. This can be the role, job, or activity they are trying to accomplish, or a problem they want to solve in their family, society, employment.

 **HOW** — How does the customer/user generally feel and thus behave, and how might it be relevant to your business or products/services to be involved in their situation.

 **WITH WHOM** — With whom does the customer/user interact with generally or based on their social groups? Who are the other contacts that can connect you with this customer/user?

 **WHERE** — Where is the customer/user mostly located or domicile – country, city, or town? Where do they like to hangout physically or online? Where else do they go in their free time or as part of their personal and social life, or where you might be able to get a hold of them?

 **WHEN** — When is the best time to contact or interact with the customer/user based on the other five attributes - WHO, WHAT, HOW, WITH WHO, and WHERE and WHEN a positive result or attention can be gained from the interaction.

---

**STRATEGY JOURNEY *Framework* Activity #7:**

Building relationships with your external customers and users as well as internal stakeholders comes from understanding how they think, act and behave. Support your business design and stakeholder management efforts by developing a customer avatar with the 6 customer persona attributes, for the main customer or user identified in your proposed Business Model or your most important and challenging stakeholders whom you need to get buy-in, to support your role and your projects in the enterprise.

*Go to www.strategyjourney.com/tools to download the template and watch the tutorial.*

# Transaction Model

The **'Transaction Model'** outlines how value is passed or exchanged between the different parties in the **Business Model**, including the service provider, the paying customers or buyers, and end users or partners. It is important to determine how many transaction sides are in a **Digital Business Model** (p. 111), as buyers and users may have different expectations of the outcomes and experiences provided by the *value proposition*.

Deciding on the *transaction model* is a key step in validating the viability of a **Business Model**, as it determines which parties need further analysis and what data needs to be collected to conduct customer modeling and service design (p. 129).

We have outlined some typical *transaction models* for you to consider:

## Business to Consumer (B2C)

The provider sells directly to the consumer who is the end user and also the paying customer. The transaction can take place via a physical or an online shop, or Mail Order Distributors may also be involved to deliver products to the customer.

**Examples:** Coca-Cola, Louis Vuitton, Nike, Boden, McDonalds, Ford, HSBC Retail Bank, Dell, British Airways

## Business to Business (B2B)

The provider sells directly to another business. Stakeholders in the customer business that can influence the buying decision include: End Users, Champions, Procurement or Administrators and the Decision Maker.

**Examples:** PwC, Deloitte, IBM, Atlassian, Salesforce, Amazon Web Services (AWS), Goldman Sacs Investment Bank, Regus Office Spaces

## Business to Business to Consumer (B2B2C)

This transaction model comes in many forms. Two examples include:

Platform or marketplaces – the provider acts as a marketplace providing the platform, both physical or online, for other businesses to trade directly with consumers. They also collect a fee for usage of the marketplace, either as a commission from the transaction or in the form of rental fees for physical space, platform users fees or advertising fees from the seller, or combinations of all four.
Examples include: Westfields, JCdecaux, Facebook, Google, Netflix, PayPal, Amazon Store, Tripadvisor, Groupon, Uber, Spotify, Crowdcube

Reseller model – the provider may buy from another business and then sell a product offering directly to the consumer with an added margin or act as a sales affiliate or broker assisting with the sales or marketing effort and taking a commission fee from the transaction.

Examples: Macy's, John Lewis, Wholefoods Supermarkets, Toys R Us, Home Depot, Best Buy, Staples, Argos, AO.com, Jones Lang Lasalle

## Peer to Peer (P2P)

Also known as Consumer to Consumer (C2C), but is in fact Consumer to Business to Consumer (C2B2C), the provider is a platform that handles the transactions between two different sets of consumers on each side, taking a fee from the transaction as well as advertising or platform usage fees from the seller.

Examples: eBay, Zopa, Twitter, Airbnb, Linkedin, Craigslist, Kickstarter

# Market Reach

'**Market reach**' describes the factors that affect a business's ability to reach customers or the accessibility of its services to customers, which can impact revenues as well as costs in a **Business Model** in today's global digital economy.

The location or jurisdiction of where customers are located can affect your business's ability to interact with and sell to your target customers, especially if the plan is to operate globally. Businesses wanting to operate globally, including virtually, must consider local or country specific government regulations covering:

- Processes to be performed locally with local staff under local employment laws and with local KPIs;
- Data privacy, information management and reporting;
- Local taxes such as VAT in Europe and GST in Australia, Singapore, etc...

There are regulations in almost every country including the USA, UK, Singapore, Malaysia, Russia, Brazil, Turkey...

Even when businesses are operating in one country or jurisdiction, there is still the matter of infrastructure.

Not all countries have high speed internet, or banking and payment facilities. In many African Countries, India, Indonesia, the majority of the population do not have bank accounts – also known as 'Unbanked' customers – making cash the main form of payment even with recent advances in mobile technologies.

Whether a business is operating in one country or several, customer relationships and culture must also be considered. These are also influenced by specific 'networks' including industry or other networks which will have their own communities and culture (p. 133). In understanding costs, it is important to factor in:

- **Language and cultural differences:**
  A business will need to consider where to locate call centers requiring staff who can communicate with specific customers.

- **Operating hours:**
  Significant time-zone differences also affect the location of staff.

- **Customer experiences and expectations:**
  In some cultures, face-to-face meetings may be required before the customer is prepared to make a purchase, or people prefer to touch and feel their products to enjoy the shopping experience.

*Market reach factors are based on the nature of the Transaction Model, but equally market reach factors may influence the transaction model and what parties as well as how parties will behave around it.*

# Wallet Size

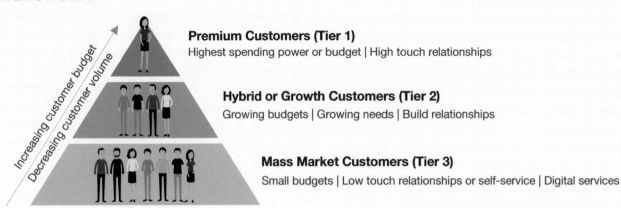

**Premium Customers (Tier 1)**
Highest spending power or budget | High touch relationships

**Hybrid or Growth Customers (Tier 2)**
Growing budgets | Growing needs | Build relationships

**Mass Market Customers (Tier 3)**
Small budgets | Low touch relationships or self-service | Digital services

*Increasing customer budget*
*Decreasing customer volume*

It is impossible to neglect the size of the customer budget when it comes to validating who the paying customers are in order to choose who to target. If your customers are consumers, then they must be able to afford your service offering(s) and where they are located, or the *market reach* affects the size of their wallets. It is the same for business customers who will have budgets driven by factors such the size of the organization by market capitalization, number of employees, and revenue or profit figures.

**'Customer Tiering'** is the technique of selling essentially the same product offering(s), with some variation in features, at different prices to different customer segments.

Both consumers and business customers typically belong to three different tiers based on their **'wallet size'** or spending power in a pyramid like structure. The number of potential customers in each tier is usually inversely proportionate to the size of their wallets, with the fewest premium customers having the latest budgets at the top of the pyramid, while the mass market at the bottom has the smallest budgets.

Premium customers tend to spend the most and have many needs and wants requiring a more high touch relationship. In the financial services and banking industry, on the B2C side, these are ultra-high-network individuals that a Wealth Management Bank like Coutts Bank would service. On the B2B side, in an Investment Bank like Goldman Sacs, the premium customers are those top global corporate businesses like General Electric, Proctor and Gamble or Huawei.

Mass market customers do have spending ability and while their wallets are relatively small, there are lots of them so they should not be overlooked. The goal in servicing mass market customers is to offer replicable and cheaper offerings that are low touch or even self-service using digital platforms where possible. Ryanair and other budget airlines provide great examples of **Business Models** who have successfully profited from mass market customers. Airbnb also offer a service now to smaller companies and entrepreneurs on a budget, while travelling for business.

In the middle, there is a hybrid tier of customers who have a growing interest in high-touch offerings, and who have growing budgets. It is often worth building a relationship with these customers as they grow or to help them with growth before they move into premium.

A business model should look to service just one tier. Of course a business can also serve multiple tiers of customers with multiple business models.

# Market Size

No business has or will ever have the whole market. Despite being the most widespread search engine in the world, Google has not been able to penetrate markets like South Korea, Russia and China for reasons including language differences, search preferences, and regulations such as in China.

There will always be competitors who offer an alternative, and customers who may opt-in to that alternative. Sometimes, alternatives may not even come from your direct competitors. For example, Facebook is not the most obvious competitor to major cigarette companies, but it is nevertheless a serious competitor, as potential customers can choose to substitute their spare time smoking cigarettes with surfing on Facebook, and getting addicted to it.

**'Market size'** is the potential number of customers that your business may be able to capture and retain as paying customers for your product offering(s).

While it may be useful to show the future vision of a **Business Model** as having the potential to capture more customers than is realistically possible especially to investors, narrowing the market size of your business to include those good paying customers only enables an objective estimate of potential revenue and costs that is achievable rather than unbelievable.

The key criteria or filters to pin down your Business Model's true market size have already been covered in the first three attributes of the Target Market Validator canvas: *Transaction Model, Market Reach, and Wallet Size.*

In the digital economy the influencing power of networks and their 'network effects' also changes the dynamic of how many potential customers can be reached by network and their budgets too, especially as new digital currencies, be it coins or tokens, begin to emerge to support new exchanges between customers in new digital marketplaces.

# Leveraging networks to expand ...

Advances in digital technology have significantly increased the impact of leveraging networks as a business competes in the digital economy to deliver value to different customers. All of today's digitally supported networks are multi-sided with the ability to operate as marketplaces (p. 111) that can provide businesses with the means to interact and transact through different *transaction models* (p. 129) with two or more types of customers (p. 121-122). This multiplying effect of being able to increase engagement, interactions, transactions, and overall connectivity with different customers on a digital multi-sided platform, at an equivalent or potentially lower running cost due to the accompanying operational efficiency gains, is known as a **'network effect'**.

In the digital economy, successful businesses use the right digitally-supported networks as part of their innovation lifecycle to grow and develop strong and long-lasting 'sticky' relationships with customers along their customer and user journeys (p. 119). The associated multiplying *network effects* enables the business to maximize the value that can be generated from their **Digital Business Models** (p. 111).

## Different Networks to use along the customer journey

There are closed networks that can be licensed as a service by different business customers and consumers for a subscription fee, as well as open networks that are free to use and are supported by a sharing economy of its own.

**Examples:**
Platform – iOS
Physical – power grid
Financial – Stock Exchanges
Transport – Air Traffic Control
Monetary - currency

**Closed
Networks**

**Open
Networks**

**Examples:**
Marketplace - eBay
Physical – telephones
Platform - Windows OS
Protocol – Ethernet
Personal – Facebook
Belief – religion

Closed networks tend to provide service solutions that are more mature along the Innovation Adoption Lifecycle (p. 99) to justify the payment of a subscription fee. While open networks tend to provide access to new *innovations* (p. 109) that are at the prototyping stage of development that require more testing through different customer co-creation techniques (p. 117).

# ... the customer relationship

### Business Function Networks
Many businesses have turned their function-based services from internet telephony, project and task management, search and research, data and content, office space, online shopping, payments and transactions, price comparison, parcel delivery, auctions, hotel booking, credit checking, video conferencing, marketing, taxis, coding, web development, virtual assistance, home automation, and many more ... into networks, that have expanded into fully fledged marketplaces. There are both open and closed function based networks with many businesses offering both via tiered pricing.

Examples:
Google, Slack, Skype, Experian, Green Bloomberg, Ebay, Tripadvisor, Amazon, Wordpress, Github, WeWork, Alexa, World Vision, Uber, FedEx, DPD, AirBnB, Coinbase

### Industry Networks
Almost all industries have formed networks (i.e. industry & trade associations) to support the different businesses as well as consumers in their ecosystem to communicate, share and trade with each other. These networks provide services to their members, usually for a fee that is charged annually and/or per transaction, and are thus non-profit businesses themselves, as well as being marketplaces. There are also Non-Government Organizations (NGOs) whose services provide: rules of engagement, transactional or payment facilities for their own marketplaces, real estate or office space, research facilities, networking events, content or data—and even their own cryptocurrency.

Examples:
PMI, IIBA), IET, Law Society, WES, CGE, WWF, Greenpeace, UNESCO, IMF, FIA, SBA, IOD, ACCA, CMI, The Lancet

### Government & Regulated Networks
Governments of different countries maintain many networks to run their social services for their citizens, and maintain security. All governments use currency networks to control the amount of currency in circulation to manage its value as well as support their economies. Government networks exist in healthcare, transport, social security, police ... and today many governments are promoting SMART CITY initiatives. Most government operated networks are closed, and controlled by rules or regulations. Governments also partner with some industries such as rail, healthcare, financial services ... to offer social services at a reduced cost to public funding, while some services have become fully privatized.

Examples:
Currency & Stock Exchanges,
National Health Service (NHS)
Universal Credit
Air Traffic Control
Crime & Forensics
Rail Networks

### Social Networks
Connectivity is one of the four pillars that drive customer behaviors (p. 48), so most people have a tribal impulse to build connections with others and form or join different communities based on a shared interest, religious, or personal connection. This impulse is what makes some networks very sticky. Many traditional social networks, such as church groups, local communities in small towns, choirs, schools, gaming, exercise, business networking, family and friends, and other common interests or hobbies have spread online via social media platforms, many with additional 'groups' functionality to service interest groups, and especially with the aid of instant messaging.

Examples:
WhatsApp, Slack, WeChat, Facebook, Twitter, Snapchat, Linked In, World of Warcraft, Pokemon Go

Different networks are offered by businesses, governments, industry groups and communities with common goals and objectives and/or to support specific business functions. All of these networks can operate in an open or closed ecosystem as well as acting as marketplaces to allow different groups of customers to interact and transact, directly or indirectly, to deepen their relationships.

# Building customer relationships ...

The rapid growth of open digital networks (p. 133), since the internet became available, has changed how businesses interact with their customers as well as how customers behave and their expectations (p. 21-22) of *value propositions*. Customers are taking control of their own buying and user journeys (p. 119), and are increasingly co-creating with businesses in order to get exactly what they want (p. 117).

This increasing trend towards *co-created innovation* (p. 118) with customers and users means that businesses are having to 'unbundle' their *value propositions*, and provide an expanded 'ecosystem' of *value propositions* that are packaged to match the expectations of customers and users based on the nature or stage of the relationship. *Co-created innovation* is part of their **Digital Business Models**.

We propose five **'proposition categories'** to group the packages or standalone products and services that match how customers want to consume value along the stages of the customer journey and as their relationship with the business develops over time:

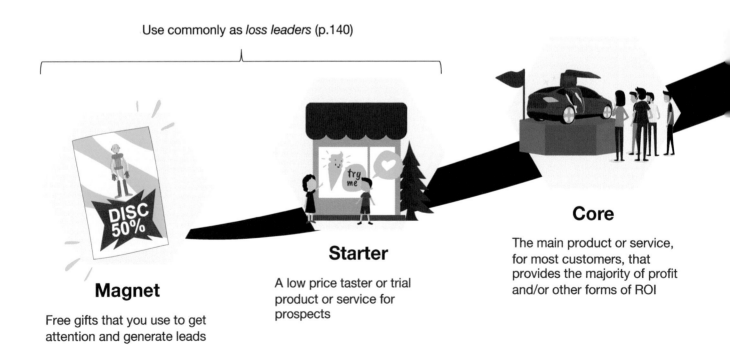

Use commonly as *loss leaders* (p.140)

**Core**

The main product or service, for most customers, that provides the majority of profit and/or other forms of ROI

**Starter**

A low price taster or trial product or service for prospects

**Magnet**

Free gifts that you use to get attention and generate leads

# ... with a proposition ecosystem

*Marketing and sales professionals often refer to this process of engaging customers and increasing the relationship along the proposition ecosystem, as a funnel or ladder. This is why it is often referred to as the 'Sales and Marketing Funnel' or 'Product Ladder'.*

## Bespoke

Highly bespoke or special one-off services that are exclusive to the the customer, with high ROI, good will and brand recognition

## Premium

Premium level product or service that exists as an add-on to the core proposition and likely to have higher margins

In a *customer co-created* (p. 117-118) modus-operandi, value is exchanged through multiple transactions along the customer journey, and the relationship between a business and a customer is built over time through these exchanges.

Whenever a product or service in the proposition ecosystem is able to meet and exceed customer expectations, it can create and increase the 'stickiness effect' with the customer to encourage them to engage, interact, and transact more with the business, to want more premium and bespoke services as trust is built. Of course, there will be customers who skip straight into 'bespoke' propositions, or who are only interested in specific 'premium' add-ons, without first trying out 'magnet' and 'starter' propositions or acquiring and experiencing 'core' propositions.

**STRATEGY JOURNEY *Framework* Activity #8:**

Develop through brainstorming the proposition ecosystem surrounding the main product/service, the core offering in your Business Model. Are there additional loss leaders as well as premium services that could be offered by the business. Highlight the 'Networks' (p. 133-134) along each stage that you could use to go to market.

# EXAMPLE: Tony Robbins's proposition ecosystem

The rise of eLearning and improved UX provided through SMAC technologies has spurred the Coaching industry to become the 2$^{nd}$ fastest growing industry in the world in 2019*, with business coaching revenue increasing to US$15 billion. It has enabled experts across almost any industry to increase their reach, income streams, as well as personal branding, through the offering of eLearning-based proposition ecosystems with a blend of personalization, to aspiring professionals and entrepreneurs.

*In this case study example, we highlight the extent of Tony Robbins's life-coaching business with his complete proposition ecosystem. See how the Business Model has evolved beyond leadership and motivation retreats for high-flyers with big budgets to a self-development empire with a portfolio of over 30 businesses including digital services worth a reported $5 billion in annual revenue as of 2016. Robbins's **Business Model**, and this 'Proposition Ecosystem' have been copied by celebrity actors, musicians, chefs, entrepreneurs and the new wave of Online Marketing Experts, Vlogger millionaires, and more … including MOOCs providers like Udacity, with different networks leveraged based on where best to connect with customers and users.*

| | **Magnet** | **Starter** |
|---|---|---|
| **Proposition Bundles** | Online Assessments & Quizzes (or 'Free Tools') starting with a 'Solution Finder' quiz<br><br>Blogs & Newsletter<br><br>Podcasts<br><br>Videos (incl. Netflix Trailer)<br><br>Breakthrough by Tony Robbins app - free access to introductory lessons from various Training Courses | Books<br>15 million volumes sold globally<br><br>Merchandise (branded with Tony Robbin Quotes)<br><br>Supplements (Energy & Health)<br><br>Introductory Free 30-min Coaching Session<br><br>Netflix Documentary |
| **Networks** | Facebook Ads<br><br>YouTube Channel + Ads<br><br>TED Talk & Netflix<br><br>IOS/Android app marketplaces | Shopify Store<br><br>Netflix Marketplace<br><br>Tony Robbins Network of Certified Trained Coaches |

**Customer Relationship is new and immature**

*Illustrative example reverse engineered by Stratability Academy*

| Core | Premium | Bespoke |
|------|---------|---------|
| Online Training Courses incl.<br>- Journals, Workbooks…<br>- Audio & Video via CD, Mobile app<br><br>Live Speaking Events<br>- Business Growth<br>- Personal Development<br><br>Training & Certifications for Tony Robbins Coaches<br>- Life Coaching<br>- Business Coaching | Private Events & Retreats (called 'Mastery University)<br>- Life Coaching<br>- Mind & Body<br>- Wealth Management<br><br>Business/Corporate Training Workshops & Programs (called Business Results Training) | Private Coaching (1:1)<br>- Life Coaching<br>- Business Coaching<br><br>Private Membership Program (called 'Platinum Partnership')<br>- Subscription gives time-limited access to different services across Tony Robbins Proposition Ecosystem |
| Shopify Store<br><br>IOS/Android app marketplaces<br>- Breakthrough by Tony Robbins app<br><br>Various Affiliated Conference Venues, Hotel & Travel, and Distribution Networks | Various Affiliated Conference Venues, Hotel & Travel, and Distribution Networks (incl. other businesses owned by Tony Robbins)<br><br>Tony Robbins Network of Certified Trained Coaches | Various Affiliated Conference Venues, Hotel & Travel, and Distribution Networks (incl. other businesses owned by Tony Robbins)<br><br>Tony Robbins Network of Certified Trained Coaches |

**Customer Relationship strengthens and matures**

# Proposition Ecosystem Pricing Strategies

**'Pricing'** is a strategic lever that determines a business's ability to make profit as well as other forms of Return On Investment (ROI). Pricing also determines if the business will suffer losses that could put it into administration which could lead to closure when the cost to run the business exceeds the income that it generates from customers.

A business can use various *pricing methods* to help it grow sustainably over time, or breakeven within a limited pre-determined budget. Start-ups need to use pricing tactics to close their first sales and reach their breakeven points when their total income has exceeded their total costs, including all of their start-up build costs, and then they can begin to turn a profit.

All businesses, and especially digital businesses, use combinations of the following three **'pricing methods'** to tactically and strategically price a *value proposition*, which can be applied to any of the *proposition bundles* in their 'Proposition Ecosystem' canvas:

---

## List price per unit

*Example bundle:
an iPhone or iWatch
will have official list
prices from the
Apple Store, but are
often sold by other
providers who may
bundle other
services such as
telephone & data
plans, health
insurance, leasing &
trade finance
contracts... with
different list prices,
margins and
discounts.*

When a business decides to offer a *proposition bundle* to the customer, then it can charged a **'list price per unit'**, which is formulated by adding up the *unit cost* of each of the unbundled product and services, plus an additional *margin*, which allows the business to make a profit through a sale of each *proposition bundle unit*. All the unbundled products and services in a business's *Proposition Ecosystem* should have a **'unit cost'**, that is the total cost to produce and deliver the *value proposition* to the end customer or user.

When a business acts as an intermediary such as broker, reseller, affiliate or agent to help sell a value proposition, this service (a *value proposition* in itself) is called a **commission** or **brokerage**.

### Setting Margins
A business can determine what *margin* it can charge, based on the value-add that is offered to the customer, as well as what the customer is willing to pay for the value-add, depending on the customer's wallet size, the market size, the market reach or network such as an online marketplace or auction site (b-14), and the overall *demand and supply* of the *value proposition* including alternates, which may allow the customer to negotiate a *discount* on the *list price*. It is also common for a business to align its *margin* and hence pricing in order to achieve specific revenue and profit targets that it has set over a period of time.

### Discounting
Discounting is a useful sales tactic used by businesses in various circumstances, including:
- Closing a sale with the customer as well as promoting goodwill and a sense of loyalty
- Shifting units of the *value proposition (i.e.* stock or inventory) more quickly, especially when there are perishable resources including time involved that shouldn't sit idle and become wasted
- Enticing the customer to make a larger purchase comprised of a higher volume of one or several different proposition bundles, including upselling of additional add-on *value propositions*.

The *discount* offered is typically a percentage of the *margin* or a fixed reduction in the *margin*.

## Recurring Income

A business can also earn 'recurring income' from any of its existing value propositions, in the following ways:

**Membership Services:**
-where a recurring fee is charged for continuous access to a shared or common service that may include usage access to specific physical or digital assets.

*Examples: gym memberships, online membership for gaming, learning and education or music content. Members may be offered the chance to pay their membership monthly, quarterly or yearly, where a smaller denomination incurs a higher total fee.*

**Lending/Renting/Leasing:**
-where fees are charged to grant temporary but exclusive access to use a particular asset belonging to the business for a fixed period of time. For longer fixed terms, the total fee may be split into several payments.

*Examples: mortgages or loans of cash, physical assets such as real estate, cars, bikes, or virtual assets such as web hosting space, advertising space or telephony line rental, equipment including tractors or computers.*

**Licensing:**
-where fees are charged to grant the customer, which is typical another business or partner, with permission to use a value proposition which is protected (i.e.: Intellectual property), to produce and generate its own income sources from third party customers, including reselling the value proposition with or without additional value-add, through white-labeling or repackaging.

*Examples: reselling of software or software as a service (SaaS), hardware repackaging (e.g.: Intel processer chips), repackaging or white-labeling of patented processes, methodologies, processes and digital assets including games, learning and education or music content.*

***In the digital economy, a clear trend has emerged where businesses who have moved to set up recurring income streams appear to be the ones with the fastest and most sustainable growth.***

## Loss Leaders

A value proposition becomes a **'loss leader'** when it is given to the customer or user for free, or when the cost to produce and deliver it to the customer or user is greater than the income that it is able to generate.

While most businesses use 'magnet' and 'starter' propositions as *loss leaders*, any value proposition, in an unbundled or packaged form can be used as a *loss leader* to attract attention and build a relationship with the customer, especially with the use of a trial period, which is often called a **Freemium Business Model**.

*Examples: free e-Books, free whitepapers, free seminars, webinars, sessions, mini-courses, etc..., trial offers for a limited time of the main services, such as 30-day free trial of a specific SaaS software.*

# What supports the business ...

No business can weather the storm of declining or no profit (p. 97), which is required to sustain a company's existence and growth ambitions over the long-term. Most starts-up fail (p. 33, 37-38) from not being able to achieve a break-even point during the company's early years, when revenue generated from sales of its initial *value propositions* is greater than the costs required to fund resources as they operate business activities to serve and deliver value to customers.  As we highlighted through the big failures experienced by Blockbuster, Kodak, Sun Edison and Lego (p. 35-36), big corporations can fail too, especially when their costs are high and they are not able to achieve the necessary customer sales to support both their ongoing business-as-usual and *business transformation* activities.

There are many ways to acquire funding to pay for the resources required to support the business (p.145-148), but over the long-term ***profit growth***, a key value measure of any business (p. 67-72), is necessary to sustain a business when excess funds can be re-invested into a business, to support its transformation challenges including future growth (p. 144).

As a *business strategy*, the goal of the **Business Model** is to contribute to ***profit growth*** 'targets'.

A good **Business Model** will incorporate a **'Growth Plan'** that defines what a company can and should achieve in target sales, with an appropriate *pricing strategy* (p.139-140) based on the *proposition ecosystem* (p. 135), which has been tailored to the target customer. It will also account for the costs in *resources* that are required to serve the end-to-end customer relationship to achieve the *profit growth* over the projected period with the 'highest demand' as will as the costs of transformation (p.144).

# ... to achieve long-term value growth

## When potential profit growth can be maximized

'Profit' can be maximized by optimizing the time that different products and services from the *proposition ecosystem* (p. 135) spend in the 'Growth' and 'Maturity' stages of the Innovation Adoption Lifecycle when 'demand', and hence customer adoption realized through sales, is likely to be at its highest if costs remain fixed. This occurs before approaching the 'Decline' stage.

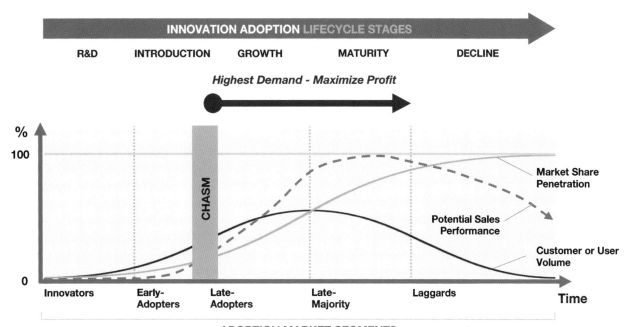

**INNOVATION ADOPTION** LIFECYCLE STAGES

| R&D | INTRODUCTION | GROWTH | MATURITY | DECLINE |

*Highest Demand - Maximize Profit*

% 
100

CHASM

Market Share Penetration

Potential Sales Performance

Customer or User Volume

0

| Innovators | Early-Adopters | Late-Adopters | Late-Majority | Laggards | Time |

**ADOPTION MARKET SEGMENTS**

**STRATEGY JOURNEY** *Framework* **Activity #9:**

Brainstorm the 'go to market' pricing method (p.139-140) that you will apply for your core offering in the proposition ecosystem. Research and estimate the effort, in time and costs to develop, produce and deliver your core offering and create a list of the key activities and costs using the guide on pages 143-144. Validate the timeframe when your Business Model becomes profitable. Does it align to a S.M.A.R.T. objective in the Mission Model? Adjust pricing and costs to derive a S.M.A.R.T. target objective.

# Costs To Run And Transform The Business

Strategy is nothing without execution. All the activities conducted by a business through its *capabilities* and the *resources* that support them, to execute the **Operating Model** and deliver a **Business Model** have a cost. To build a successful business that can sustainably deliver value to customers and stakeholders, it is important to understand what makes up this cost - that is the **'cost structure'** for *strategy execution*, to realize business outcomes.

## Types of costs in the business

All businesses will have ***running costs*** versus ***transformation costs*** with different characteristics.

### Running Costs

These are the costs to continuously execute the *capabilities* that support existing *value propositions* for stakeholders, and especially paying customers. They are needed to pay for *resources* that keep the business open, by conducting 'business as usual' activities, and may form a significant part of a company's **'working capital'** - its liquid funds in cash - to support everyday activities.

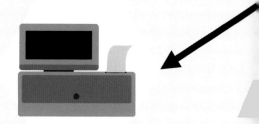

The cost to run everyday business activities is comprised of the following two cost types:

### Fixed Costs

These are costs that don't change over the short-term such as monthly or annually, and are required to run the business regardless of the volume of output or number of *value propositions* produced. Examples include rent, salaries for employees, utilities to support infrastructure both physical and virtual, property taxes on fixed assets, insurance, and maintenance costs including amortization on intangible assets and depreciation on tangible assets.

### Variable Costs

These are costs for goods sold so they vary based on the level of business activity required to produce the business's *value propositions* and change according to volume driven by supply and demand. Examples include direct cost for materials, commissions paid to partners along the value chain for outsourced *capabilities* and activities, and the labor costs to support additional production not covered by the capacity offered from fixed cost *resources*.

**Business Models** with high mandatory fixed costs are generally more challenging to start, and to run and maintain with the need to generate the necessary income or other funding to support operations. Thus, it can be difficult to justify and dedicate surplus funds towards *business transformation* activities.

## Transformation Costs (Change Costs)

These are the costs to transform the business and pay for the activities and *resources* that design the strategies and execute the changes in the **Operating Model** to create and enable the new or updated **Business Models** and *value propositions*. They cover brand new features, modifications, updates and improvements as well as the managing and governance of the *transformation journey* itself which is often underestimated. Start-up costs are a form of 'change costs'.

The costs to conduct *business transformation* and especially *digital transformation* can be astronomical or considered to be good value, depending on the size of the business and the approach taken by an organization through its **Transformation Model**. They can be split into three cost types:

### Strategy Design Costs

The whole point of a having new *business strategy* is to look at what needs changing in the business and to create a better future, in order to keep delivering value to stakeholders in accordance with the *mission*, *vision* and values of the business. So there is a cost for *resources* to design new and better strategies and solutions, comprised of fixed and variable staff or consultant costs for design, architecture, and engineering talent - supported by sales and operations - who are responsible for defining new activities, *capabilities*, *value streams,* and *value propositions*.

### Strategy Execution Costs

These are costs that are specifically dedicated to *business transformation* initiatives, projects and the change management resources, including the people who will carry out the change-specific business activities to implement the changes in the business's **Operating Model,** as well as any tools required to support *strategy execution*. The costs are calculated based on the scope of the problem being solved, and hence the time and *resources* required to support the implementation of the solutions that will transform the *capabilities* involved.

### Strategic Management Costs

These are costs to manage *business transformation* initiatives. It is the cost of *resources* to support the governance processes, including any people and tools that will enable the business to make the best strategic decisions on what strategies to implement, when, and how. This includes the tracking of transformation activities to ensure they deliver within specific timeframes and budgets. *Business transformation* activities can be complex and disruptive to 'business as usual' activities, requiring strong coordination via a plan and roadmap that is aligned to deliver a 'return on investment'.

It is important to provide a scope of potential *transformation costs* when designing a new **Business Model** or when making changes, as this enables an organization to determine what investments it needs to make to fund these changes to the **Operating Model** to deliver the **Business Model** strategies.

# Funding Strategy Execution & Growth

It takes money to make money and create value. This is the hard truth that hits every business owner, CEO and his or her *business design* team, whether the business is a small start-up, a big incumbent multinational corporate, non-profit charity or public sector organization. Nothing happens and businesses shut down, if there's no **funding** to pay for a business to run itself and transform.

A **Business Model** needs to be executed to grow value. Execution happens through **funding** the business to develop and deliver the *value propositions* to *customer segments* and *value is measured for* all stakeholders. Good execution allows value to grow in the business.

*Funding* provides 'working capital' and a certain amount of 'cashflow', that is liquid or easily accessible 'cash' to provide contingency for unforeseen costs, to get all the *value streams*, *capabilities*, *assets*, and *networks* working so that the business runs. It must also be sourced and available, to enable the business to carry out its *strategy execution* activities and achieve its target *Business Growth Plan*.

*We have summarized some relevant 'funding sources' for the three types of businesses\*:*

- *Start-up businesses: that are in their early stages of forming and possibly pre-revenue, and micro or relatively small*
- *High growth scale-ups: which are typically small and medium size businesses (SMEs) that have a proven record of sales and some assets*
- *Incumbent corporates and institutions: that may have surplus profit, and want to expand or diversify in new markets*

*\* Funding sources listed are not exhaustive and indicative of the type of funding typically available to businesses with similar characteristics, but there are exceptions, and funding sources are not necessarily exclusive across different business types.*

Self-funding including help from friends and family (interest free loans), provide other future investors evidence of 'skin in the game' and enable the owners to have more control of the company. How does a business make these limited funds last?

Business activity from small and medium businesses can represent approximately 50% of the economies, so many governments from all of the world provide various grants to small businesses and start-ups to stimulate their economies. The process to access funds can be slow and bureaucratic.

Banks do offer loans for small businesses, but it can be difficult to get a bank loan for most pre-revenue start-ups, given the high risk of failure. Many small businesses and start-ups have turned to peer-to-peer (P2P) lending networks and lines of credit from third party lenders, that offer borrowings at much higher interest rates.

Pre-sales from one or a few major customers, or using crowdfunding to attract 'innovators' and 'early-adopters' who are prepared to co-create, can help to cover development costs. Once the value proposition is finished, sales can multiply and the small business can start to accelerate growth.

## Bootstrapping (self-funding)

## Small Business Grants

## Funding sources for start-up businesses

## Pre-Sales & Crowdfunding

## Loans & Line of Credit

## Partnerships & Bartering

It can be advantageous for small businesses and start-ups to partner with each other or bigger businesses, to reduce costs and accelerate growth. Partnerships include the sharing of expertise, resources, networks, or exchange of services not no cost that may then result in a split in revenue from the joint value proposition, or involve licensing and white labeling.

## Incubators

There has been significant growth in the number of incubators or accelerators and catapults ...funded by government and industry bodies, business communities, universities, and other big businesses, often in partnership, that provide funding and support via an ecosystem of complementary services for start-ups to grow.

## Venture Capital

Venture Capital (VC) funds come in larger sums, starting from 1 million, so they an really help to accelerate a small business or start-up's growth. VCs do take a lot of equity and control, in order to provide a fast ROI, in some cases compromising the mission, vision and values of the business. VC deals can also take a long time to close.

## Angel Investors

Angel investors are wealthy individuals who have previously grown and/or sold very successful businesses,. As well as providing funding between $25,000 -$250,000 they can also provide their expertise and access to their networks to support a start-up to grow. Angel networks help to curate the best start-ups by industry or subject for investors.

Expensive equipment including machinery, tools, and technology that are required to support the growth or running of the business can be financed through this form of loan, where the assets purchased are not paid for up front but over the lifetime of the lease in installments.

### Asset Finance

The business raises capital by using the director's personal, existing pension pots, as collateral and to act as a guarantee for the loan, which is paid back with interest. It comes in two known forms: a commercial loan and an unlisted share investment, which is more suited to asset light businesses.

### Pension-Led Funding

### Partner Credit Lines

With proven sales, assets, and expertise to offer, high growth businesses can form partnerships more easily with other business that provide complementary services in the same value chain (p 153). Partners can provide credit lines where payment for services (e.g.: with suppliers or distributors) is differed till a later date, thus increasing working capital and cashflow.

### Mini-Bonds

A business issues un-secured mini-bonds to raise funding from a group of individual lenders, who are usually their customers. The customers may receive discounts or preferential services for free in addition to a potential higher premium when the loan reaches full term. They can redeem the loan before the full term for a lesser return or sell their bonds.

Many more government grants tend to be available to help high growth scale-ups to expand, including specific education grants for research of new sciences, innovation of new technologies, export grants for expansion into international markets, and grants for environment conservation, and social responsibility.

### Government Grants

## Funding sources for high growth scale-up businesses

### Private Equity

Private equity is a non-publicly traded investment fund that acts as a limited partnership with a range of investors including large institutions, venture capital, university endowments, and angel investors (p. 146). The private equity manager takes some or all equity ownership of the scale-up to ensure that funds provided are used properly in the right areas to give the best ROI to investors.

Loans, overdrafts, and credit cards are more accessible to businesses that have managed to build a market of customers, and can show a growth trajectory via a solid business plan. High growth business can acquire loans from banks, peer-to-peer lending or debt-based crowdfunding networks, and investment funds.

### Commercial Loans & Credit Cards

### Venture Debt & Invoice Financing

A high growth business will have developed and accumulated assets that it can leverage to raise funds through venture debt to fund specific projects. Invoice discounting or factoring is also available, as a business can draw funds against its sales before the customer has actually paid from a finance company or online platform, thus increasing its working capital.

Incumbent larger businesses may sponsor specific research and development (R&D) projects in collaboration or partnership with governments where grants may be available, especially when projects are aligned to environment conversation and social responsibility. In certain industries or areas where a government may have an agenda that includes specific public policies, including policies from international are regional governing bodies, an incumbent may align itself or comply with these policies in order obtain or gain their share of specific subsidies available.

Businesses, especially incumbents, often reinvest profit and other financial income such as interest, dividends and capital gains from its assets and holdings** (i.e. deposits, shares and other securities owned), that is self-generated capital to support business transformation efforts for future growth. This requires a capital surplus of course, and means that the business does not pay dividends to its shareholders.

In addition to eliminating specific business activities and most of the associated operating costs, apart from logistics management, which is even easier with the support of tools using the latest digital technologies like AI, incumbents may have significant partner credit lines that allow them to operate activities over long periods without having to pay for services till much later, thus eliminating the burden from having high amounts of working capital and cashflow. (E.g. Amazon)

## Government Subsidies & Grants

## Internal Funding including Reinvested Profit, Interest & Capital Earnings

## Funding sources for incumbent businesses

## Partner Credit Lines

## Hybrid Securities

Incumbent businesses may also raise capital, with the help of an investment banker or broker via hybrid securities that combine the characteristics of both debt and equity securities* such as preference shares or options, convertibles or warrants. Most hybrid securities are more complex, with different structures, risks and benefits. Hence they need to be managed by approved financial institutions like banks, as as well as being regulated by financial authorities.

## Debt Capital via Debt Securities

Similar to smaller businesses, an incumbent can also raise capital to fund business activities from loans and other debt securities, such as bonds, debentures deposits, notes … Holders of the security are are entitled to repayment of the principle plus interest, over an agreed term, when the security then matures. Debt securities may be protected or secured by an an asset of the business, also known as collateral, which can be sold in the event of a default, or be unsecured.

## Equity Capital via Share Issue

All businesses can and may issue more shares, that is common stocks* to raise capital funding for financing business activities. Investors buy these shares in the hope that their value goes up and there is a capital gain, as the value of the business goes up. Shareholders do have voting rights on how the business should operate. Many larger incumbent businesses are publicly listed on a stock exchange, thus allowing their shares to be traded, that is bought and sold. When a stock is publicly listed, then its share price is tracked openly and subject to fluctuations influenced by general market or economic trends and movements.

*Common stocks or shares are also called Equity Securities.*

*** Holdings may include Cryptocurrencies or Crypto-assets.*

# Growing value from business assets

The overall value of a business, including the organization that supports it, can be derived from the sum value of all its assets. This is why asset growth is a key 'value measure' and a goal or objective of many businesses as outlined in their **Mission Models** (p. 83).

An **'Asset'** is what the business owns, that can help it to grow the value (p. 67) that it produces and delivers to different stakeholders, in both the short term and long-term future.

As part of its *business strategy*, a business needs to indicate WHAT assets it requires to support its **Business Model** to achieve *profit growth* (p. 141), and whether it will organically build, produce, or grow these assets, or buy them from other organizations through Mergers and Acquisitions (M&A), within its **Operating Model**.

## Types of assets owned by a business:

### Tangible Assets

Objects or things owned by a business that need to be stored securely using physical infrastructure, and/or maintain physically in a location, in order to be used/re-used to produce output and value-added outcomes and experiences that can be delivered to customers and stakeholders when required.

**Examples**:
Staff, real estate, including land and buildings, equipment, including computers, phones, tractors, cranes, cars, vans, robots, other machinery, packaging including paper, glass, plastics, toys, consoles, commodities including cash, gold, silver, tin, rice, wheat, oil, gas ...

### Intangible Assets

Non-physical things owned by a business that may need to be protected legally as intellectual property with trademarks, patents, copyright, or contractually, to account for their value, and/or stored virtually, in order to be used/re-used to produce output and value-added outcomes and experiences that can be delivered to customers and stakeholders when required.

**Examples**:
Ideas and knowhow, brand, time, networks, software, data and information including conversations, and other customer data, other digital assets including currency, financial instruments or special purpose vehicles, crypto-assets, and specific processes including skills and capabilities developed by the business ...

## The role of assets in the business

The role of an asset is to act as a resource in the organization as part of the business's **Operating Model**. The job of an asset is to support the business to deliver output and in doing so, provide value-added outcomes and experiences through its *value propositions* to customers and stakeholders.

Assets can also be *value propositions* in themselves that are sold to a customer. An asset that can be sold quickly and easily to convert its value into cash is considered to be highly liquid.

Typically, the more valuable its assets, the more a company is worth. Its business value (p. 67) increases and this is reflected through its share price on a stock exchange if the company is publicly listed, and/or its business valuation in the event of a sale or Initial Public Offering (IPO), when shares are listed for the first time on a stock exchange.

Different assets can be valued based on the potential value they might provide for a business at a point in time. For example, the value of the business's brand when it is of good standing and highly reputable is significantly higher than the re-sale value of one of its commodity products held in stock in a factory. Banks, asset managers, venture capital firms, and their lawyers and financial accountants can use different calculations to determine the value of an asset, based on its *asset category* (p. 151). It is useful to know an asset's category and its potential value when deciding what assets need to be built or bought as part of the **Business Model** design process.

## Value of digital assets

Many digital assets that are formed from different types of data and information have increased significantly in value, especially digital platforms, as a result of their potential to derive future value from future sales and *profit growth* with the aid of digital technology and **Digital Business Models**. As we highlighted on p. 19 with Facebook's acquisition of WhatsApp and Instagram, data has very much become a commodity and currency in its own right. Larger businesses are willing to buy smaller companies and competitors for their data or *Platform Business Model* (p. 111) at a premium, in order to acquire its digital assets. Similar acquisitions include Amazon's purchase of Twitch for $1 billion in 2014, and Google's purchase of YouTube for $1.65 billion in 2006.

**STRATEGY JOURNEY *Framework* Activity #10:**

Make a list of all your assets, including tangible and intangible asset such as digital assets, and categorize them using the guide on page 151. Are there assets that are not currently listed in the business's annual accounts? Add any future assets that are work in progress.

# Value Held By Different Assets In The Business

The equity value of a business can be calculated based on how assets in its possession stack up in value. There are many ways to calculate the value of an asset, and hence the equity value of a business at a point in time, which are used by different asset management and venture capital firms as part of their M&A deals.

We have summarized the following asset categories with different magnitudes of value that are used and combined to support the business models of digitally-driven businesses. These all contribute to the equity valuation of a business:

**BRAND**

A good **'brand'** is an intangible asset, that holds the most value for a business, as it is what provides an invisible multiplier to the value of all of the business's other assets. It is the most difficult to build quickly and to maintain over time, as it is formed from the perceptions of different stakeholders of how the business behaves through its actions, as well as the quality and value of its *value proposition*. A poor **'brand'** can devalue the other assets in a business with a negative multiplier.

**NETWORKS**

Use of **'networks'** including partners with their network effects can significantly increase a business's value through the improved ability to reach and transact with customers. When a business builds a **'network'** that it owns and controls through its own proprietary technology to support its connectivity with and/or between customer and partners as a multi-sided platform, it has a very valuable asset that enables it to multiply all its interactions and transactions, and the value that it can produce and deliver, as well as grow.

**INTELLIGENCE**

A business with **'intelligence'** assets has the ability to exponentially increase the value that it can produce in the future. The *'intelligence'* is held by data, and calculated based on the volume, quality and convertibility of this data. Data convertibility includes future predictions, and future re-use within or as *value propositions* that can be sold to customers. Intelligence value is further increased through intelligence capabilities, where the business has unique processes to leverage and multiply the data.

**CAPABILITIES**

The ability of a **'capability'** to increase both the quality and volume of business outputs with speed over a period of time, to sustainably increase the value add produced by the business's *value propositions*, is what makes it an asset. The value of a **'capability'** as an asset to the business is primarily based on the quality of its processes that are executed through people and systems, and heightened by its uniqueness, when it cannot be copied by competitors, such as a patented process or special secret formula eg. KFC

**CULTURE**

The **'culture'** of a business is an asset in its own right that attracts followers, in the form of co-creating customers and good staff, who are value-driven towards adding value and growth by getting involved in *business transformation*, innovation, and future income-generating activities. Strong positive culture is comprised of talented staff, supported by good training for people to flourish in their job roles. It indicates the business's ability to adapt to changes, and the likelihood of strong future performance and value.

**COMMODITY**

A **'commodity'** is an asset that the business has in abundance, ready to be re-sold easily to the mass market, with the amount of stock and the price driving its value. It includes physical assets like the latest iPhone or sacks of rice ready to ship to the customer, or it can be a more intangible virtual asset in the form of a repeatable service, such as the ability to process a PayPal payment or transaction, that can be sold to customers in volume online.

## Example: The Assets That Account For Udacity's Growth And Unicorn Status*

In February 2018, while e-Learning start-up Udacity may not have reached profitability yet since launching in 2011, its former CEO Vishal Makhijani hinted at the company's goal of an impending IPO, when he disclosed a doubling of revenue to $70million, as well as the assets that form Udacity's business model, to help justify its future valuation. Udacity may have a $1billion valuation to give it a Unicorn status based on the money it has been able to raise through investors to the value of $165million up until 2015, but what are the real assets that could contribute to its valuation at IPO?

**High quality, job ready professional training backed by strong brands**
- Over 18,000+ graduates, many having gained employment or are sponsored by big industry leading brands like Google, Facebook, IBM, Mercedes-Benz, Amazon, AT&T …
- Courses are accredited through collaborations with Top Universities (e.g.: MIT)

**Proprietary network and multisided platform built with the latest technology**
- Mentor matching connects top talents with top experts
- Content from nanodegrees is backed by state-of-the-art code & project grading platform
- Industry-connected alumni network and community

**Data on over 8 million students in over 200 countries (as at 2018) and growing**
**Data on the jobs market for technology skills in the latest trending sectors including AI, AR, AV, Blockchain …**
- Strong student growth in China, India, Brazil, MENA and many more. …

**World class learning on the latest technology co-created with the most innovative technology firms, including specialization in *Autonomous/Self-driving Vehicle Technology***
- The latest content and learning techniques are co-created through extensive partnerships with the biggest brands (e.g.: 50,000 Google employees trained, 500 engineers at Infosys trained …)

**A culture of innovation focused on providing democratized education to uplift, empower and transform students to connect them with the best jobs**
- 400+ employees including freelancers as well as partners and collaborators in over 100 countries
- Have helped to fund over 100,000 scholarships annually

**Free and Paid Nanodegrees courses available in over 200 countries**
- Over 30+ Paid Online Nanodegrees available in two formats: certified or self-training with 50,000+ enrolled students, who have submitted over 300,000 projects in 2017 alone
- New blended learning programs available in 14 different cities in 9 countries
- Thousands of free learning materials, available on demand or via live webinars

*\* Data as at 2019 has been sourced from Udacity.com and other public sources in order to illustrate asset categories only.*

# What delivers the value propositions

The goal of the **Business Model** is to enable a business to maximize the net gain or 'margin' in *profit growth* as well as *asset growth* from delivering its *value propositions* to customers. To achieve this 'margin', the total cost of the **Business Model** should be less than the total gain in value, including sales revenue and assets built up over time. The **Business Model** needs to specify what resources are required in the **Operating Model** to perform the business activities that will produce and deliver its *value propositions* effectively to customers, over the period. This optimal value-driven enterprise must specify the **Value Model** that will drive how its **Operating Model** will deliver its **Business Model.**

The **'Value Model'** describes what constitutes value for an enterprise and its customers, encompassing where the value is created, the exchange of value between different stakeholders, and most importantly, how to find new opportunities to create value in the wider global business ecosystem.

The **Value Model** directs WHAT value-added outcomes and experiences customers receive to form their *value propositions*, and hence WHAT *value streams* are required to support their delivery. These *value streams* support the enterprise's overall *value chain* (p. 64, 153-156) by directing resources and the business activities to perform optimally, in order to deliver the desired 'margin'. *Value streams* are implemented or executed through the enterprise's **Operating Model** where they may also need to be transformed to remain optimal, through the **Transformation Model**, so they are the connectors that join·the·dots in the business along the stages of its strategy journeys.

# How value streams work in the business to deliver the value

A business delivers its *value propositions* to its customers, through its *value streams*.

**'Value Streams'** are the internal *value propositions* that join together to create an 'end-to-end solution' or external *value proposition* with a set of value-added outcomes and experiences for the customer. They fulfill customers' expectations in exchanged for payment via a transaction.

A *value stream* is often called a 'business service' because it delivers an end-to-end service to the organization with a set of value-added outcomes and experiences for stakeholders or internal customers (p. 121). A *value proposition* is often called a 'service offering' as it serves external end customers with an 'end-to-end solution'. A *value proposition* can rely on many *value streams* to deliver its outcome.

*Value streams* are supported by an organization's *capabilities* (p. 179), which are sets of *resources* in the business's **Operating Model** that are optimized to perform a specific set of business activities efficiently. This produces and contributes the outputs required to effectively deliver the outcomes and experiences of the *value streams,* as well as the *value propositions* that they support to customers.

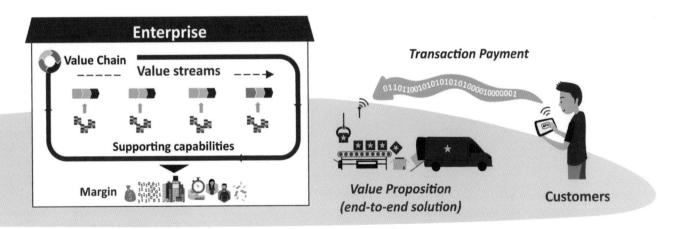

'Service Design' *is the* process that defines the *value streams* to deploy in the business to support its **Business Model** and deliver the *service innovations*. To realize these new and improved *value streams,* changes in the *capabilities* that form the enterprise's **Operating Model** are required and need to be implemented through business transformation.

'Transformation Design' is the process that defines what modifications need to be made to the **Operating Model** capabilities, to implement the *value stream changes* that will deliver the new and improved *value propositions* to customers. Finally, *value* is delivered through the outcomes achieved when *business transformation* has been successfully implemented through a managed 'transformation journey'.

# What Value Models yield ...

With many different types of value (p. 67) to deliver in an ever-changing and increasingly open digital ecosystem (p. 95) influenced by rising customer expectations (p. 21-22), today's companies can differentiate by being able to deliver more value better and faster to customers and stakeholders through their **Value Model**.

## How to configure and optimize the Value Model

Businesses of all shapes and sizes can differentiate and build business advantages over competitors and non-competitors (p. 103) through the process of *service design* (p. 115-116) to influence and transform their **Value Models**.

**'Service Design'** encompasses 'value modeling' where a business configures its *value streams* to achieve *service innovations* with Unique Selling Points (USPs) that enable it to produce more valuable solutions for customer and stakeholders. This enables the business to optimize its *value chain* while leveraging as well as influencing its *value ecosystem*.

Today, the increasing trend is for digitally savvy customers to configure their own **Value Models** from self-connecting digital services that are available from open networks such as the Cloud to solve their problems along their customer journeys, to form their own *value streams*. With this change in behavior, service differentiation comes from the user journey where sticky user experiences are created to influence customers through their user expectations. These **Service Value Models** are where the latest service innovation opportunities exist, and hence where enterprises should focus their *service design* efforts.

## Value Chains

The 'value chain' describes the collection of business activities to design, produce, market, deliver, and support the firm's products in sequence and operates as a pipeline to produce a margin or net gain in value. It relates to how the entire enterprise operates as a single entity, unit, or whole. Value is configured and optimized from HOW different *'business functions'* who perform the activities (p. 179) are integrated to work seamlessly together. Learn how *value chains* were conceived by Michael Porter in 1985 on p. 181.

# ... business advantages

## Value Ecosystems

The 'value ecosystem' describes the wider collection of value-producing business activities performed by the other parties in the business ecosystem surrounding an enterprise. It relates to how a business can partner with other parties including marketplaces, regulators, other competitors and non-competitors to leverage their *capabilities*, which are better and faster than equivalent existing *capabilities* to fill a gap in its *value chain* or specific *value streams*. Value is configured and optimized from HOW external *capabilities* are combined into internal value streams to create 'network effects' (p. 133) and to support the overall *value chain* of the business.

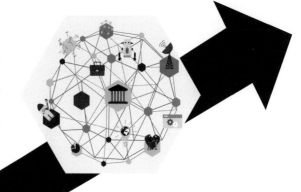

*Configuring value streams through* **'Service Design'** *is where an enterprise can differentiate its service innovations with USPs. It is also where customers are self-connecting digital services to define their own* **Service Value Models** *along their customer journeys.*

## Value Streams

A 'value stream' describes the end-to-end collection of business activities dedicated to producing a desired result or set of outcomes and experiences for the customer, including external customers and internal customers or the stakeholders of an organization (p. 121-122). The process of 'value modeling' involves identifying specific activities that satisfy customer and user expectations through their experiences of the *value proposition* that is delivered through the combining of *value streams* (p. 154). Value is configured and optimized from HOW the outcomes and experiences provided by *value propositions* meet or exceed the expectations of customers and users – with 'stickiness effects' (p. 119).

# Extending the service lifecycle ...

The practice of **'Service Innovation'** is to discover and implement new and improved *service offerings* that enable the business to achieve 'growth'. In most businesses, the primary goal of its *service innovations (new service offerings)* is to gain traction along the **Innovation Adoption Lifecycle** and cross the 'chasm' to reach the 'growth' stage (p. 99).

However as illustrated on p. 99, if and once an innovation has reached 'growth', it will naturally and organically begin to mature and approach decline. This 'decline' stage, typically indicated through a noticeable decline in sales, is when the service and the business are most susceptible to disruption from new or alternate *service innovations* introduced by competitors and non-competitors, or even the business itself, as illustrated in the Kodak and Blockbuster examples from page 35. So as well as achieving a 'growth' stage, *'Service Innovation'* must also include strategies and tactics to keep the business in a constant 'growth' state.

An enterprise must first choose its *service innovation* strategy or 'game plan' where there is the potential for 'growth' and 'market adoption' of its service offerings by customers in order to direct is 'customer modeling', 'service design' and 'transformation design' efforts (p. 115) This 'market adoption' strategy is the strategic lever that directs what customer segments and customers journeys to analyze where new and improved service offerings including feature upgrades, can be introduced to build the 'stickiness effects' that can extend the customer relationship.

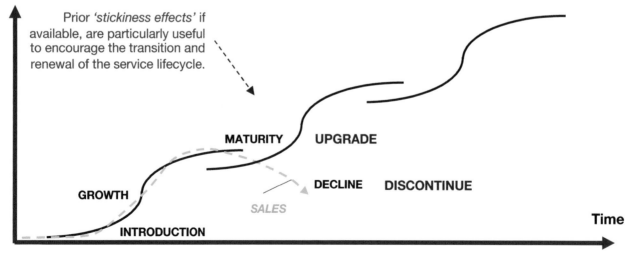

# ... through Service Innovation

First introduced in 1957, Ansoff's Matrix* is one of the best tools to help you determine an appropriate *service innovation* strategy to direct an enterprise's **Operating Model** transformation efforts. It describes four different ways to transform a business through its product or service offerings to different markets, to enable it to grow and/or sustain its existence from possible disruption. It also indicates the relative levels of risk in achieving or failing to achieve a Return On Investment (ROI) from the business transformation effort.

## Ansoff's Matrix*

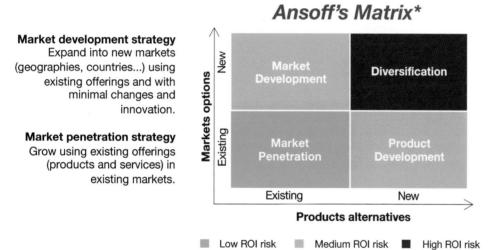

**Market development strategy**
Expand into new markets (geographies, countries...) using existing offerings and with minimal changes and innovation.

**Market penetration strategy**
Grow using existing offerings (products and services) in existing markets.

**Diversification strategy**
Grow market share by introducing new offerings in new markets.

**Product development strategy**
Create new products and services targeted at existing markets to achieve growth. This involves extending the product range to the firm's existing markets.

*\* Ansoff's Matrix was introduced by Igor Ansoff, a Russian-American engineer, scientist and mathematician who is known as the father of Strategic Management via the Harvard Business Review paper, Strategies for Diversification in 1957.*

Ansoff's Matrix guides you to choose a high level 'game plan' based on the enterprise's existing resources and risk appetite, to direct your *service innovation* efforts in one of its four quadrants: Market Penetration, Market Development, Product Development or Diversification.

When once you have decided on the 'game plan', then the next step is to consider the 'gameplays' and choose a 'priority play' by which to commence the service innovation process, involving what customer segments to analyze, customer journeys to disrupt and serve, and what value streams and capabilities in your **Operating Model** to transform.

# Service Innovation Strategies & Tactics That Grow The Business

In the digital economy where organizations and the services that they offer can become obsolete and irrelevant in a little as 10 years (p. 12), it is clear that enterprises must reach beyond existing and current 'growth' and innovation strategies that enable market penetration, and invest more rigorously in their Service Innovation practices where they are capable of service and enterprise extensions and diversification.

In **THE STRATEGY JOURNEY method**, we have extended the strategies from Ansoff's Matrix to help you go beyond a **'game plan'** and consider different 'gameplays' and choose the 'priority play' to apply to your *service innovations* – with the **Service Innovation Matrix**.

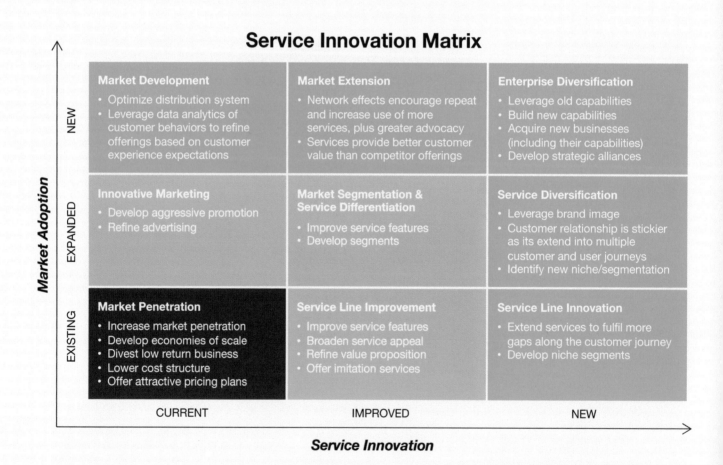

## Service Innovation Matrix

**Market Adoption** (vertical axis)
**Service Innovation** (horizontal axis)

### NEW

**Market Development**
- Optimize distribution system
- Leverage data analytics of customer behaviors to refine offerings based on customer experience expectations

**Market Extension**
- Network effects encourage repeat and increase use of more services, plus greater advocacy
- Services provide better customer value than competitor offerings

**Enterprise Diversification**
- Leverage old capabilities
- Build new capabilities
- Acquire new businesses (including their capabilities)
- Develop strategic alliances

### EXPANDED

**Innovative Marketing**
- Develop aggressive promotion
- Refine advertising

**Market Segmentation & Service Differentiation**
- Improve service features
- Develop segments

**Service Diversification**
- Leverage brand image
- Customer relationship is stickier as its extend into multiple customer and user journeys
- Identify new niche/segmentation

### EXISTING

**Market Penetration**
- Increase market penetration
- Develop economies of scale
- Divest low return business
- Lower cost structure
- Offer attractive pricing plans

**Service Line Improvement**
- Improve service features
- Broaden service appeal
- Refine value proposition
- Offer imitation services

**Service Line Innovation**
- Extend services to fulfil more gaps along the customer journey
- Develop niche segments

CURRENT — IMPROVED — NEW

Legend:
- Low disruption risk, strong business agility
- Medium disruption risk, medium business agility
- High disruption risk, poor business agility

The **Service Innovation Matrix** enables you to consider different **'gameplay'** options by which to deploy your enterprise's *service innovation* and *business transformation* efforts. It enables you to explore specific *service innovation* strategies and tactics that will increase market adoption, versus the level of *service innovation* with associated business transformation activities.

There are nine service innovation strategies with associated tactics will direct how you conduct 'service design' as well as 'transformation design' to execute *business transformation* in the **Operating Model**:

- Market Penetration
- Innovative Marketing
- Service Line Improvement
- Market Segmentation & Service Differentiation
- Market Development
- Service Line Innovation
- Market Extension
- Service Diversification
- Enterprise Diversification

The matrix's nine quadrants guide you to weigh the level of *service innovation* against likely market adoption rates, by considering the disruption risks to the business, when any of its core service offerings are approaching or already in the 'decline' stage of the **Innovation Adoption Lifecycle** (p. 99), especially if the enterprise took no action. This analysis is also useful when conducting 'competitor analysis'.

During your analysis and as part of decision making on how an enterprise invests its funds to achieve a Return On Investment (ROI), it is important to account for the level of *business agility* currently in the enterprise based on existing resources available, as well the level of *business agility* that can be built in the future from its *service innovation* and *business transformation* efforts.

The *Service Innovation* strategy and tactics (Service Innovation Quadrant) chosen as the 'priority game play' for your enterprise should drive the decision making around what gaps in the business to address, including 'Customer Gaps', 'Service Gaps', 'Capability Gaps' and 'Transformation Gaps'. In **THE STRATEGY JOURNEY method**, these 'gaps' are discovered during the *'service design'* and *'transformation design'* design processes, as part of 'value modeling' and addressed by the business through implementation of *business transformation* changes in the **Operating Model** along the transformation journey.

**STRATEGY JOURNEY *Framework* TIP #8:**

It is useful to find out the existing Service Innovation strategies and tactics already deployed by an enterprise, to discover its 'game plans' and what 'game plays' are already in motion. So use the Service Innovation Matrix to map specific projects in your enterprise already underway or looking for investment funding and try to map your competitors too.

# What gaps in the customer journey...

The issues that customers have and experience in their quest to solve their problems are not the same as the issues that exist within an enterprise. Businesses instead turn customers' issues into opportunities to service them better, through using their service solutions. This is why there are two types of gaps to discover, in the **'Service Design'** process to understand where opportunities exist to add value and then create outcomes that deliver the value.

In **THE STRATEGY JOURNEY** *Framework*, we recommend two methods to model these gaps: (1) value can be added in the customer journey; (2) value can be produced by a service innovation, including new service offerings as well as service improvements; Together these define an enterprise's **Value Model** as well as customers' **Service Value Models**:

**Customer Gaps**

**'Customer Gaps'** are gaps in service as perceived by a customer along their customer journey to solve a big problem and achieve an end goal. Customers are exposed to different services that present them with potential solutions, partial or end-to-end that they can buy to help them resolve the pains and achieve gains along their customer journeys.

The 'Customer Gaps' exist when there are either no existing services or inadequate services that do not meet customers' expectations in addressing their pains and gains along their customer journeys.

To discover 'Customer Gaps', it is necessary to map the customer journey, covering how customers think, act and behave along the different stages of this journey, and how they could become buyers or users of existing or new services. Once identified, an enterprise can decide if these 'Customer Gaps' warrant the effort to develop and deliver new and improved service offerings, through analysing the 'Service Gaps'.

# ... provide **service opportunities**

**Service Gaps**

**'Service Gaps'** are the potential new value-added service offerings or service improvements, that could be introduced to address the 'Customer Gaps' identified within the customer journey.

The 'Service Gap' is the new service opportunity, delivered through either new or improved service offerings including feature add-ons, that the enterprise could offer to customers along their customer journey, which they can buy and use. It is the service solution with outcomes that meets or exceeds the customer's expectations as a buyer and a user of the service that will be purchased and used. Providing a great buyer experience as well as a remarkable user experience is how an enterprise can build 'stickiness' in its relationship with its customers.

To discover what 'Service Gaps' can be turned into new and improve service innovations and features, it is necessary to analyse how the customer as a user, thinks, acts and behaves along their user journey. The customer should be co-creating (p. 117) with the enterprise through trialling and using the service.

# Different Customer Journey Paths For Buyers Versus Users

When conducting 'value modeling' in the *Service Design* process, it is useful to distinguish the role of the customer as a buyer versus a user as their paths are not the same. The stages in the path experienced by a buyer have different 'goals' to that of a user who is experiencing the service as a recipient. It is this difference that causes two distinct experiences with outcomes which need to be communicated or shared, especially when the buyer and user are not the same individual. Even when the same individual is both the buyer and user of a service, the dots always need to be connected, especially in order to create and amplify *'stickiness effects'*.

*We provide the following guidance to help you define effective buyer and user journey paths, including how to join·the·dots between them to facilitate 'stickiness effects' in your services:*

## Buyer Journey

The buyer journey can only commence when the potential customer and prospective buyer becomes 'aware' of their problem.

A buyer moves through six stages along their customer journey from being problem unaware to solution advocacy;

- Awareness
- Discovery
- Selection
- Onboarding
- Satisfaction
- Advocacy

Effective marketing and sales strategies are able to move the buyer along their customer journey quickly during the customer acquisition stages, to covert the prospect into a real customer who is willing to buy a solution, through closing the sale at the 'selection' stage when the buyer transacts with the business.

During the customer retention stages following a sale, the goal is to keep engaging with customers to build a relationship that will maximize **'Customer Lifetime Value' (CLV)**. The 'onboarding' stage is crucial for developing this longer-term relationship of trust where stickiness effects play their part in how far this relationship goes to convert more future sales through 'advocacy.'

## User Journey

The user journey may exist before or after the buyer journey commences, based on the customer's 'prior experience' with any thing related to the service offering.

A user moves through six stages along their user journey from their anticipated experience to their prospective experience in a future use case*:

- Anticipated Experience
- First Experience
- Reflective Experience
- Repetitive Experience
- Retrospective Experience
- Prospective Experience

Effective marketing is able to utilize the user journey of a related experience to make the customer aware' of their big customer problem, and thus enter the buyer journey. This can be achieved through **'co-creation techniques'** (p. 117), especially when the user and the buyer are the same person. But even when they are not, the relationship can be established. For example, a child user may only be able to access services with the permission of their parent.

Along the user journey stages, the objective is to influence the user's attitude through their **'User Experience' (UX)** of the service offering, by establishing context and encouraging repeat use to embed learned behaviors. The goal is to create immediate, short-term and long-term *'stickiness effects'*.

*\* Based on User Experience Lifecycle Model by Anna E. Pohlmeyer, Martin Hecht, and Lucienne Blessing*

# Deriving Service Experiences Through The User Journey

An originating Customer Journey is problem-based and agnostic of any specific service or service provider. It is when the customer considers potential services that they may use, that they undergo a Buyer Journey. So, it can only be defined based on the customer's perception and captures how they think, act, and behave. This is an important distinction from the User Journey which is based on the adoption of an actual service. In the User Journey it is possible to use innovation techniques to differentiate the service and the associated brand of the enterprise, along the User Journey. The goal in designing for the User Journey is to deliver remarkable 'sticky' experiences for the end-user as they begin use a service offering from a specific service provider.

**Customer Experience (CX)** and **User Experience (UX)** are not the same thing and when combined to influence how an end-user feels along their User Journey to create the 'stickiness effects', they can also impact how a buyer feels along their Customer-Buyer Journey (p. 119).

*We provide the following guidance to help you distinguish your UX designs from your CX designs to create 'stickiness effects' in the User Journey:*

## Customer Experience

Customer Experience (CX) is the reflection of how a customer feels about an enterprise and how it operates to deliver its services.

CX encompasses everything about the enterprise, from its purpose including its Mission, Vision, and Values, as well as how it operates along any specific User Journey for any of its service offerings, and as apart of any Customer Journey, where it has touchpoints with the customer.

The UX provided to a user during each User Journey will accumulate to influencer the CX of the customer, either positively or negatively.

An accumulation of good CX created along numerous User Journeys, is what creates 'Brand Stickiness Effects' that can influencer buyers along their customer journeys in how they think, act and behave towards future services from an enterprise.

*E.g. Branding can influence potential customers to try or avoid the services from a company and the likelihood of purchases.*

Constant communication and data exchanges between the
CX and UX of the buyer and customer along their User
Journey, can influence behaviors during the Customer
Journey. Existing attitudes from the Customer Journey can
also influence the attitude of a user in the pre-use stage of the
User Journey.

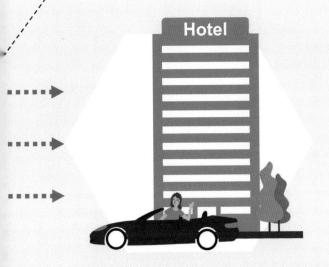

## User Experience

User Experience (UX) is the reflection of how an end-user
feels about a specific service offering as they navigate
through the User Journey stages from pre-use to post-use,
and the possibility of re-use.

UX encompasses the concerns of the user, that is things that
matter to the individual along the User Journey specific to a
service, and how the solution of outcomes and experiences
provided measure up against the user's expectations.

The ability of the UX provided by the service to not meet or
exceed the user's expectations while they navigate the User
Journey is what creates 'Service Stickiness Effects', both
positive and negative.

Whether the user and buyer are the same individual or not, there is a feedback loop, that is
communication from the UX of the user to influence the overall CX of the buyer. Similarly, the UX can be
influenced by any attitude towards a service from any prior CX influences on the buyer side.

*E.g. Higher prices and prior brand value can raise expectation's as well as mitigate the impact of mistakes and errors.*

# Establishing Buyer Journey Goals Along The Customer Journey

The buyer journey is triggered and driven by the underlying big problem and end-goal of the customer. It is motivated by the values and thinking patterns that form their mindset (p. 123-124). Once this starting point is established, it is necessary to help the individual* to achieve each of their 'mini-goals' in each stage of their journey to facilitate their readiness to move into the next stage. These **'buyer journey goals'** form the basis by which to engage and interact with customers. They support 'co-creation' and create the foundational data points for directing the entire 'service innovation lifecycle'.

*We provide the following guidance to help you establish and define the 'goals' comprised of 'pains' and 'gains' that direct the customer along their buyer journey, as well as the key data metrics to monitor and act on in the customer relationship management (CRM) lifecycle:*

## Selection

## Discovery

## Awareness

**Key metric: lead capture rate**

What 'pains' trigger the customer to realize they have a problem that needs work for them to solve and achieve their end-goal with the 'gains'?

**Key metrics: 'touchpoints' rates**

What additional 'pains' is the customer undergoing when they begin to search for ways to solve their problem, and what quick win 'gains' do they need to make them feel that they have a potential solution for further consideration?

**Key metrics: conversation rate, drop-off rate ...**

What remaining 'pains' are stopping the customer from moving forward with a potential solution? What 'gains' does the customer need to help them make their decision to select a specific solution option and proceed with the transaction?

*The 'selection' stage is when the customer may dropout of their customer journey based on the priority of their problem. So 'urgency' or 'priority' is a key 'pain' and 'time saved' is a key 'gain.*

*In the B2B transaction model, the final purchasing decision is taken by an individual while being influenced by other individuals in the organization, so it may be necessary to establish the goals of each of these stakeholders.*

## Advocacy

Key metric: referral rates

What associated 'pains' experienced by the customer's circle of contacts, with up to six degrees of separation, might impact the customer enough, or that the customer can relate to on reflection to cause them to take action and refer or recommend a potential solution to the perceived problem? What additional 'gains' does the customer want to receive or expect for supporting others in 'pain'?

## Satisfaction

Key metric: satisfaction rates

What ongoing 'pains' in the customer's lifestyle or work life (i.e.. business as usual) could they experience that they would attribute to the service either directly or indirectly? Are there any ongoing benefits that act as 'bonuses' to give them 'gains' that they could attribute to the service to elevate their satisfaction with the service?

## Onboarding

Key metric: cancellation rate

What are the concerns or doubt-based 'pains' that could cause the customer to change their mind and pull out if permitted or become dissatisfied with the service if not dealt with properly? What 'gains' could the service provide to encourage satisfaction and begin to create 'stickiness' with the customer?

*The 'onboarding' stage is crucial to developing 'stickiness effects' as it triggers the **'User Journey'**.*

*It is also when customers may cancel a service and ask for a refund if they are dissatisfied with the level of support they receive.*

# Customer Experience Factors That Influence Buying Decisions

Customers may be feeling stressed, worried, eager, angry, excited, bored... or they could be in denial about how they feel when faced with a problem and end-goal on their customer journeys. Understanding how customers think, and then act or behave is the objective of customer journey mapping... to learn what factors will influence and move the customer along their journey of problem-solving into a buyer seeking to purchase solutions to their problems.

The Customer Experience (CX) of different service providers and brands through touchpoints in the Customer Journey is how an enterprise can develop a relationship with their customers and convert them into buyers as well as advocates.

*We provide the following guidance on the key CX factors\* to consider when collecting customer journey data, that can be analyzed to gain insights on how an enterprise and its services could influence the buying decision and establish stronger customer relationships:*

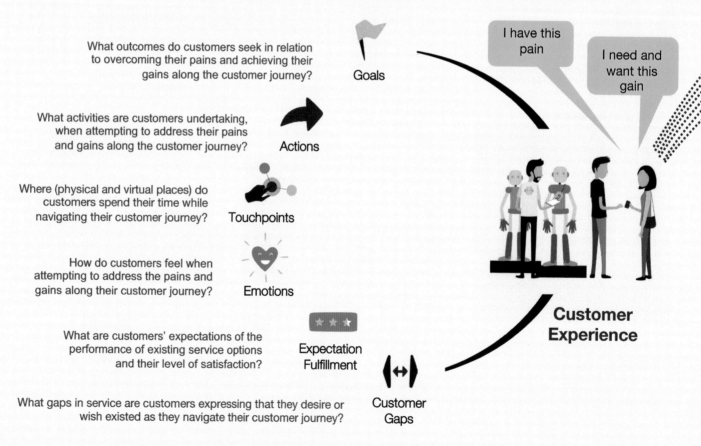

What outcomes do customers seek in relation to overcoming their pains and achieving their gains along the customer journey?

**Goals**

What activities are customers undertaking, when attempting to address their pains and gains along the customer journey?

**Actions**

Where (physical and virtual places) do customers spend their time while navigating their customer journey?

**Touchpoints**

How do customers feel when attempting to address the pains and gains along their customer journey?

**Emotions**

What are customers' expectations of the performance of existing service options and their level of satisfaction?

**Expectation Fulfillment**

What gaps in service are customers expressing that they desire or wish existed as they navigate their customer journey?

**Customer Gaps**

I have this pain

I need and want this gain

**Customer Experience**

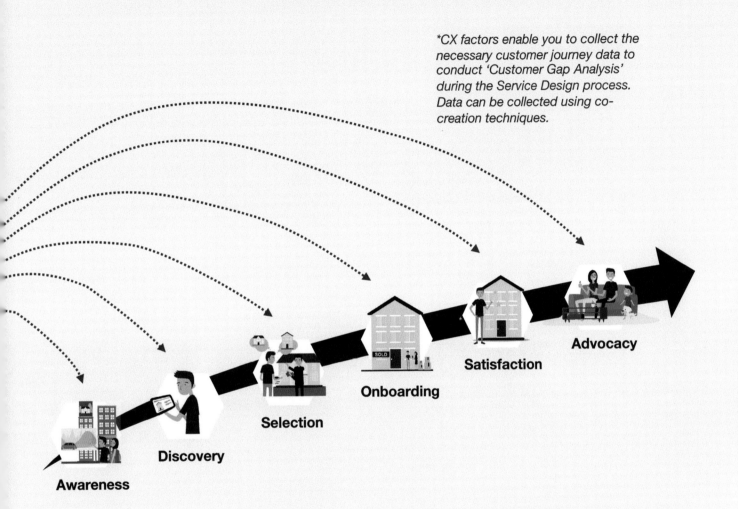

*CX factors enable you to collect the necessary customer journey data to conduct 'Customer Gap Analysis' during the Service Design process. Data can be collected using co-creation techniques.

**Advocacy**

**Satisfaction**

**Onboarding**

**Selection**

**Discovery**

**Awareness**

---

**STRATEGY JOURNEY *Framework* Activity #11:**

For the main customer problem and pain points identified in Activity #6, that your business wants to serve better and faster through its service offerings, identify the goals of customers as they navigate along the six stages of their customer journey, from awareness to advocacy. Indicate along the customer journey stages where your core offering has touchpoints with customers and where they are 'Customer Gaps'.

*Hint: Conduct this fast track analysis of 'Goals', 'Touchpoints', and 'Customer Gaps' in the current state. A complete customer journey mapping case study is available in the HOW section where we illustrate the steps to apply* **THE STRATEGY JOURNEY** *Framework to design the target state as part of 'Customer Gap Analysis'.*

# Designing A Sticky Service Experience Along The User Journey

The success of service design comes from encouraging, motivating, and facilitating a 'repetitive experience' of a service along the stages of the User Journey, as well as a 'prospective experience' through re-use that cycles back to an 'anticipated experience' of a future service.

*We* provide *the following guidance on key 'user journey data attributes' to capture and measure along the user journey stages\* about the user's mindset and behaviors to help you develop 'stickiness effects' for both a service and a brand:*

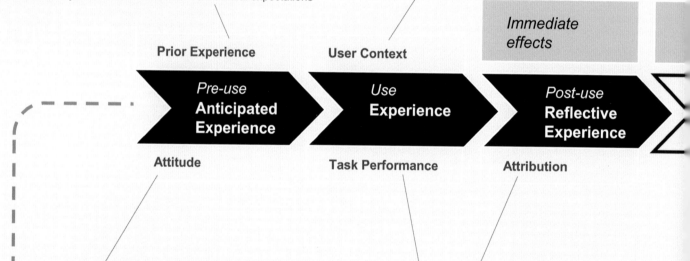

**Prior Experience**
Unlike the customer journey experienced by a buyer, the user journey may have commenced at any time based on the customer's prior experience of any thing that is perceived to be related to or associated with a service offering. Prior Customer Experience (CX) and User Experience (UX) of the service or the brand may also raise or lower the user's initial expectations

**User Context**
User context is the situation or circumstances behind why the user begins to use the service and may even persevere or will they give up easily. User Context is based determines what measures influence the User Experience (UX) because it may directly or indirectly set user expectations.

**Attitude**
The nature of a user's attitude, positive or negative, towards the service, and its parent brand, can significantly influence the rest of the User Journey path. Attitudes are common influenced by the challenges customer face to solve their problems along their customer journey paths.

**Task Performance & Attribution**
Task performance will dictate the user's attribution of service value. Users will consider utility and usability factors, which determine the usefulness of the service (v-19). As first impressions count, these facts can create 'immediate effects' that determine if the user will repeat use or give up and walk away.

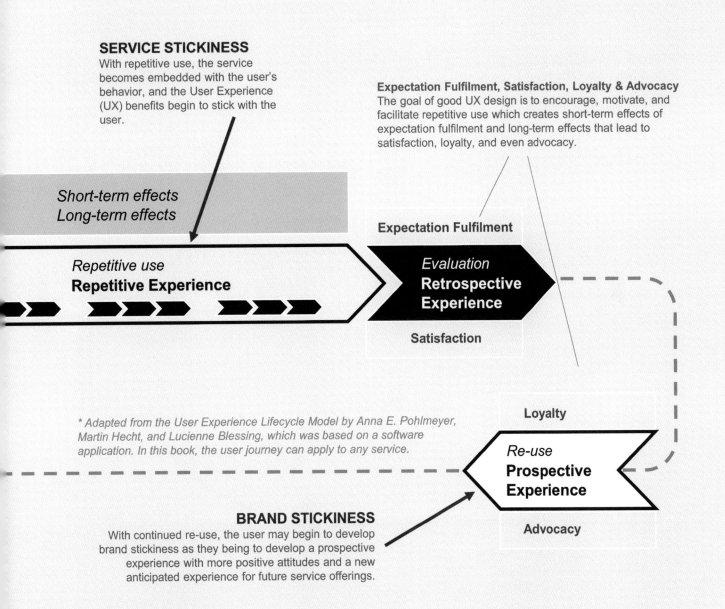

**SERVICE STICKINESS**
With repetitive use, the service becomes embedded with the user's behavior, and the User Experience (UX) benefits begin to stick with the user.

**Expectation Fulfilment, Satisfaction, Loyalty & Advocacy**
The goal of good UX design is to encourage, motivate, and facilitate repetitive use which creates short-term effects of expectation fulfilment and long-term effects that lead to satisfaction, loyalty, and even advocacy.

Short-term effects
Long-term effects

*Repetitive use*
**Repetitive Experience**

**Expectation Fulfilment**

*Evaluation*
**Retrospective Experience**

**Satisfaction**

*\* Adapted from the User Experience Lifecycle Model by Anna E. Pohlmeyer, Martin Hecht, and Lucienne Blessing, which was based on a software application. In this book, the user journey can apply to any service.*

**Loyalty**

*Re-use*
**Prospective Experience**

**Advocacy**

**BRAND STICKINESS**
With continued re-use, the user may begin to develop brand stickiness as they being to develop a prospective experience with more positive attitudes and a new anticipated experience for future service offerings.

# User Experience Measures That Build Stickiness Effects

Customers are naturally attracted to shiny objects that make them want to try a new service innovation. However, adoption only comes about when they have experienced the service innovation for the first time, and begin to engage in further experiences, repeatedly, until it sticks. When users become advocates along with marketing efforts, this can encourage even more customers to adopt the new innovation. The User Experience (UX) of a service innovation through touchpoints in the User Journey is how you can build these 'stickiness effects.'

*We provide the following guidance on key UX measures\* that address user concerns during the User Journey stages to help you measure your UX designs and the levels of value that they deliver to the end-user:*

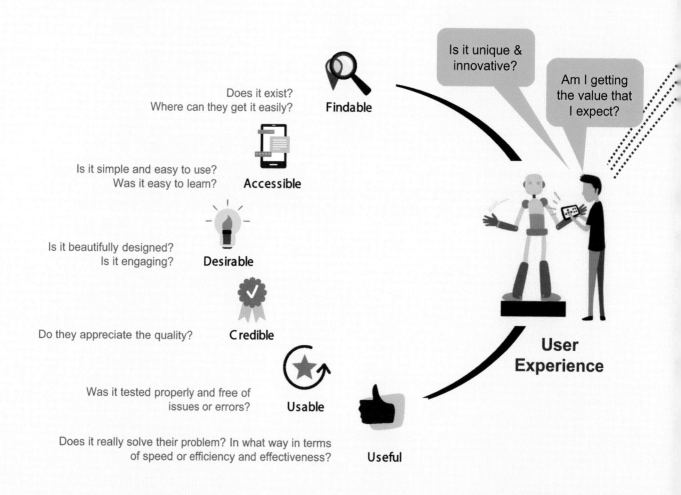

Does it exist?
Where can they get it easily?
**Findable**

Is it unique & innovative?

Am I getting the value that I expect?

Is it simple and easy to use?
Was it easy to learn?
**Accessible**

Is it beautifully designed?
Is it engaging?
**Desirable**

Do they appreciate the quality?
**Credible**

**User Experience**

Was it tested properly and free of issues or errors?
**Usable**

Does it really solve their problem? In what way in terms of speed or efficiency and effectiveness?
**Useful**

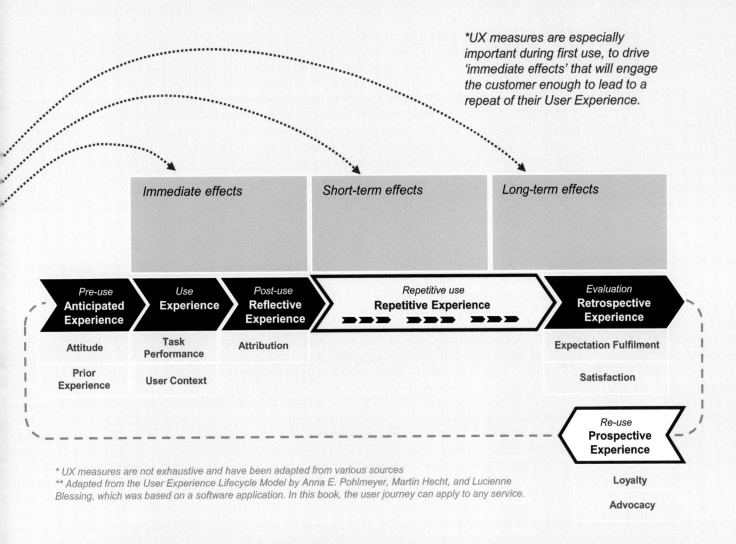

*UX measures are especially important during first use, to drive 'immediate effects' that will engage the customer enough to lead to a repeat of their User Experience.*

| Immediate effects | Short-term effects | Long-term effects |

**Pre-use** *Anticipated Experience* — **Use** *Experience* — **Post-use** *Reflective Experience* — **Repetitive use** *Repetitive Experience* — **Evaluation** *Retrospective Experience*

Attitude

Task Performance

Attribution

Expectation Fulfilment

Prior Experience

User Context

Satisfaction

*Re-use* **Prospective Experience**

Loyalty

Advocacy

\* UX measures are not exhaustive and have been adapted from various sources
\*\* Adapted from the User Experience Lifecycle Model by Anna E. Pohlmeyer, Martin Hecht, and Lucienne Blessing, which was based on a software application. In this book, the user journey can apply to any service.

## STRATEGY JOURNEY *Framework* Activity #12:

Create a survey to ask customers questions of how they feel along their user journey for your core service offering, following the data attributes from page 167-168. Add questions to collect any user data on your customers' repetitive use and/or re-use rates.

*Hint: Conduct this analysis of the current state or situation for your core offering. Reflect on how this user journey affects the customer journey that you developed in Activity #11 based on any stickiness effects that exist. Identify if is there a lack of stickiness effects in the user journey?*

# EXAMPLE: How Netflix's stickiness effects disrupted Blockbuster*

*Building on the earlier example that highlighted how ignoring the digital customer journey busted Blockbuster (p. 35)...*

We know a brand has established a strong position in customers' mind when its name becomes a verb, like Google, Uber, Skype or Zoom. And one such brand that cannot be ignored in this digital age is Netflix. Netflix has come a long way, starting from an online DVD rental service to the world leader in the streaming industry. The company completely changed how people watched movies and consequently destroyed the throne of Blockbuster, once the giant brick and mortar video rental store in the U.S. In 2000, Blockbuster turned down a $50M offer to purchase Netflix. 10 years later it found itself put out of business under the reign of Netflix.

Netflix has mastered the art and science of digital transformation on its strategy journey by nailing its understanding of the customer journey and implementing a remarkable user journey full of stickiness effects.

## Before Netflix, the age of Blockbuster...

Back to the late 20th century, when Netflix was just a small start-up, Blockbuster dominated the video rental industry and managed to get exclusive deals with big Hollywood studios to rent new DVD releases after cinema showings ended. At that time, households required a videocassette recorder (VCR) to watch videos, and Blockbuster rental stores were people's frequent destination for movie selections.

Customers went to Blockbuster stores not because they enjoyed the experience but just because it was the only choice for them to watch new movie releases. Consider the time spent by a family driving to a nearby Blockbuster store, going through hundreds, if not thousands of DVDs on the shelves without a catalog or any recommendations from store attendants, getting eyestrain from reading the titles, and arguing with your kids what to watch. New releases were promoted however were charged out at a premium.

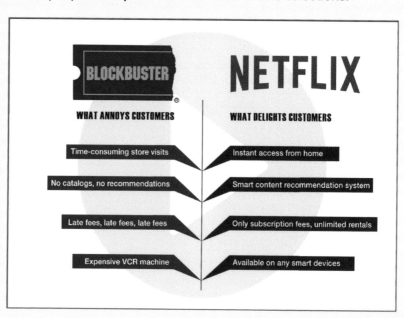

Customers had to clean the VCR machine's video head regularly and replace their machines at considerable cost when the format moved to DVD. If they forgot to return the Cassette/DVD on time (because life gets busy) they had to pay the store an exceptionally high late fee. Late fees comprised of a large part of Blockbuster profits. It was an unpleasant experience that actually drove people away from the business.

## Then Came Netflix – a Market Disruptor

As a former Blockbuster customer, Netflix CEO Reed Hastings thoroughly understood the issues with that customer journey, and he initially started Netflix as a mail-order DVD subscription service to eliminate the lengthy in-store visits and annoying late fees. To make up for the lack of physical customer interaction, Netflix offered lower prices (monthly subscription fees for unlimited rentals) and implemented efficient order-processing computer systems. After just a few years Netflix steadily grew its revenues and got Blockbuster on guard.

Nevertheless, it was when Netflix launched its video streaming service that saw the end of Blockbuster. Again, Netflix took a deep dive into the problems experienced by customers as users in a consumer journey and foresaw the future demands for instant-access entertainment at the convenience of Internet devices in that journey. With the new streaming service, Netflix customers and users could browse a detailed digital movie catalogue, make a selection and immediately press play with no need for a physical DVD. This has proved to be a highly sticky user experience, that has grown Netflix's streaming service to account for one-third of downstream Internet traffic during peak hours in the U.S.

In 2013, upon discovering the potential hype of binge-watching, Netflix started to produce in-house content, known as Netflix Originals, and released all the episodes at one time. Its first original series, House of Cards, still remains one of the best dramas on Netflix. Netflix took on customers' desire for personalization and came up with the smart content recommendation system which was backed by machine learning. Each customer now has a customized experience on Netflix based on their personal habits and preferences. This is where Netflix built up its sticky service to get customers as users of the Netflix platform  addicted and keeps them coming back for more.

Netflix's popularity was evidenced by impressive numbers even before the COVID-19 pandemic: circa. 150M users, almost double the runner-up Amazon Prime; two-thirds of Netflix users share their accounts with others, increasing the actual viewers by 2.5 times; 10 hours spent on Netflix weekly by average U.S. users; 23 languages used and 57% of international users; etc… Netflix has drastically grown its international content in the library too, especially as the COVID-19 pandemic and social distancing requirements have halted the film making industry from producing more content.

# Scaling Business to deliver value ...

Businesses have existed for thousands of years. Since the 1700s they have endured four separate Industrial Revolutions (p. 13-14), surviving and thriving, mostly through scaling their **Business Models**.

Growth is achieved following the innovation of a *minimum viable proposition* (MVP) which reaches the 'chasm' in the Innovation Adoption Lifecycle (p. 99). The business must be able to scale its *resources* to support growth. This resource scaling occurs via its **Operating Model** where *business transformation* (p. 81) is undertaken to span the chasm and realize the growth potential of its **Business Model**, delivering value as defined in its **Value Model**.

The **'Operating Model'** describes HOW the business runs, through all its business activities, to support the design, build, testing and delivery of its *value propositions* to customers, including internal customers or stakeholders (p. 121-122). It comprises processes, data, technology systems, and people, the component *resources* supporting the organization in different locations, both geographic and virtual, that are responsible for delivering business activities.

The goal of the **Operating Model** is to support the business to scale by organizing its resources and structuring the business activities that they perform to deliver more value. From designing new *business strategies* to the execution of those strategies across the entire enterprise better and faster, the **Operating Model** provides both the operational efficiency and *business agility* (p. 51-54) that will support growth in the business as well as keeping it sustainable.

# ... with the Operating Model

## What activities and resources form the Operating Model

All organizations operate with an overall *value chain* (p. 153-156) that describes how the business has chosen to manage and organize its business activities in order to deliver a 'margin'. The business activities in the *value chain* are executed by the component *resources* in the **Operating Model**, which are organized into *capabilities* performing different *business functions*. The *capabilities* support the *value streams* that deliver *value propositions* to customers and internal stakeholders, effectively and efficiently.

Some organizations use the *value chain* to diagrammatically depict different viewpoints of its **Operating Model** at point in time, with additional details layered over the *value chain*, like an architecture blueprint. When a business undergoes *business transformation*, it is making changes in HOW it operates to move from its **Current Operating Model (COM)** to its **Target Operating Model (TOM)** - two viewpoints of the **Operating Model**.

## Operating Model Canvas*

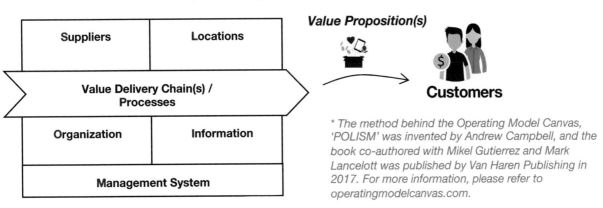

* The method behind the Operating Model Canvas, 'POLISM' was invented by Andrew Campbell, and the book co-authored with Mikel Gutierrez and Mark Lancelott was published by Van Haren Publishing in 2017. For more information, please refer to operatingmodelcanvas.com.

The *Operating Model Canvas** (OMC) is a good organizational design tool, to help you illustrate a specific high level viewpoint of the **Operating Model** by describing WHAT *key activities*, *key partners* and *key resources*, in a business enable it to deliver different *value propositions* to customers and according to different **Business Model** strategies.

---

**STRATEGY JOURNEY** *Framework* **TIP #9:**

Use the Operating Model Canvas to quickly outline WHAT makes up your enterprise's Current Operating Model (COM). *Go to* www.strategyjourney.com/tools *to download the template and watch the tutorial.*

# What resources create a ...

'**Capabilities**' are the building blocks of *resources* from a business's **Operating Model**, which have been optimized to perform different set of business activities that produce outputs for an organization. Many organizations refer to their *capabilities* as *business functions* and may use the terms interchangeably, as the term '**business function**' describes WHAT purpose and/or primary outcome is performed and/or delivered by a set of business activities.

## Component resources in a capability building block

The component *resources* in a '**capability**' building block are how, where, when, and by whom a set of business activities is conducted. They produce the outputs required by the business to deliver its *value streams* as directed by different **Business Models** (p. 154). They comprise processes, data, people, and technology systems, located in different geographies and that virtually make up the **Operating Model**.

**PROCESSES**

'**Process**' is how the business mixes all the necessary business activities and sequences them through the different *capabilities* in its **Operating Model** to enable the organization to run in an operationally efficient manner. This produces the best quality products and services to customers, while also delivering other internal or supporting *value streams* at the most optimal cost versus benefit provided.

**DATA**

'**Data**' or '**Information**' is what the business collects, uses, and learns from continuously through its business activities to produce and deliver value to customers and stakeholders. It enables the business to measure performance and apply changes. It can be used to analyze and predict the future performance of *value propositions* with the aid of technology, and to support *business transformation* and *innovation*.

**PEOPLE**

'**People**' with different skills are responsible for performing different sets of business activities (i.e. business functions) in the business to deliver its *value propositions* to customers. Staff spend time delivering customer-facing versus non-customer-facing business activities, or innovation, impacting the costs of operations in an organization. Staff interactions with customers can also impact the quality of the customer experience.

**SYSTEMS**

'**Systems**' supported by the most relevant, as well as best, technology available, should be used by a organization to improve the quality of its outputs, and increase the speed of and cost to execute its business activities, where appropriate, to produce its *value propositions* and associated value-added outcomes. When benefits outweighs costs, slow manual processes operated by people should be automated by systems.

**LOCATION**

'**Location**' is where the business chooses to operate its business activities in different combinations using the four component resources of processes, data, people and systems, supported by the appropriate physical and/or virtual infrastructure. It is chosen based on a combination of factors including cost and availability of quality resources and/or customers, overall accessibility (i.e. regulations) and potential network effects (p. 133).

# ... capability in the business

## Making valuable assets out of resources with capabilities

A **'capability'** is formed when different *resources* in an organization are combined to perform a specific set of business activities to an optimal level of performance that can be measured through KPIs, such as productivity, quality, capacity, competitiveness and other operations performance measures. *Capabilities* have the ability to create value through the outputs and outcomes as well as experiences that they produce and deliver.

This ability to measure the performance of a *capability* and the value that is creates, which allows it to be compared with other *capabilities* especially those owned by competitors, is what makes it an asset that is owned by a business (p. 149-150). The value of a *capability* as an asset to the business can be calculated from the performance of its processes, which holds data, that are executed through people and systems. This value is heightened by the *capability's* uniqueness especially when it is part of a *Unique Service Proposition* that cannot be copied by competitors, such as a patented process or special secret formula (eg. KFC or Coca-Cola).

Organizations may engage in buying or licensing *capabilities* from other organizations who offer their *capabilities* as a service. Buying or licensing a *capability* can help an enterprise to fill and hence mitigate capability and resource gaps in its **Operating Model**, which will help to support its **Business Models** to scale and speed up business growth (p. 141).

## Developing competitive advantage with capabilities

Organizations compete through the performance of their *capabilities* and the value-added outcomes and experiences that the *capabilities* produce, to support the business's *value streams* and *value propositions*.

A **'Unique Selling Proposition' (USP)** is created by utilizing one or more superior *capabilities* within *value streams* to form a superior *value proposition*. So developing better and faster *capabilities* as well as using *capabilities* in a better way that make *value streams* and *value propositions* perform better and faster, is how an organization can differentiate itself with a 'competitive advantage'.

> **STRATEGY JOURNEY** *Framework* Activity #13:
>
> Brainstorm and identify a list of all the *capabilities* that are required to support your core offering in the **Business Model** and indicate those that are run internally through your staff and/or systems, versus those that are outsourced. Focusing on your core offering, align and sequence the relevant *capabilities* into your core *value stream* and mark them as *'core capabilities'*. How many of these *core capabilities* are internal versus external? Identify the *core capabilities* that are responsible for delivering your core offering's USP.

# Aligning organizational resources with the value chain

Most organizations organize their *resources*, and hence structure themselves, to operate based on their *value chains* as it is how they intend to make profit, scale and grow. The *value chain* outlines the 'pipeline' of business activities that support an organization's primary **Business Model**. This is why most traditional **Business Models** are 'pipelines' (p. 111)

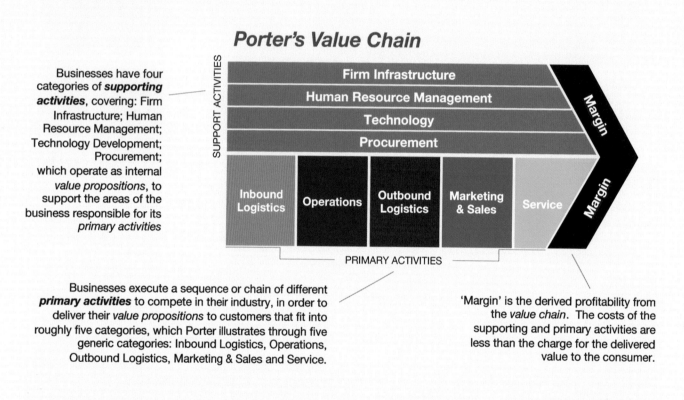

## Porter's Value Chain

Businesses have four categories of **supporting activities**, covering: Firm Infrastructure; Human Resource Management; Technology Development; Procurement; which operate as internal *value propositions*, to support the areas of the business responsible for its *primary activities*

SUPPORT ACTIVITIES

Firm Infrastructure
Human Resource Management
Technology
Procurement

Inbound Logistics | Operations | Outbound Logistics | Marketing & Sales | Service

Margin

PRIMARY ACTIVITIES

Businesses execute a sequence or chain of different **primary activities** to compete in their industry, in order to deliver their *value propositions* to customers that fit into roughly five categories, which Porter illustrates through five generic categories: Inbound Logistics, Operations, Outbound Logistics, Marketing & Sales and Service.

'Margin' is the derived profitability from the *value chain*. The costs of the supporting and primary activities are less than the charge for the delivered value to the consumer.

Michael Porter came up with the concept of *value chains* in 1985, following the huge success of the first three Industrial Revolutions (p. 13-14). He provided a generic map of **primary activities** and **supporting activities** within an organization that form the building blocks for the design, development, delivery, and servicing of a product to customers in order to derive a margin.

**Porter's Value Chain** has been used extensively to describe major industries of the late 20th century. It quite accurately describes the *value chains* companies in the manufacturing and automotive companies, such as Toyota and Ford, who have thrived for decades on the success of their *value chains* which connect with their 'supply chains'. This is the process where multiple business partners (p. 121) participate together across an industry or business ecosystem (p. 95), that is a *value* ecosystem (p. 156), to fulfill a customer request.

## Driving value with 'Vertical' versus 'Horizontal' business lines

The *primary activities* in **Porter's Value Chain** form the *value streams* that deliver the **Business Models** of an enterprise, operating as a pipeline to deliver the margin, while *supporting activities* operate as *resources* that are optimized to reduce costs. Many organizations operate with these **'Vertical'** and **'Horizontal'** business lines that are designed to support traditional *Pipeline Business Models*.

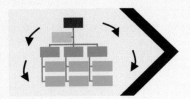

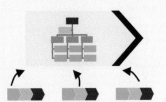

### 'Vertical' business line

When an organization aligns its *capabilities* into *value streams* that deliver *value propositions* to customers who are external to the business (p. 121) as depicted by Porter through the sequence of *primary activities*, it is said to be operating vertically with *capabilities* bound by a **'Vertical'** organizational structure to form a **'Vertical' business line**.

In 'Vertical' organizational structures, a top-down approach from senior management is taken to drive and deliver value through the **Business Model** – to deliver the margin. Business decisions are made at the top of the hierarchy and filter down through the organization into the different *capabilities* who perform the business activities as part of a *business function*.

### 'Horizontal' business line

A **'Horizontal' business line** describes a **'Horizontal'** organizational structure when *capabilities* are organized into *value streams* that deliver internal *value propositions* to other stakeholders in the business (p. 122), as depicted by Porter through *supporting activities*, where the role is to support all the organization's *'Vertical' business lines*, equally.

In a 'Horizontal' organizational structure, a *'Horizontal business line'* operates as a set of *resources* with a cost to the overall business in the organization's balance sheet and impacts the business's ability to deliver a margin.

### Converting Horizontal businesses lines into Vertical businesses lines

A *'Horizontal business line'* may choose to operate vertically by extending its *capabilities* to include marketing and sales, as well as servicing and developing a new **Business Model** to deliver *value propositions* as defined by the **Value Model** to both internal and external customers. For example, this is how the Amazon Web Services (AWS) business was formed, from extending its internal 'web services' business function into an entire business line offering 'webservices' to business customers. This is an increasing trend amongst many companies to convert their *internal value propositions* into external *value propositions* in their attempts to overcome disruption from the digital economy and stay relevant.

# Example: The *value chain* supporting the higher education industry

The Higher Education industry has been dominated by big traditional institutions with many years of history and tradition in delivering quality education, such as Harvard, Cambridge, Wharton, Stanford, Oxford, Massachusetts institute of Technology (MIT) and many more higher education organizations. Organizations have been competing for many decades through their rankings from industry bodies. The **Business Model** of higher education institutions has remained primarily the same with strategies focused on making changes to their **Operating Model** based on what enables them to rank well, as well as delivering steady revenue and profit. The *value chain* for a typical higher education institution operates as a pipeline (p. 96) involving six primary activities* where *capabilities* and *value streams* are formed to deliver the value to customers, that is paying students: Design, Recruit, Enroll, Deliver, Graduate, and Improve.

| DESIGN | RECRUIT | ENROLL |
| --- | --- | --- |

**'Design'** encompasses the *capabilities* involved in an education *value proposition* curriculum creation. This includes but is not limited to *value streams* aligned to support content creation, such as Market Research and Planning, Curriculum Design & Customization, Professional Learning and Accreditation.

**'Recruit'** encompasses the capabilities involved in bringing students to the platform/institution to undertake an education course. This includes but is not limited to value streams aligned to Agent Management, Sales (Domestic and International Student Recruitment), Scholarship Management and Prospective Student Engagement.

**'Enroll'** encompasses the capabilities to take a prospective student through the processes to enroll for an education course. It encompasses value streams such as Matriculation, Allocation and Placement and Unit enrolment so that the student is setup for their course with specific specializations.

In today's digital economy (p.95), the traditional **Pipeline Business Models** of higher education institutions are increasingly being disrupted by new entrants, such as Udacity, Udemy, Coursera and many others that leverage new **Digital Business Models** to offer professional education services to adults.

Six Primary Activities undertaken by higher education services enterprises
*Adapted from Caudit.edu.au*

## DELIVER  >  GRADUATE  >  IMPROVE

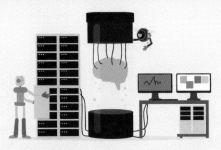

**'Deliver'** encompasses the capabilities to both deliver the education course and assess the students. This includes, but is not limited to, value streams such as the Learning Service (Teaching Material Preparation and Delivery), Content Administration, Customization and Scheduling & Timetabling.

**'Graduate'** encompasses the capabilities to assess and award students with qualifications. This includes, but is not limited to, value streams such as Eligibility Assessment, Degree & Qualification Award, Ceremony Management, Alumni Relationship Management.

**'Improve'** encompasses the capabilities to assess and improve the education curriculum. This includes, but is not limited to, value streams such as Quality Management, Performance Management, Program and Unit Disestablishment, which overall manage the evolution of the quality of the content and the delivery of the education.

**STRATEGY JOURNEY** *Framework* **TIP #10:**

It is useful to locate existing industry value chains to help you identify the value streams and capabilities that support any enterprise or organization. *Go to strategyjourney.com/tools for more information, including links to other generic industry value chains.*

# What gaps in the Operating Model ...

All services are delivered to customers (buyers and users) by enterprises big and small, through their *value streams* of interconnected *capabilities* (p. 154) from their **Operating Models**. When new services or improvements need to be delivered, relevant capabilities in the value stream must also change through business transformation (p. 81). The effort in time and resources required to implement business transformation will depend on the relative gaps in maturity (p. 187-188) of existing capabilities from how they operate today to how they need to perform to support the new services.

The goal of a *'Transformation Design'* process (p. 154) is to identify what *'Capability Gaps'* exist in an enterprise that are required to support its key *value streams* and how the enterprise will address these gaps, through analyzing its 'Transformation Gaps'. Successful business transformation of the **Operating Model** that will enable an enterprise to deliver its new and improved *value propositions* (service innovations) to customers and realizing its **Business Model**, requires both gaps to be addressed.

**Capability Gaps**

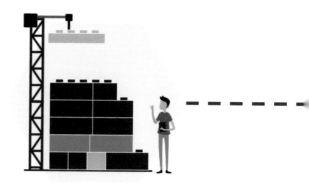

**'Capability Gaps'** are the gaps in the **Operating Model**, that make an enterprise incapable of delivering a service, and its service gaps.

The 'Capability Gap' is the missing/inadequate *capability* that is required to support the end-to-end value stream of a service. Most *capabilities* form part of more than one *value stream* and the service offering that it delivers, so addressing 'Capability Gaps', as part of the 'Transformation Design' process can improve the *business agility* (p. 51-54) of an enterprise and its **Operating Model**. When significant gaps in *capability* are improved through business transformation, there can be a network effect of supporting multiple services and solving multiple problems both internally in an enterprise and for customers.

# ... require business transformation

**Transformation Gaps**

'**Transformation Gaps**' are the changes that need to be made to the specific components in a *capability* in order to address the 'Capability Gap' in the **Operating Model**. The changes modify the operation of the capability through changes in any of process, data, people or systems in the different locations both virtually and geographically that the capability exists.

Each '**Transformation Gap**' describes what needs to be changed as well as how the change needs to be executed. '**Transformation Gaps**' can vary in size or complexity as they depend on many factors relating to the current maturity level of a capability versus the required target maturity level to support the new or improved service offering in the **Target Operating Model** (p. 187-190). Addressing '**Transformation Gaps**' involves business transformation projects and activities in the enterprises 'transformation journey', that are managed via the **Transformation Model.**

# Evolution Steps Towards Digital Operating Model Maturity

Successful *service innovation* can be hard to achieve especially when an enterprise seeks to diversify how it operates (p. 158) to combat the increasing challenges from a fast changing digital economy. To be able to maintain and continuously increase the value-add that it can deliver to customers and stakeholders through its service innovation efforts an enterprise needs a high level of maturity in its own business transformation *capabilities.* This ensures it is able to operate with the necessary *business agility (p. 51-54)* to develop better and faster service solutions, keep learning, adapting and improving how it operates with speed to market.

**'Maturity'** is used to objectively assess how developed the components of an **Operating Model** are, in how they perform to deliver and produce value for an enterprise, covering an entire capability and the component resources that form it.

## The Five Maturity levels of Operating Model capabilities

### Siloed

*Capabilities* are bespoke, undocumented, specific to a single process and/or service using non-standardized processes and data. They are also supported by independent or adhoc systems that are unsecure.

Eg. When a potentially corruptible excel spreadsheet is used to run a business with no backups.

### Tactically Integrated

*Capabilities* are better defined and integrated for end-to-end or front-to-back business use cases in limited instance(s) via data mapping and systems interfacing. Technology applications are used to define process and SOPs. Customer experience is technically improved.

Eg. New systems that duplicate existing processes are added into individual products, with hardwired data mapping.

### Process-Driven

*Capabilities* have characterized processes and data. There is a process-led definition of all aspects of the capability aiding and improving integration between process steps end-to-end or front-to-back. Repeatable reliable processes improve customer service to support expectation fulfilment along during service delivery.

Eg. A single CRM system is integrated to manage and track multiple pipeline and customer servicing processes.

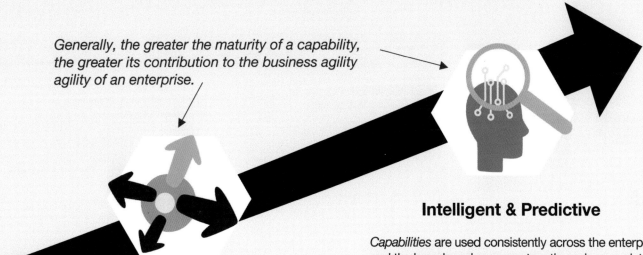

*Generally, the greater the maturity of a capability, the greater its contribution to the business agility agility of an enterprise.*

## Intelligent & Predictive

*Capabilities* are used consistently across the enterprise and the broader value ecosystem through more data-driven touchpoints such as via API integration, with the objective of capturing and using big data to predict and improve business agility and customer service requirements. There is the capability to measure and fine tune customer stickiness and drive future trends in customer behaviors that will facilitate business growth through increasing Customer Lifetime Value (CLV), especially with increase used of data driven digital transformation techniques and technologies such as artificial intelligence (AI).

Eg. Amazon Alexa network which operates on the AWS cloud, with big data and AI capabilities incorporated, Microsoft AI services, any many SaaS services deployed on Cloud Architectures that have incorporated IBM Watson or other AI modules.

## Modular & Optimized

*Capabilities* are modular and re-usable in different configurations using standardized processes, data, systems, and people roles exist to drive scalable output with monitoring for continuous improvement. **Operating Model** components in the capability are consistently used and repeatable providing process integration across the enterprise to optimize business agility (p. 51-54) and better and faster customer service.

Eg. All capabilities including third party apps are integrated within a service architecture such as AWS or Google Cloud, with well defined APIs and operational characteristics.

**'Maturity levels'** can be used as part of the *'Transformation Design'* process to determine the extent of the changes required to transform a *capability* in its current state to the level required in the **Target Operating Model**. They identify the 'Transformation Gaps' that could exist in a 'Capability Gap'.

---

**STRATEGY JOURNEY** *Framework* **Activity #14:**

Review and rate the current level of maturity for the capabilities in your business that support your core service offering and value stream (from Activity #13). Use the maturity index on pages 189-190 to identify the level of maturity at a more granular level, in the Operating Model components.

# Operating Model Capability Maturity Index

| | Siloed | Tactically Integrated |
|---|---|---|
| **CUSTOMERS** | • Sales teams focused on revenue<br>• Minimal customer/client segmentation<br>• No clear understanding of the customer journey<br>• Inter-business rivalry for customers<br>• Limited focus on customer experience post sales | • Limited cross-selling of products and services<br>• Concept of customer journey and customer service le▮ recognized<br>• Set-up of adhoc customer service teams<br>• Disjointed and fragmented effort to improve customer▮ experience |
| **STAFF & PARTNERS** | • Subject matter experts<br>• Culture is adversarial with mutual distrust<br>• No formal change management procedure<br>• I will do my job, you do yours | • Cross-functional process teams usually led by IT<br>• Limited understanding of cross departmental process▮ needs & dependencies (i.e. limited understanding of f▮ to-back or end-to-end service flows) |
| **PROCESSES** | • Static business processes<br>• Product and/or functional silos<br>• Geographic silos<br>• Department focused<br>• Informal communications within departments<br>• No standardized monitoring or reporting | • Limited process reengineering and cross-functional process coordination (manual one-time efforts)<br>• Systems drive baseline process definitions<br>• Limited understanding of front-top-back value chain a▮ value streams<br>• Limited standardized reporting and monitoring |
| **DATA & INFORMATION** | • Data definition is specific to the needs of individuals or small teams within product/function/location…<br>• Significant use of spreadsheets rather than databases<br>• Significant reconciliations and data cleaning effort Major risk of data breaches/regulatory non-compliance | • Multiple data-sources, project or system driven<br>• Some data alignment via mapping where systems are▮ integrated<br>• Adhoc/fragmented/manual data control to meet regulatory requirements<br>• Major reconciliations effort and cost |
| **SYSTEMS** | • Independent systems<br>• Islands of automation<br>• Integration only within business functions<br>• Legacy enterprise systems<br>• Business critical systems implemented using office software (Excel) | • ERP systems starting to support cross-functional integration<br>• Point-to-point partner integration<br>• Increasing usage of automation within teams and business functions<br>• cross-functional initiatives (systems focused) |
| **LOCATION** | • Multiple disparate locations<br>• Bespoke business functions per location<br>• bespoke process and systems per location<br>• in house operations<br>• Customer access across all locations | • Locations connected to support tactical process integration<br>• Technology layer integration across locations<br>• Increased location data reconciliation requirements<br>• Some co-ordination across customer access location▮ points |

| Process-Driven | Modular & Optimized | Predictive & Intelligent |
|---|---|---|
| nproved customer segmentation and cross-selling / ome service tiering defined by customer segment / ormal customer service teams across the value chain / upported by standard processes / ollection of qualitative feedback from customer on / xperience/interactions | • All customer journeys and SLAs defined & implemented<br>• Customer experience is embedded in all processes in the enterprise to measure customer experience<br>• Commence build of single customer view | • Predictive modeling based on customer behaviour<br>• Pro-active and pre-emptive customer servicing using single customer view<br>• Customer experience is a competitive advantage<br>• Customer communication & feedback is continuously used to improve processes |
| ervice and/or Process leaders/owners define, deploy, / nhance & maintain core processes / unctional teams focused on high quality/specialized / xecution / ntroduced customer experience as performance / easure | • Cross-selling & re-use of services is incentivized<br>• Lean organisation focused on optimizing process definitions & execution<br>• Ongoing process training for employees<br>• Customer experience is a performance measure | • Partner/vendor selection includes process & cultural attributes<br>• Ongoing training for employees & partners<br>• Customer centricity if part of cultural DNA |
| ransitioned from functional to process focused, including / anagement structure, execution teams and / erformance evaluation / usiness process outsourcing prevalent / rocess led design / rocess standardized reporting and monitoring | • process integration across the enterprise<br>• continuous process improvement program<br>• Outsourced non-core business processes (reduce cost and increase quality)<br>• End to end service based reporting and monitoring | • Total process integration across the value streams and with connected value ecosystem<br>• Key services flow seamlessly across firewalls<br>• Ability to influence customer journeys outside the enterprise & customer interactions with supported channels |
| obal data sources and logical data model / ata management teams, data standards and / overnance set-up / nproved data quality & control to support reporting and / ecision making / utomation has reduced data reconciliation effort | • Enterprise golden data sources available<br>• Majority of internal systems use data standards<br>• Data transitions managed by well defined process<br>• Exception management is process & data driven<br>• Minimal reconciliation efforts<br>• Data intelligence actively utilized to support business | • Golden data sources used throughout the enterprise & with partners<br>• All systems use standard data sets (with local variations)<br>• Standardize data to support process data analytics & business intelligence (i.e. predictive modeling)<br>• Easy to add new data, control and reporting |
| rocess-led thinking on initiatives driving systems / duced usage of Excel & tactical solutions / ystems & instances consolidation per business function / streamline processes & information management / ultiple simple workflow solutions | • business process management (BPM) lead architecture & system solutions to integrate and operate processes as services<br>• enterprise monitoring & control across value streams & Operating Model capabilities<br>• system architecture for the enterprise<br>• AI systems utilized to support service enhancement | • business process management (BPM) solutions operate services end to end<br>• Systems infrastructure supports service integration with external partners and customers across the ecosystem/value system<br>• AI systems prevalent throughout services |
| apabilities standardized in key locations / rocess led design connecting locations / ome business function outsourcing / ustomers access services through defined access / oints / ocation strategy approach | • Location based centers of excellence in process and service<br>• operating model determined location strategy to optimize service delivery and efficiency<br>• use of outsource and near shore and virtual<br>• Customer access and service experience led | • Intelligent and predictive location strategy based on future business and operating model<br>• Modular capabilities with redundancy across operating locations<br>• Agile service and capability deployment across operating or new locations<br>• Locations optimized for customer experience |

# Leverage value ecosystem services ...

In every *value stream* operating within a business there will be capabilities that are supported in-house or sourced from third parties. Sourced *capabilities* act as **'sub-services'** in the enterprise as they are service offerings provided by other players in the wider business ecosystem that surrounds the business - its **'value ecosystem'.** During business transformation (p. 81), an enterprise can choose to address its **'capability gaps'** on its own or through sourcing and/or partnering with other players from its *value ecosystem*. This decision to build and improve services in-house or source and integrate services externally is a part of the **'Transformation Design'** process.

Increasingly, in our digital economy, the trend is for enterprises to partner with other service providers from their *value ecosystem* in order to deliver better and faster services to customers and end-users. This is achieved through sharing and leasing of the latest technologies and networks (p. 133) as *'services'* from each other (i.e. Cloud Services and Software as a Service). In turn this enables an enterprise to focus its resources and efforts internally on *capabilities* that differentiate its own services, delivering a *Unique Selling Proposition (USP),* that gives it a competitive advantage. In the *value ecosystem*, former competitors may become strategic partners through alliances, as the 'race' in the 'game of business' is to provide valuable outcomes first and foremost to customers and users.

Examples of how value ecosystems work:

- Financial Services players provide funding for companies in almost every other value ecosystem.

- Most IT departments in companies across multiple industries leverage the web services provided Amazon Web Services (AWS), and other similar Cloud service providers.

- Almost all OEMs in the automotive industry leverage the same set of suppliers and differentiate through marketing.

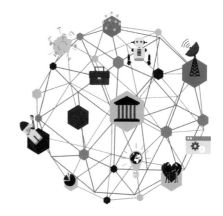

Any service provider can have one or more roles in the *value ecosystem* of a service provided by another service provider, and thus operate in multiple *value ecosystems*. All internal *capabilities* a company possesses with a unique position and competitive advantage, relative to the other players in each *value ecosystem*, are opportunities for a new service offering.

# ... in the Operating Model

## Different players in the Value Ecosystem

Every service will have a *value ecosystem* consisting of players which should be assessed to find possible partners to fill 'capability gaps' within the service's *value stream*. Sourcing of external capability will provide the opportunity to extend a service's unique *capability* or *capabilities* 'upstream' and 'downstream' realizing a competitive advantage. Integration of value ecosystem players improves an enterprise's *business agility* (p. 51-54)

*We have classified ecosystem players into the following ecosystem roles to help you identify them during service design and as part of value modeling:*

### 'Upstream' ecosystem

Upstream ecosystem players provide inputs into the *value stream* of a service to support how effectively and efficiently it operates.

They include:

- Dependencies
- Suppliers (in the supply chain)
- Enhancers

### 'Downstream' ecosystem

Downstream ecosystem players support the outputs from the service and its delivery to the end-user and customer by extending the *value stream*.

They include:

- Customer/Users (especially during co-creation)
- Channels
- Distributors

It is the role that a sub-service provides that determines if the ecosystem player is supporting a service upstream or downstream to fill a 'Capability Gap'. Any ecosystem system player could potentially fulfill multiple roles if they have valuable capabilities with USPs that the ecosystem requires. Thus they would be able externalize/extend these capabilities into services for other ecosystem players.

In today's digital economy, 'Competitors' and even 'Disruptors' may end up as partners especially downstream to support other players to reach customers and end-users better and faster using their networks with *'network effects'* (p. 133).

*E.g. You can leverage the Amazon Marketplace or Alexa app, as well as IOS and Android app stores to access customers.*

# Value Ecosystem Player Roles

Every enterprise and their specific target service offerings are surrounding by one or more Value Ecosystems with players that possess and provide capabilities that they could leverage to mitigate their 'capability gaps' in their Operating Models. Some of these players may provide their USP capabilities as service offerings to support specific supply chains. Many of these USP capabilities can also play a different role in additional supply chains that have not yet been identified.

*We have provided a list of these other value ecosystem player roles where it is possible reinvent how a USP capability can be used in different value streams from alternate industries and within new service innovations:*

## Suppliers

Complete component products or end-to-end sub-services involving labor and/or systems from external third party partners that are required to produce and create your target service offering.

## Dependencies

Services with specific *capabilities* provided by controlling or other government or regulatory bodies and organizations that are mandated to form part of your target service offering. And where there may be rules, regulations, and procedures to comply and integrate with.

## UPSTREAM

## Enhancers

Specific capabilities where there is a joint venture with an external party to develop and improve the capability together involving Intellectual Property (IP) or some increase in value to an asset that supports the target service offering.

## Disruptors

Service offerings that can replace and take over the time spent that customers and users on an existing activity in their customer journey and/or the user journey of the target service. Indicate what activities are being made redundant or obsolete. For example digital photos have replaced film.

**DOWNSTREAM**

### Channels

The different ways or mechanisms to interact with customers and users directly as part of your end-to-end service offering, including specific networks (p. 125).

### Customers/Users

The segments of customers and users who form your target market, who have been validated as viable commercially to support Business Model growth, and whom you will need to deliver value through the User Journey to solve their problems along their Customer Journey.

### Competitors

Similar or comparable alternative service offerings to the target service offering from rivals in the marketplace.

Hint: Indicate the extent of what makes this alternate service different where possible.

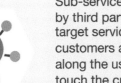

### Distributors

Sub-service capabilities offered by third parties that enable the target service offering to reach customers and users indirectly along the user journey, and that touch the customer journey.

**STRATEGY JOURNEY *Framework* TIP #11:**

When your enterprise has a 'Capability Gap' with a significant difference in maturity between its current state and the target state that is required to support a new service innovation, you should explore partnerships with other value ecosystem players to fulfill the gap. Identify if they can be integrated through an API to support data exchange.

# EXAMPLE: Tesla, a platform for the wealthy and an energy network

What kind of company is Telsa Inc? Is it a car company, an energy company, a manufacturer, a research and innovation service, a data analytics company, a financial services provider, or an aspiring luxury brand?

In the seventeen years since it was founded in 2003, with the support of celebrity entrepreneur and Elon Musk, Tesla Inc. (formerly Telsa Motors) has successfully transformed itself several times.

It has undergone a metamorphosis from a small pioneering electric car manufacturer to a global manufacturer of broader use EVs, global charging infrastructure, renewable energy production and storage, financial services and data intelligence.

Tesla has focused relentlessly on service and product design with customer experience as a differentiator. These coupled with best in market capability utilizing the latest technologies have helped it become a market leader.

The product and service strategy has built a platform for the wealthy, with a connected set of value propositions for its customers, and partners, including:

- Luxury cars for sale and lease
- Connected data and automation services
- Global recharging infrastructure and lounges
- Vehicle Maintenance services via subscription
- Financial services in the form of loans and purchase lease plans
- Domestic and commercial solar energy capture & storage
- City grid energy planning and data

## Operating Model Transformation is at the heart of Tesla's recent success

Operationally, Tesla has transformed at key stages in its history. New operating models have powered the business model changes that built Tesla into a technology R&D leader, volume product manufacturer, global distributor and iconic brand.

The Model S was Tesla Motors plan to scale manufacturing to deliver a volume product. Prior to the production and global distribution of the Model S in 2012, Tesla purchased the NUMMI manufacturing plant in Fremont CA from GM/Toyota in 2010. This plant supported a transition from the small scale production of the 2008 Roadster years. Making NUMMI operate for the Model S represented a significant change in operating model where sourcing and supply chain agreements were key to ramping production along other industrial scale processes. Also in 2012, a new service was developed and rolled out to support the Model S launch – the Supercharger network. Developing this network involved assessing and engaging partners around the world taking a Tesla commoditized design and developing stations across relevant markets.

The Model X was delivered in 2015 and in 2016 the mass market Model 3 was announced. Further scaling for these products dictated a significant change in operating model moving to a center of excellence approach concerning energy technology and the first Gigafactory came on line on 2016. In 2017 Tesla announced a set of domestic and commercial energy capture and storage products using Tesla battery technology.

Tesla cars, with their autonomous driving features, which create a luxury, time saving, and scientific or technology driven (ie. Gadgetry) customer experience for the wealthy and aspiring wealthy, have become a container for several of the company's ecosystem of connected services. As an autonomous data driven value proposition, each Tesla car is indirectly co-creating with customers, as its automated sensors inside and on the car are continuously collecting data about car usage, and behavior patterns around transportation, which can all be re-used through Telsa's other services, including current and future value propositions. Through data and this network of services, the car effectively becomes a value making machine.

The company's announcement in 2018 that it is transforming to become an energy company, was part of its strategy and operating model plan from the beginning. It is clear that Telsa's strategy is to grow its subsidiary, SolarCity, where it is reinvesting surplus profits into its battery and solar technology value propositions, as it bids to gain a major foothold into an even larger and very lucrative network, in the form of the power grid or energy supply grid, a global network formerly dominated by industry leaders of oil and gas power.

*Based on research conducted by Stratability Academy using public information - sources available in References section*

# What capabilities enable …

All strategies and tactics defined by the **Mission Model**, **Business Model** and **Value Model** amount to nothing if they are not executed through implementation of changes in the **Operating Model** of an enterprise. Strategy execution is required to achieve *business transformation* including *digital transformation* and the value added outcomes that come with it. When executing *business transformation*, an enterprise undergoes a **'transformation journey',** with many transformation challenges that it must overcome, to reach its **Target Operating Model**. The path to achieving this future state requires considered planning, as well as coordination and co-operation during execution via a **Transformation Model.**

The **'Transformation Model'** describes the effort in time, resources, costs and the governance of the roadmap associated with the transformation journey of an enterprise, as it executes changes to its *capabilities* and improves its *business agility*, for continued value delivery to customers and stakeholders, and future business growth.

An effective **Transformation Model** that can manage the logistics of an enterprise's transformation journey with *business agility*, delivering the best possible value-added outcomes for a business and its customers, is enabled by the following four additional 'transformation capabilities':

## Governance

Governance describes the method by which an enterprise manages why, what, how, where, when and with whom it should transform to keep creating, producing and delivering value for all parties – its stakeholders including customers. It supports effective business transformation through a roadmap of activities that coordinates how the enterprise will achieve its quick wins as well as strategic outcomes, while transforming its Operating Model, to provide the best possible Return On Investment (ROI). Strong leadership that can communicate changes effective and pull staff along the transformation journey to participate in continuous business transformation is also essential for effective governance.

# ... effective **business transformation**

## Data Science

Effective use of data as an input and enabler to the enterprise's *business transformation* is essential support the governance of its change initiatives and projects to provide the best possible Return On Investment (ROI). Insights gained from collecting, mining, analyzing big data in an enterprise can support investment governance decisions on why, what and how it should address the different gaps in its customer journeys, and the capabilities in its **Operating Model**. With strong data science, an enterprise is able to monitor its performance and its risks, to incorporate better predictive and intelligence analytics into its decision making process for more effective **business transformation** that can adapt to different threats quickly.

## Co-creation

Strong 'co-creation' enables an enterprise to achieve *business transformation* in its **Operating Model** capabilities to deliver services to customers, users and stakeholders within the organization better and faster. 'Co-creation' facilitates more comprehensive analysis of how services should, could and do deliver value. It supports the data science where more thorough or unique solution options are produced from having collected and analyzed a bigger data set (big data), that actually considers thick data from customers behaviors along their customer and user journeys. It adds customers and users into the equation and their decision making process to support the decision making by leaders in an enterprise.

## Culture

With many different transformation challenges to overcome in a digital economy (p. 9-10) that demands better transformations faster, the governance of an enterprise's business transformation efforts, can be plague by an organizational culture that is 'fixed' and resistant to changes. The development of a culture of learning in staff and in how the enterprise operates to proactively and intelligently make decisions involving changes is an essential ingredient for effective *business transformation*. When this 'growth mindset' is part of the DNA of an enterprise and encapsulated in how it governs itself, then the enterprise has the ability to outperform others through its 'culture of learning' that supports continuous transformation.

# What does it take to govern ...

Enterprises use many different methods to govern how they should execute their *business transformation* activities. These methods may need to be modified according to their 'game plans' (from their **Mission Model)** to achieve 'quick wins' in the short-term as well as the long term gains of the **Target Operating Model**. The **Transformation Model** joins the dots by describing how an enterprise will execute changes in its **Operating Model** in order to deliver its **Business Model** and **Value Model**.  The **Transformation Model** may employ of one or more of these different methods and the governance will evolve as the enterprise tries, tests and deploys new ways to change.

## Transformation Viewpoints

The business transformation effort as described by a '*Transformation Roadmap*' must resource numerous projects comprising the required transformation activities and coordinate their performance and execution to achieve the milestone goals and strategic objectives in the **Mission Model**. Depending on the 'capability gaps' that exist in the **Operating Model**, changes may be substantial and so *business transformation* can be complex involving many distinct projects. Significant investment may be required for the changes to be made and the projects and investment may need to be coordinated as programs of work..

**'Enterprise View' should comprise management dashboards that can drill into the detailed views**

Governance must support the decision making process around what gets invested to form the enterprise's portfolio of work. This is why the **Transformation Model** has many viewpoints in how it directs, tracks and reports on changes.  Within the model the investment required to fund programs and projects is validated before budgets get released and execution commences. There are three viewpoints by which to invest funds and resources, track the progress of transformation changes and monitor the performance of changes once executed to calculate the Return On Investment (ROI).  These are '*Portfolio View*', '*Program View*', and '*Project View*'.

Portfolio Views can be combined to form an '*Enterprise View*' summarizing how all programs and projects are performing and delivering. All views can be linked and combined through 'Management Dashboards' and the data that supports them. For smaller organizations with less investment funding, a 'Program View' may not be required, as it is likely that there are fewer resources to coordinate in less complex projects. So there may just be one 'Portfolio View' which is also the 'Enterprise View' and far fewer 'Project Views' for these smaller organizations.

# ... business transformation

Many medium and larger sized enterprises may organize their 'corporate strategy' and 'change management' functions and teams around these different viewpoints comprising:

- a **'Strategy & Architecture' Function** operating at the *'Enterprise View'* level
- a **'Portfolio Management' Function** operating at the *'Portfolio View'* level
- a **'Program Manager'** coordinating many projects through the *'Program View'*
- a **'Project Manager'** coordinating the specific activities and tasks to execute changes through a *'Project View'*

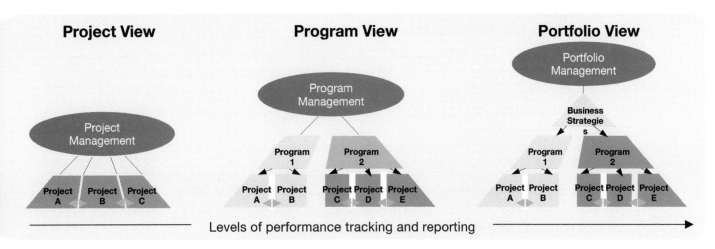

Levels of performance tracking and reporting

Each viewpoint may have its own roadmap, funding or budget, and resources, in terms skilled staff and systems to enable its operation. The different overseeing business functions or teams also meet regularly to make decisions on actions to take based to control the execution. These change based on the problem context and the different 'game plan' options available including risk assessment outcomes. The actions taken follow the steps in the 'priority gameplays', which together form the enterprise's transformation journey. These meetings may occur as small project-based meetings or where more coordination across functions and/or management levels is required, they become 'design authorities' which some larger organizations like to call 'steering committees'.

Larger enterprises are likely to also introduce a hierarchy within their organizational structure to coordinate allocation of resources and how decisions are made. This can introduce a level of bureaucracy slowing down progress when executing *business transformation*. Smaller and medium size firms may be less structured, which has its pros, in supporting agility, and cons, as a lack of structure on complex transformation programs can lead to chaos and failure to deliver any outcomes of value. Taking the effort to design a **Transformation Model** that is fit for purpose is how an enterprise strikes a balance to deliver effective *business transformation* with the best possible *business agility* – this is the responsibility of the *'governance capability'*.

# Transformation Governance Techniques

We recommend two transformation governance techniques which suit 'service innovation' projects that lead to *digital transformation* for your consideration in defining the **Transformation Model**:

## Change Development Lifecycle

The 'change development lifecycle' is a formal governance process for managing how the different stages of an enterprise's initiatives or projects move from idea through to solution execution. It is typically comprised of stages that individual project teams need to navigate to achieve a specific business transformation milestone on the transformation journey.

Decision making along the change development lifecycle may be governed through checkpoints to review proposed activities and well as the ongoing progress of projects. Decisions will also be made on when and how to START, PROGRESS, OR STOP projects responsible for executing a stage in the change lifecycle.

In **THE STRATEGY JOURNEY** *Framework*, we recommend five *'change development lifecycle'* stages to govern effective *business transformation* with five checkpoints.  We also advocate key business transformation activities that facilitate the enterprise to transform with *business agility*:

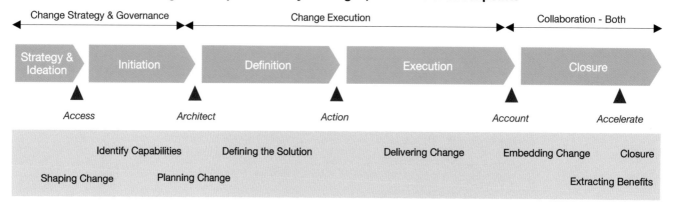

**Change Development Lifecycle Stages, Activities & Checkpoints***

Effective business transformation is difficult to achieve without strong leadership that is supported by effective communication that will persuade people to accept change. The five stages of the 'change development lifecycle' require a parallel communication strategy such as the Kotter's Change Methodology* comprised of eight steps to lead, communicate and embed change (p. 205) in an enterprise.

*\* Designed to incorporate best practices from the Waterfall Model and Kotter's Change Methodology*

# Using a Design Authority to support planning

A 'Design Authority' is a formal structure that supports the planning and governance of change initiatives and projects before, during and post changes. Agreed checkpoints are used when assessing projects. This formalizes the achievement of specific standardized milestones in the 'change development lifecycle'.

The Design Authority is typically responsible for providing guidance to decision makers and supporting change management teams concerning their business transformation activities along each stage of the change lifecycle, whilst managing and monitoring a centralized plan of all transformation projects and activities. It may incorporate a voting and approval process for budget releases on individual projects at formal meetings held at each checkpoint. With these responsibilities, a 'Design Authority' will need to be supported by strategy & architecture, as well as portfolio and project management functions in an enterprise.

For Design Authority meetings to be effective, they must have an agenda that is based on a prioritized pipeline of items needing design recommendations and decisions. It is important that sufficient pre-work studying and reviewing the items under consideration, where data is collected, and analyzed for insights, is completed before the formal meetings.  This ensures that recommended decisions in the form of 'game plans' and 'gameplays' can be made to allow *business transformation* by a project or program of projects to progress along the stages of the change lifecycle. The outputs of a design authority also form data points (control points) for tracking the performance of projects with regard to meeting their Return On Investment (ROI), as well as the effectiveness of the enterprise's transformation governance capability.

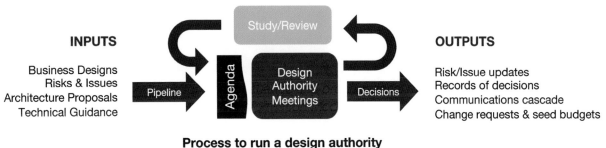

**Process to run a design authority**

Go to *strategyjourney.com/tools for a list of change and organizational management methodologies that you can apply in the design of the Transformation Model including the Nudge Theory used by governments to shift thinking and behaviors of large groups of people and Holacracy which is used by some smaller start-ups companies such as Zappos.*

# Transformation Implementation Techniques

*Digital transformation* is delivered through *service innovations* that are heavily dependent on technology systems and software development. In *Service Innovation* projects, we recommend leveraging different methodologies including two popular software development methodologies: Waterfall Model and Agile…

## Waterfall Methodology

The Waterfall Model is a project management lifecycle for software engineering first documented in 1970 by Royce that describes the sequential stages of the software development process, moving from concept, through design, implementation, testing, installation, troubleshooting and ending with operation and maintenance. Royce discovered the methodology while trying to find ways to cut costs on his projects and make them more predictable, while working on space-flight systems at TRW.

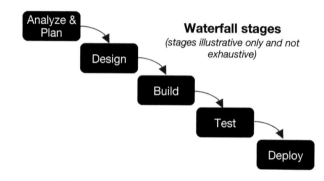

**Waterfall stages**
*(stages illustrative only and not exhaustive)*

The Waterfall Software Development Lifecycle (SDLC) method was used for about thirty-five years and through the 1970s and 1980s to organize and provide a structured approach to managing big projects across many industries including civil and mechanical engineering. After this some enterprises with the need for Rapid Application Development (RAD) of software began to move to more agile methods in order to speed up the software development lifecycle using more iterative steps to gain continuous improvements in shorter sprints.

## Agile Methodology

The Agile Methodology for software development was born in 2001 at a meeting by software leaders who codified 12 principles in an Agile Manifesto. Its development came from frustrations faced by software leaders who found the Waterfall Model too rigid because projects would freeze in time from further work, if a preceding stage such as 'functional design' was incomplete, thereby preventing the coding and testing stages from commencing.

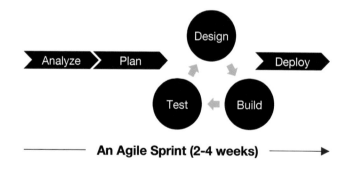

**An Agile Sprint (2-4 weeks)**

This meant that the innovation process for software engineering which was significantly different for big civil and mechanical engineering projects that required less changes, could not add iterative improvements and test changes to validate the functional design was fit for purpose with users of the software. Today most software development projects use the Agile methodology to iterate their application development in short sprints. Iterations are made usually between 2-4 weeks in order to incrementally add features to new software apps. Agile development or variations of it, is considered best practice for effective User Experience (UX) design, especially for the development of SaaS applications.

# Directing Business Transformation with a 'Transformation Roadmap'

In **THE STRATEGY JOURNEY** *Framework*, we recommend that different methods are combined and even expanded or evolved to fit the purpose, goals and objectives of an enterprise and its projects in the **Transformation Model**, in order to achieve *business agility*. It is important to consider different methods and what kind of outcomes they provide, based on the needs and wants of customers and users, in relation to a problem and their customer journeys, which is directed by an enterprise's overall 'game plan' and 'gameplays'.

The *Strategy Journey Paths (HOW Chapter)* guide you to apply a service-led approach rather than a solutions-led approach, that combines the data-driven principles for *business transformation*: Value-Driven, Customer Co-created and Network Connected. These principles are applied through the Five **Strategy Journey** Models: Mission Model, Business Model, Value Model, Operating Model and Transformation Model.

The **Transformation Model** is where you join·the·dots through the execution of *business transformation,* which is described by using 'Transformation Roadmaps' in order to communicate and direct 'WHAT' and more importantly 'HOW' the enterprise shall change.

As well as identifying 'WHAT' capabilities in the **Operating Model** are prioritized and sequenced for transformation to achieve specific milestones goals and S.M.A.R.T. objectives a good 'Transformation Roadmap' should also describe who is involved in the co-creation process to design, test and deploy the new or improved *service innovations.* It should also detail how the different projects and their tasks and activates are mobilized, sequentially or in parallel. This requires considerable planning and strong communication before the enterprise is considered ready to implement changes. Change execution should be monitored and tracked against strategic goals and objectives.

PMI Project & Program Management Best Practice

| DEVELOP PLAN | ANNOUNCE | IMPLEMENT |
|---|---|---|

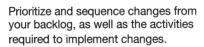

Prioritize and sequence changes from your backlog, as well as the activities required to implement changes.

Mobilize staff through effective communication, that will motivate them to participate in change implementation.

Track implementation progress and risks, and adapt how changes are applied, while iterative service solutions.

The Project Management Institute (PMI) a professional body of over 400,000 transformation management practitioners outlines three stages for best practice Project & Program Management: Develop Plan, Announce and Implement. These three best practices need to be applied in the **Transformation Model**.

# Transformation Mobilization Techniques

In the 'art of war' and the 'art of gamification', strong planning must be supported by effective mobilization of resources with the right mindset.  These must be deployed into the right places before a business is are considered ready to take on the fight. Mobilization of an enterprise's resources requires an effective communication strategy that will motivate people into action.

## Kotter's Change Methodology

John P. Kotter is a Harvard Business School Professor who first introduced his 8-Step Process to successful change in his 1995 book, 'Leading Change', which has seen been updated in subsequent books including 'The Heat of Change' (2002) and 'Accelerate' (2014). Kotter's Change Methodology was the first to focus specifically on the mobilization of changes through people and their response and approach to change.

Kotter's 8-step process splits into three stages responsible for:

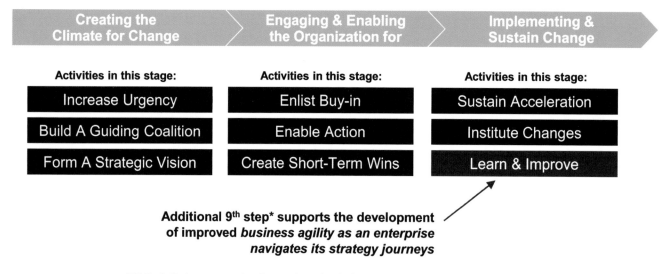

| Creating the Climate for Change | Engaging & Enabling the Organization for | Implementing & Sustain Change |
|---|---|---|
| Activities in this stage: | Activities in this stage: | Activities in this stage: |
| Increase Urgency | Enlist Buy-in | Sustain Acceleration |
| Build A Guiding Coalition | Enable Action | Institute Changes |
| Form A Strategic Vision | Create Short-Term Wins | Learn & Improve |

**Additional 9th step\* supports the development of improved *business agility as an enterprise navigates its strategy journeys***

\* Kotter's 8-step process has been adapted to include additional 'Learn & Improve' step by **THE STRATEGY JOURNRY** *Framework*

In **THE STRATEGY JOURNEY** *Framework*, as well as aligning Kotter's Change Management steps to the 'Change Development Lifecycle' that develops an enterprise's *business agility*, we have extended the 8-steps to include an additional 9th step – **Learn & Improve** – where the enterprise and its people also learn from their experiences in implementing change, in order to course correct and improve the way the enterprise transforms iteratively in the future.

# Using a Persuasion Campaign

Along with planning and implementing changes during *business transformation*, it is essential that enterprises also communicate effectively to mobilize people to change. This mobilization of change following Kotter's 8-Step process as well as the additional 9th step to 'Learn & Improve' can be implemented using a persuasive marketing campaign or '*Persuasion Campaign*'.

As illustrated through what some might have considered to be surprise results in the 2016 US election that made Donald Trump president, and the UK Brexit Referendum, an effective 'Persuasion Campaign' has the ability to mobilize a lot of people who may have been indifferent or undecided when it comes to they way they vote, into a specific action.

In their article, 'Change Through Persuasion' (hbr.org, 2005), David A. Garvin and Michael A. Roberto describes the ***Four Phases of A Persuasion Campaign***, with the process commencing before as well as running in parallel with the turnaround process to develop the 'Transformation Plan' and implement the activities in it -  and continues long after implementation is completed.

* Adapted from 'Change Through Persuasion' by Garvin and Roberto to incorporate **THE STRATEGY JOURNRY** *Framework*

In **THE STRATEGY JOURNEY** *Framework*, the **Transformation Model** encapsulates the 'Persuasion Process'. The four phases are used to influence the mindsets of people or staff in the enterprise through different communications, preparing them for change as well as reinforcing and embedding the right behaviors as the enterprise navigates its strategy journey. The 'game plan' which supports the **Mission Model** and 'gameplays' form the plan and the 'Transformation Roadmap' outlines the path for implementation. Following completion of each strategy journey lifecycle, transformation simply starts again. So the objective is also to build *business agility* which is embedded in the enterprise through a *culture of learning*.

# What data drives transformation

Transforming a business is a significant financial undertaking with significant downside from numerous threats and risks. The **Transformation Model** has to be well conceived and deliver on business needs based on what problems or challenges it should tackle.  There are many challenges (transformation scenarios) that instigate the need for change as discussed on pages 9-10.

Transformation investment must focus on what priorities need to be addressed to deliver the objectives of the *business strategy*. A piecemeal approach to prioritization driven by the most vocal stakeholders or a shotgun 'blanket' type approach attempting to address everything will not deliver the desired outcomes.

How does a business prioritize which transformation scenarios to address first and how should each of the transformation challenges be addressed – what is the transformation path?

The answer is found through different types of data that characterize the business and its challenges: Customer Data, Transactional Data, Performance Data and Transformation Data.

*Insights from objective, intelligently sourced data directs successful innovation*

### Customer Data

We have already established that it is paramount to model customers  (p. 125-126) in order to service their customer journeys effectively.  Customer Demographic, Customer Profile and Customer Journey data are all essential to establishing what is it that a business should be servicing to satisfy customers.
All of these different forms of **'Customer Data'** enable service innovation to discover and implement new services that will stick with customers, and increase an enterprise's ability to scale their Customer Lifetime Value (CLV).

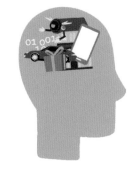

### Transactional Data

User interactions with the business via the 'Transaction Model' that the **Business Model** supports produces '**Transactional Data'**. The most common form of data that businesses collect is payment data in the buying and selling process. Payments are what businesses need to track in their accounts and report to the tax department. *Transactional Data* also includes 'interaction data' which is more valuable as it captures the customer's interaction with an enterprise's service(s), thereby also telling us more about customer's behaviors – it is additional *Customer Data*.

## Performance Data

**'Performance Data'** is calculated based on how an enterprise performs its business activities relative to the targets indicated by its S.M.A.R.T. objectives in the **Mission Model**. It is only relevant if there is enough of it from having collected, mined, used and analyzed the other two forms of data – *Customer Data* and *Transactional Data*. If these other forms of data are not present as input, then the *Performance Data* is absent of any real value.

*Performance Data* becomes more valuable when it is tracked in order to learn from it and what has changed, or not changed – and this is when it becomes *Transformation Data*. **Transformation Data** is the data that helps the business to make decisions as it is based on what has changed or needs to be changed in the performance of a process or interaction with respect to a service or product. This is the data that will enable prioritization of *business transformation* by informing its strategies and tactics in its 'game plans' and 'gameplays', thereby supporting an enterprise's investment and transformation governance decisions.

*Performance Data* can also be monitored and tracked across a group of enterprises in an industry or location such as country or region to provide insights into the overall performance of an industry or economies.

---

### Example: How intelligent data created and continues to transform Amazon.com

*Building on the earlier example that highlighted how two sets of data gave birth to Amazon...*

In the early 1990s, Jeff Bezos used market data detailing the increasing adoption rate of the internet by consumers to conceive his idea for an on-line book store. This trend in Transactional Data coupled with rich consumer market data on requirements for knowledge services and convenience (Customer Data) prompted Bezos to setup Amazon.com from his garage in 1994. This intelligent use of data to connect needs and trends in consumer retail provided him first mover advantage in internet retail services.

Amazon's initial focus on retail allowed other data led startups to capture first mover advantage in other types of services. Netflix harnessed advances in scalable internet streaming technology to create first mover advantage in video streaming to the consumer in the home. Again consumer internet adoption figures and home movie demand data identified the opportunity. Netflix dominates this market for streaming but Amazon is building a following via its Prime TV & Video Service offering hoping to capture market share from its omni-channel architecture and broad understanding of consumer needs.

Amazon's recent purchase of Twitch was driven by intelligent market trend data highlighting the popularity and profitability of open on-line gaming streaming services - a market where other proprietary gaming networks such as Sony Microsoft & Nintendo have established offerings.

# What data-driven capabilities enable ...

In the digital economy a business has to immerse itself in information in order to innovate and transform successfully. Becoming *data-driven* means building the capabilities to identify, source and utilize data in all aspects of a business's strategy setting, product and service development, client base development and operations. There is a lot of data on the customer, market, transactions, operations, economic, any industry ecosystem ...) as summarized by the three types of data (p. 207-208) that can be associated with operating a business.

In a data-driven enterprise, the objective is to reach and operate continuously at 'predictive and intelligent' level of **Operating Model** maturity (p. 187-188). A business differentiates itself and increases the value that it can create, produce and deliver, as well as its own valuation (p. 150), by investing in the capabilities that enable it to operate with this level of maturity.

## Operating a Data-Driven Enterprise

All stakeholders in a business (p. 122), whether senior executives, business management, change management, engineering & technology or operations need to utilize data in relation to:

- **Mission, goals and objectives directing the business**
- **Business Model and measurement of performance**
- **Customer value and customer interaction** (the end to end customer journey)
- **Services in the Operating Model** (the end to end service serving the customer journey)

This data that you define through applying the *Strategy Journey Paths* to join·the·dots in the Five Models of **THE STRATEGY JOURNEY** *Framework*, enables a more cohesive and continuous approach to *business transformation* by enabling *Service Innovation* (p. 115) to transform the **Operating Model** of a business while building *business agility* in the enterprise. All of this data and the intelligence that can be generated from it, must be supported by data-driven capabilities and technologies, which have increasingly becoming mandatory for operating a Data-Driven Enterprise.

# ... business transformation

**Service Innovation**

**Big Data**
**(incl. Data Management)**

**IoT Wearables**
**(incl. with AR & VR)**

## What does Data Science involve?

**Data Science** is a practice that requires and includes many data-driven capabilities to operate effectively in an enterprise. The composition of many interconnected sub-capabilities that have their own benefits depending on what transformation challenges they support in the business, is the reason why it is difficult to know what to invest in, when it comes to building an overall data science capability or practice in an enterprise. There are many technology solutions and services that require data and apply data science within their use cases.

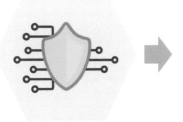

**Cyber Security**

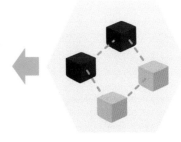

**Blockchain**

**Cloud Service Architecture**

**Artificial Intelligence**
**(including data analytics)**

**Platforms, Marketplaces & Service Applications**

# Mandatory Data-Driven Capabilities That Enable Data Science

These capabilities are paramount to being able to operate with a data driven approach. They are fundamental to being able to source, manage and store data as well as have agility for connecting services to generate it in an efficient, effective and scalable manner;

## Big Data

'Big data' is a term that describes the large volume of data that a business consumes, creates or is inundated by on a day to day basis. The concept of big data gained momentum in the early 2000s when industry analyst Doug Laney articulated the now-mainstream definition of big data as the three V's:

**Volume**: Organizations collect data from a variety of sources, including business transactions, smart (IoT) devices, industrial equipment, videos, social media and more. Cheap storage in data lakes and Hadoop have eased storing this data..

**Velocity**: The Internet of Things (IoT) data streams in to businesses at an unprecedented speed and must be handled in a timely manner. RFID tags, sensors and smart meters mean these torrents of data arrive in near-real time.

**Variety**: Data comes in all types of formats – from structured, numeric data in traditional databases to unstructured text documents, images, emails, videos, audios, stock ticker data and financial transactions. Much from social media.

**\*In one minute**

277,777 Instagram stories posted

511,200 Tweets sent

4,500,000 YouTube videos watched

4,497,000 Google searches conducted

18,100,000 Texts sent

188,000,000 emails sent

Big Data is the driving force behind the latest digital technologies including:
* artificial intelligence (AI);   adaptive learning (a form of AI);
* blockchain;   augmented reality (AR).

Having a Big Data capability means having the expertise and infrastructure in place to identify, source, categorize, clean and present the data for business use.

*\* Adapted from visualcapitalist.com/big-data-keeps-getting-bigger*

Big data management is the organization, administration and governance of large volumes of both structured and unstructured data. The goal of big data management is to ensure a high level of data quality and accessibility for business intelligence and big data analytics applications.

Publicly available data comes from massive amounts of open data sources like the US government's data.gov, the CIA World Factbook or the European Union Open Data Portal. Other big data may come from data lakes, cloud data sources, suppliers and customers.

By 2025, over a quarter of data will be real time in nature and IoT real-time data will account for more than 95% of it. Insights will be generated via new technologies like machine learning and natural language processing. Protection and security of sensitive and private information is crucial.

# Cloud Service Architecture

Cloud service architecture (CSA) defines the overall cloud computing services and solutions that are implemented in and across the boundaries of an enterprise business network. CSA deals with the diagnosis, analysis, design, deployment and integration of cloud services, allowing organizations to operate their businesses within the cloud.

The service architecture approach considers the core business requirements and matches them with a possible cloud solution implemented in a public or private/hybrid cloud. CSA defines the structured guidelines, procedures and constraints of deploying a cloud solution within an enterprise.

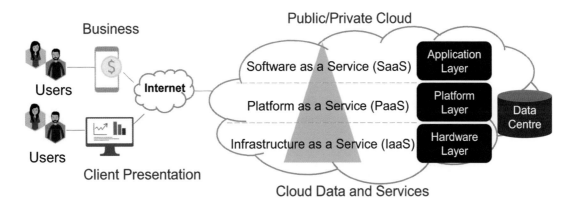

Cloud computing is a major player in the Internet of Things (IoT) supporting the operation of huge numbers of 'smart' home use and commercial devices and applications. Like grid computing, cloud computing reduces costs by maximizing the use of existing resources. The difference is that in cloud computing, an app doesn't access these resources directly. Instead, it accesses resources indirectly through a service, which in turn engages the physical resources necessary to respond to the app. Cloud is essential when actions require significant or scalable computing and data storage power. Cloud supports huge numbers of IoT, domestic and commercial cloud services data sources in a standardized manner with programmatic access and is a key enabler of Big Data.

Building a Cloud Service Architecture capability to govern the design, development and use of cloud based services provides a business with a rapid and scalable means to deliver enhanced service functionality in a cost effective manner. The CSA will guide customer and business services development in a structured and managed way through the use of connected cloud services, big data and business unique selling point services.

# Data-Driven Capabilities That Empower Transformation

Building upon the mandatory capabilities these provide a means to understand the value of the data that you have built through your data driven enterprise, make business development decisions using it, decide what features to build using it and to protect it as it is a key business asset.

## Business & Artificial Intelligence

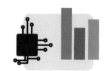

Business intelligence (BI) utilizes software and services to analyze different forms of business data and transform it into actionable insights. These insights are used to inform strategic and tactical business decisions.

BI tools access and analyze sets of data and present analytical findings in a variety of formats to provide intelligence about the current state of the business. Typically, specific BI data reports, dashboards, graphs, charts and maps are generated relevant an area of business. BI is descriptive telling you what's happening now and what happened in the past to get to the current state.

Business analytics (BA) is a collective term for data analysis techniques that are predictive. These techniques incorporate projection analysis to provide a perspective on what may happen in the future. They are prescriptive in that they present the actions that should be undertaken to create better outcomes for the business. (BA are usually thought of as that subset of the larger category of data analytics that's specifically focused on business.)

Artificial intelligence (AI) is a further category of analysis of data. AI makes it possible for machines to learn from experience using large data sets and adjust to new inputs and perform humanlike tasks. Most AI examples today, from chess-playing computers to self-driving cars, rely heavily on deep learning and natural language processing (NLP). Using these technologies, AI algorithms can be trained to successfully complete specific tasks by processing large amounts of IoT data and recognizing patterns in that data.

The importance of big data doesn't revolve around how much data you have, but what you do with it. BI, BA and AI can be applied to Big Data to provide insights to;
- customer journey enhancements and customer behavioral factors
- service cost reductions and service speed improvements,
- new product and service development opportunities and optimization of offerings
- smart decision making for tactical and strategic business moves

Using high-powered analytics, a business will be able to perform operational tasks such as:
- determining root causes of failures, issues and defects in near-real time.
- generating bespoke offers at the point of sale based on the customer's buying/browsing habits.
- calculating credit/loan assessment approvals in minutes.
- detecting fraudulent behavior before it has an impact on the business.

# Cyber Security

In the digital age, an online presence and online servicing is a minimum entry level requirement to conduct business. However, an increasing level of sophistication of customers and the technology means a tailored, frictionless and sticky customer experience is what generates a business edge in a competitive service world. Leading services leverage mobile, big data, analytics and AI and are built in a hybrid manner using Cloud Service Architecture utilizing IaaS, PaaS, SaaS combined with bespoke development. These solutions provide sophisticated functionality to the customer and the business. They also generate huge amounts of valued customer and business data. This data is a core asset of the business and consideration of protecting this from cyber security threats warrants a focus on building a Cybersecurity capability to consider Application security, Network security, Cloud security & Internet of things (IoT) security.

Cybersecurity capability encompasses the creation of;
- cybersecurity Governance & Risk management Frameworks
- risk identification and management processes
- risk mitigation assessment process
- risk detection processes
- incident response processes
- resilience capabilities for recovery
- Chief Information Security Officer role and security operations function

**5 key forms of cyber threat**
- Phishing
- Ransomeware
- Distributed Denial of Service (DDoS)
- Computer virus
- Attack Vectors, drive-by, MITM, Zero-day…

Building cybersecurity capability maturity will enable a business to move from a compliance and certification based mode to a fully risk based model working at an enterprise level to support business operations.

# Service Innovation (including Transformation)

Service Innovation is a process applied by businesses (as a strategic tactic) to their business models, operations or operating model in order to execute and achieve business transformation.
Innovation can either be incremental, through varying degrees of change, or a fundamental transformation to a business. It can serve to disrupt a business or a market.

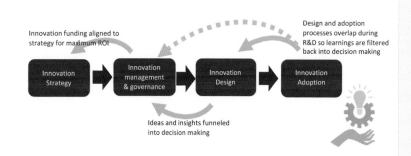

# Use Cases That Require A Data-Driven Enterprise

The world is dominated today by companies that have got their data driven organizations working in a market leading way. These use cases highlight where huge success can be found with data driven approaches supporting digital business models, mass market IoT devices and disruptive technologies.

## Platforms, Marketplaces & Service Applications

Platforms require a cohesive approach to data and data management. Businesses built around a platform such as Facebook, YouTube or Google require data to be at the heart of their architecture and services. Their business models are constructed around data and content data that is amassed, characterized and packaged for use in marketing/sales or to sell behavioral data derived from it.

Marketplaces depend on data to ensure a smooth, cohesive and seamless experience of services provided to customers and users. Amazon and Alibaba operate omnichannel marketplaces using multiple channels supported through their multisided platforms. They are extending these to offer financial services value propositions to customers along their existing customer journeys. Big Data and a being a data driven enterprise is at the core of enabling the marketplace and its extension.

Service applications (SaaS) such as Salesforce utilize data centric services to ensure that their cloud operated service can be configured to individual consumer needs. Each instance then supports data centric services for the consumers own customers.

## Internet of Things Wearables (including Virtual & Augmented Reality)

IoT is the extension of internet connectivity into physical devices and everyday objects. These devices are embedded with electronics, internet connectivity and sensors. They can communicate and interact with others over the internet, integrate with 3rd party services and be remotely monitored and controlled.

VR is the term used to describe a three-dimensional, computer generated environment which can be explored and interacted with. IoT innovators in smart cities are integrating VR into urban planning for smart cities. AR is the blending of virtual reality and real life. AR is converging with IoT. In industrial or medical applications data from hundreds of sensors can be visualized simultaneously, overlaying relevant and useful information from the environment through a headset to aid surgery or maintenance.

Fitness trackers and healthcare monitoring devices are used to support health insurance policies. Vitality offers an Apple IWatch with some of its policies and offer rewards based on policyholders attainment of health and exercise goals. Combined with the mobile app Vitality uses a data driven approach to incorporating streaming IoT health data to make decisions and offers to policy holders.

# Blockchain

A blockchain is a linear, time-ordered, list of of transactions (grouped into blocks) linked together, hence forming a chain. These blocks are secured by cryptographic methods to prevent fraudulent attempts to tamper with the data, and replicated on every computer participating in the blockchain network, wherever these computers are in the world. The participants of the network are incentivized to validate the transactions and bundle them into blocks. For this they're rewarded in the form of new coins, transaction fees, or by becoming a stakeholder and having a say in the evolution of the network. Blockchain is the technology that powers *bitcoin*. Each new bitcoin transaction is stored in a block that gets added to a chain of existing records, so it serves as a public ledger of all transactions. Updates are validated through a public verification process.

Blockchain provides a means to bypass traditional trust intermediaries, such as banks.  Blockchain relies on trust in the environment where the participants transact directly (peer to peer) between each other, without knowing each other, and therefore implicitly trusting each other. This trust derives from the properties of the blockchain: immutability, transparency and reliability. Removal of intermediaries will decrease friction and costs in business transactions, and also decrease any risks of the data being tampered with, either by mistake or fraudulently, once the data is stored on the blockchain.

The role of blockchain technology is clearly as a secret power-up tool, in the Operating Model of an enterprise, where it has the ability to increase the business agility of the organization, allowing it to create value better and faster through its processes and data.

When blockchain technology is applied to the right business use cases, you get productivity and business intelligence at the same time through further application of Artificial Intelligence (AI).
Successful business use cases for blockchain are
Crypto currencies - Bitcoin
Cross border payments – Abra Everex
Real Estate – Dubai land registry is blockchain enabled
Accounting and Audit – Fizcal
Digital Identity – Civic, Shocard

**STRATEGY JOURNEY *Framework* Activity #15:**

Review and rate the current level of maturity using the Index from pages 189-190 of your enterprises 'data-driven capabilities and use cases' as described in pages 210-216. Are there any proposed *service innovations* that require a higher level of maturity? Indicate the 'gap' by identifying the level of maturity required in the **Target Operating Model** that is required to support the new service innovation.

# EXAMPLE: Vitality takes a data driven approach to health insurance

Founded in South Africa under the name Discovery, Vitality is the world's first health insurer to create its own network for wellness solutions. This has brought an explosion of growth since its launch in 2016 with a 39% improvement in its overall financial performance in recent years.

It has grown by 127% across its global network of partners in 16 countries and has a 25% ownership of China's largest comprehensive insurer, Ping An Health. Since the launch of the new network-connected services, in just over a year, Ping An Health achieved a 66% improvement in profitability.

The Vitality group has leveraged many data-driven capabilities across its global network, to offer what has become its core *value proposition*, the Vitality Shared-Value Insurance service, which is constantly co-creating with customers, to add value to the customer experience through data analytics that leverages AI technology.

All of the group's transformation activities have been focused on building out this service, which is supported by a customer app and platform.   Whilst the Mission and Vision may be the same as other healthcare insurance businesses, to offer the best health services to their customers, the **Business Model** and **Value Model** have been designed to be digitally crafted from the ground up.

This digital differentiator has been paramount in driving the recent success and growth of the business and is attributed to a laser focus on digital *service design* and **Operating Model** transformation.

The service connects customers with their data to provide intelligence to them about their health. Additionally, the platform connects customers with further complimentary services provided by third parties across the entire health and wellbeing ecosystem including hospitals, pharmaceuticals, gyms and holistic services.

This novel service also utilizes the latest consumer technology as access points to the management of their policies or for monitoring if desired. Some service offers unlock discounted access to complimentary technology used to manage interaction with Vitality.

IoT devices including the Amazon Alexa Echo, Google Home, Apple iWatch, and Smartphones can be used to connect with customers and to help them measure and monitor their health. These platforms access broader ecosystems and allow customers to connect with third party providers in a global multi-sided platform.

For Vitality, value is captured and provided through the data acquired about customers. This data is enhanced through the application of AI to suggest further complementary or discounted health services that will improve the customers health and well being. For some services there are rewards with cuts to monthly premiums and access to bonus third party services based on healthy behaviors, leading to an overall money saving sticky experience.

*Based on research conducted by Stratability Academy using public information - sources available in References section*

## STRATEGY JOURNEY *Framework* TIP #12:

A quick win to achieve business agility and go to market is to leverage different network connected services and platforms or marketplaces, to reach and serve customers. Make sure you use these platforms for the right purpose based on your level of access to specific data. For platforms and networks that provide limited data, while also control your pricing, such as Kickstarter, Udemy or Amazon, launch and test new products and services with them only. Consider building your own or whitelabeling for core service offerings so that you have better control of your data, and the ability to analyze it for multiple Business Models and other future use cases.

# What runs and transforms the business

Similar to a house, any building or skyscraper, a business is a structure comprised of multiple layers of different resources, that work together to deliver the different forms of value to its customers and stakeholders externally and internally. So no single business is exactly the same as another, from the different perspectives and viewpoints of its interested parties.

To successfully operate a business and to transform it through business transformation, you need to know what makes the business what it is, what builds or supports it, what does it do … everything that forms its underlying architecture. This foundational architecture of a business is what gives it the ability to deliver the value added outcomes, as it navigates through the Five Stages of **THE STRATEGY JOURNEY**.

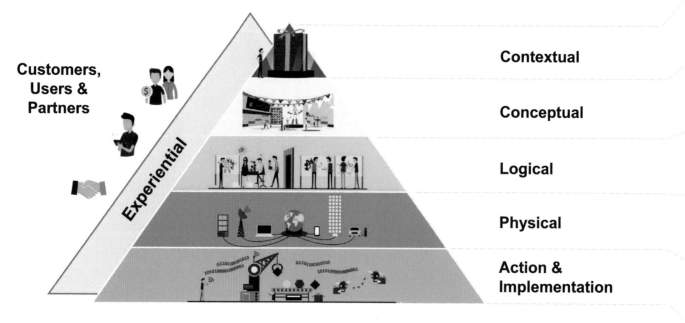

An enterprise has *five 'internal' architecture layers** that enable it to function and transform, through different interconnected business activities that enable data and information to be transferred and shared by the different *resources* and *stakeholders* in the organization as it goes about capturing, producing and delivering value. These internal layers are connected with a *sixth 'experiential' architecture layer* where co-creation (p. 117-118) takes place with different external customers, and the value is received and experienced. The joining of these architecture layers through data provides a 'service-led' viewpoint of how an enterprise delivers value to its customers and stakeholders through problem solving.

*\* Adapted from the Zachman Framework conceived by John Zachman in the 1980s at IBM. The Zachman Framework provides an ontology or structured way of viewing and defining solutions in an enterprise (www.zachman.com).*

Where senior executives including the CEO, and members of the board, supported by the Heads of Businesses, Strategy and Research, would review the competitive landscape and the problems faced by the business, agree priorities and define the scope with which the organization will operate in the **Mission Model**, including what *value propositions* it will serve to market, based on the **Value Model** directed by the market, and the business transformation activities that it will conduct over a period of time in order to achieve specific targeted value-driven goals and objectives.

Where the Heads of Businesses, who are responsible for a product or service ownership and their business management teams, would design the **Business Model** strategy, that outlines what value streams, resource capabilities, distribution networks, funding sources, assets are required to deliver value added outcomes to targeted customers and for the business. Designers must also identify gaps in the customer and user journeys by which to gain a competitive advantage to create sticky services and serve customers according to their **Value Model**.

Where the appropriate process design, architecture and transformation teams, define how the business changes in the **Transformation Model** from its current state of operating to it **Target Operating Model (TOM)**, with appropriate levels of governance, that enables changes to be orchestrated and executed with a good level business agility (p. 46) to support speed-to-market. Transformation effort is designed to execute changes in accordance with the **Value Model** as directed by customers, and to deliver desired outcomes of the **Business Model** and **Mission Model**.

Led by engineering and supported by technology, it is where the *value propositions*, that is, the products and services are physically designed, built, produced and delivered in different locations, to different types of customers (p. 121-122), as part of validating and iterating the **Value Model** and **Operating Model** through co-creation and network connectivity and in accordance to the **Transformation Model**. It includes management of infrastructure including assets required to produce and deliver the *value propositions*, and to support the activities of sales and operations.

Where and when sales, operations and servicing teams, supported by engineering and technology, as well as other functions such as human resources, and finance action and implement the necessary value streams (p. 154), capabilities (p. 179) and business-as-usual activities in the **Operating Model** to support delivery of the value added outcomes to its recipients, that is the different types of customers, as well as internal stakeholders from other functional areas (p. 121-122). This is where revenue, profit and most of the other value measures in the **Mission Model** are achieved.

**RESPONSIBLE STAKEHOLDERS:**

*C-Suite & Senior Executives*

*Business Management*

*Change Management*

*Engineering & Technology*

*Sales, Operations & Servicing*

# The stakeholder roles who must ...

While technology advances have certainly helped to solve many problems and changed how the world works through greater network effects, it is people, especially, an organization's **'internal stakeholders'** who make the difference. These role are pivotal in creating the necessary priorities and impact for business success in a highly competitive digital economy. People in roles are responsible for their actions in a business and accountable for taking risks and making decisions on what are the right business activities to be undertaken. In a world of fast advancing artificial intelligence technology, machines still have to be programed to perform specific actions, including informing on risks or taking decisions.

Service innovation is improved through co-creation (p. 117), when staff, and customers are able to work together toward the stages of the 'Change Development Lifecycle' as well as the 'Innovation Adoption Lifecycle' to create, produce and deliver value-added services with the best supply and demand fit.

## Defining co-creation roles for business transformation

The challenge and what will set a business apart from others is in how it organizes its people ... staff or employees ... to work **cohesively** together and co-create its services, based on their roles across the five architecture layers of an organization (p. 219) and as the business navigates through other challenges faced along **THE STRATEGY JOURNEY**, to transform with agility, accountability and action.

Good communication between different teams and colleagues is essential for creating a cohesive and efficient organization that is capable of transforming with *business agility* (p. 51-54). This involves different people with different skillsets and roles, working together to inform each other of specific decisions and actions, that support coordination of business activities, and governance of resources and investment, with as little conflict or friction as possible.

# ... co-create to deliver transformation

Performance improves better and faster when people have the right skillsets to support their roles, so it is important that a business invests in its people. It is common sense to equip an individual through training, or to hire a trained expert to perform specific business activities as this is likely to produce better results faster. Customer and users too can be trained, to improve their user experience of services and hence their overall customer or brand experience of a business.

But the right functional skillset doesn't not include how an individual should work with strangers, on complex business transformation programs and projects. People will need to learn how to work together, and as they learn they are likely to face friction and conflicts, as well as making mistakes. These challenges during co-creation, can be mitigated by defining and communicating people's roles when they are performing specific transformation activities including strategy and service innovation, using the following four role characteristics, also known as the *RACI*:

### Responsible
What work or business activities, that is processes, including those aided by technology systems are performed by this role?

### Accountable
What decisions and any associated risks and actions that follow from it, is this role ultimately accountable for making?

### Contribute/Consulted
On what business activities and actions should this role be consulted for feedback and should this role contribute to via their feedback?

### Informed
What decisions or actions does this role need to know about, in order to perform its own responsibilities at its best?

It is vital that roles have appropriate boundaries and handovers based on what they are accountable for, responsible for specific business activities, as well as whether they should be consulted for feedback.

It is also important when staff are co-located in a smaller business but becomes significantly more important when staff are remotely deployed in cross-country or international teams as part of a national or global organization. There are many companies that operate almost entire remotely, especially technology firms such as Twitter who have move to this way of working since the COVID-19 pandemic crisis.

Staff and employees should be empowered through their roles with the right levels of responsibility, accountability, contribution and information, and trained with the right skillsets, to allow them to perform at their best and in doing so, support the business to perform at its best including *business transformation*.

# Organizing & Managing Stakeholders During Business Transformation

Managing a transformation portfolio, program or project can be challenging when there are many people with different roles and personalities. When individuals work in any team or cross team environment that requires collaboration, naturally conflicts occur, because people are different in the way they think, act and behave, which is driven by their 'mindset' - and there are many mindset styles to work with (p. 123).

When deciding how to fill roles in a team or any organizational structure, it is important to classify stakeholders, on their activities and tasks which they need to perform functionally, their RACI role, and other characteristics that determine how to manage an individual and how people should work with them.

Some stakeholders can significantly influence how the business is operated (e.g. a regulator) and some may be politically more influential in the circles of power. Others will drive projects, rebel against actions that violate their beliefs or wait for instructions and follow orders, without making the effort to think and apply more intelligence to their words and actions. All these characteristics can impact the deliver of results in any business activities but especially during timebound business transformation programs and projects that have tight budgets.

## Ways to classify stakeholders

Classifying and characterising stakeholders via their interest and influence in a business is a good way to establish who requires managing closely to ensure the success of a transformation versus those who only need monitoring or to be kept informed. Different levels of influence and interest require a different engagement approach.

We have provided a list of criteria for you to evaluate how to organize and manage different stakeholders on business transformation projects:

- Stakeholder Group
- Ability to disrupt the change
- Current understanding + Required understanding
- Current commitment + Required commitment
- Required support
- Level of authority
- Level of influence
- Type of concerns

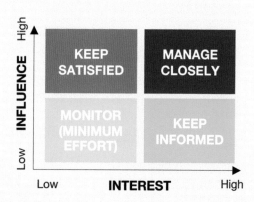

Classification criteria can be used to organize teams or to help you work out how to manage and influence stakeholders who might be more difficult to work with, and/or resistant to change.

# Principles for engaging stakeholders

Once stakeholders are classified into one of the four quadrants that indicate what you need to do manage them, the next step is to engage them in the right way to develop your co-creation relationship. An engagement strategy may need to be developed to help you communicate in the right manner with each set of stakeholders, or even individuals. A stakeholder engagement strategy should incorporate the following engagement principles:

**Audience**
**WHO**

The stakeholder is seeking to understand as well as to be understood. Does the individual require more time to think and consider how they should act or react. Do they feel more comfortable with guidance and training or they prefer autonomy and independence?

**Medium**
**HOW &**
**WHERE**

Is it necessary to be proactive and engage early as the stakeholder likes to be the first to be informed, and to provide their opinion. So should you seek a personal meeting one-to-one or make a general announcement via a live video conference, or use an email?

**Message**
**WHAT**

Most stakeholders prefer simple, relevant, concrete (not abstract) messages where possible, and will ask for more detail when they feel they need it. It is important to tailor messages to the stakeholder, when they need to be managed closely, including both the contents of the message as well as its tone of communication.

**Outcomes**
**WHY**

Be purposeful with follow through so it is important to repeat your engagements until they stick, while being mindful of someone's time and avoid annoying them or even offending them unwittingly. Be clear on what's in it for them, as well as the collective, in the team or the entire organization, that is what is their contribution to success.

An engagement strategy may need to change based on the stage of the 'Change Development Lifecycle' (p. 201) and as well as adapting to other ecosystem influences (p. 93-94) that can impact an individual stakeholder's mindset.

**STRATEGY JOURNEY *Framework* TIP #13:**

When managing a team or staff, and especially on any transformation projects and activities, always outline who is responsible versus accountable for specific activities and who needs to contribute or informed. Also explore the influence and interest of stakeholders to decide how they need to be managed and then consider how best to engage them to get the best result possible based on their mindset styles (p. 123).

# Building A Growth Mindset Business For Long-Term Success

A business who wants to achieve long-term success at a future point in time, in its 'target state' and accelerate both the speed and effectiveness of its business transformation efforts with *business agility*, needs to invest in training and coaching to support its leaders, managers, and employees … all of the business's stakeholders, including its customers … to think, act and behave, with a **'growth mindset'**, as they participate in co-creation to innovate services and deliver value together.

**Growth Mindset**
describes a person who considers that their abilities can be evolved through determination and hard work.  A person with a *growth mindset* believes that there is always room for growth and improvement through learning and development.

As outlined on p. 123-124, *mindset* motivates and drives the behaviors of customers and employees, to play a big role in influencing how a business operates and transforms.

The idea of a *fixed* and *growth mindset** is developed by Professor Carol Dweck from Stanford University. Professor Carol categorizes two very different poles on the mindset spectrum that characterizes our basic belief about how people see themselves. An person can have a fixed mindset on one occasion and a growth mindset on another occasion. Every person is a mixture in a spectrum between the opposite poles and where they are in that spectrum can change dynamically based on different triggers that affect the person.

When a person is in the *fixed mindset* and faced with a difficult situation, he or she wants to prove their ability to fix the problem to look smart, and will argue their way to prove they are right even when they know it is not the best option.
At other times, when in the *growth mindset,* the same person is prepared to try and experiment with different solutions even if it may fail and may not look good to others.

It is impossible to be successful in business transformation if the stakeholders involved in the initiative are of or in a *fixed mindset*.

*\* Also published in Mindset: The New Psychology of Success (Ballantine Books 2006, Updated Edition in 2017) by Carol Dweck*

## Fixed Mindset

describes person who believes in their innate traits, like intelligence or talent, are constant. A person with a *fixed mindset* will spend their time proofing and protecting their intelligence instead of growing it, and also considers their inherit talent will help to achieve success without much work.

Whether it's members of the team responsible for delivering the change, or the recipient, that is customers or users of a new innovation or solution, when there are people of a *fixed mindset*, this causes conflicts that will hinder the transformation initiative from being successful. Many of these *fixed mindset* behaviors are highlighted on p. 43 which discusses how *poor transformation culture* is the real root cause of transformation failure ... something to be eradicated in an enterprise.

Having a *fixed mindset* versus a *growth mindset* is different from the mindset style (p 123) of a person which is formed by their values and beliefs (that do not change). It is possible to influence or change someone to have a fixed or growth mindset, through different methods of engagement within an environment, and at a point in time, such as a 'Persuasion Campaign' (p. 206).

The type of mindset that exists overall in an enterprise at a point in time, plays a significant role in how its leaders will shape its **MISSION MODEL** by which to drive the business forward into the future. Developing and operating with a growth mindset is how direction can be set to foster the right culture, a *culture of learning* (p. 44, 198), across all other architecture layers of an enterprise and as a business navigates **THE STRATEGY JOURNEY** stages to innovate new **Business Models**, discover new **Value Model** gaps and opportunities, identify and define changes to make in the **Operating Model**, and apply or execute changes with the **Transformation Model**.

**STRATEGY JOURNEY** *Framework* **TIP #14:**
When engaging stakeholders, consider if they are of a fixed versus a growth mindset at that point in time, to adjust how you deliver specific messages, especially the method of delivery and the tone of that delivery.

# What business culture facilitates...

In any transformation exercise within a business there is a significant chance for things not to go as expected unless there is planning, communication, strong leadership and importantly, a culture of handling and adopting change.

Culture in a business is a defining attribute of how the business operates. Culture relates to the beliefs and behaviors that determine how a company's employees and management interact and handle the operation of the business. Culture is develops organically over time. In some businesses it can be progressive and enabling when staff and leaders are operating with a growth mindset (p. 226). A *culture of learning* (p. 198) evolves with events that bring new experience into the business such as a significant merger or acquisition or a change in the senior leadership team. Both of these potentially add to the progressiveness of the culture as new staff arrive into the business. New staff bring new capabilities and experiences from other businesses or from disciplines outside of the normal business scope, and also new data. Over time the culture evolves as different values, beliefs and ways of working are slowly integrated.

## Consequences of a Non-Transformative Culture

Culture can also be very static and resistant to change, as highlighted by the characteristics of Poor Transformation Culture (p. 43).

A change resistant culture can effectively block successful transformation from occurring as employees are not open minded to the benefits of change - for themselves as individuals or the business at large, nor in changes to the way things have always been done.

When the employee happens to be in a senior leadership position this presents a very strong influence on the way a business operates as junior staff will operate as their leader does. The result is a lot of bureaucracy, and mind games played out in the enterprise's politics. People might be spending most of their time fighting for projects, inventing activities and wasting time and money on redundant activities. There is often negative value in the enterprise, from opportunities costs, or fines as problems when not attended to properly with effective *business transformation* that will deliver the necessary changes, can exacerbated from moles to mountains.

This kind of 'fixed' mindset (p. 225) culture creates frustrations in those employees who are of a 'growth' mindset (p. 226) and open to learning from others and make changes in order to grow the value they gain from learning, as well as from changing. And it cause not only conflicts but also attrition when staff leave an enterprise as they have lost their ability to add value.

# ... effective business transformation

## Developing a Transformation Culture through Leadership

To be sustainable, transformation has to be fostered and developed so that it becomes part of a business's standard way of doing things and be fully supported by the culture. The value of this is significant in the digital age when success depends on being first to market with new innovative approaches – or fast following the market leaders.

A business should champion transformation from the top levels of management and instil the transformation way of thinking in the leadership structure. Leading by example will drive the staff to think and act differently.

Strong senior leadership needs to operate via new ways of working, to demonstrate that an enterprise's leaders believe things should change from the top down. This enables a new way of working to filter down the management structure. Direct reports then see how senior management are operating and put it into practice themselves. These 'growth mindset' principles will, over time, make the new way of operating the normal way of operating and thus it becomes part of the firm's DNA.

As well as 'leading by example', strong leadership also includes 'putting your money where your mouth is' where investments are made to build and enhance transformation capabilities through educating existing staff who understand the business whilst also looking to recruit experienced staff from outside the business to run key functions such as the innovation process and the *business transformation* function.

The new ways of approaching transformation that are developed internally or brought into the business need to be given the space to develop and grow with low personal risk to the individuals involved. Learning through 'fast failure' is a proven means of rapidly improving capabilities and experience. 'Fast failure' can be practiced as part of Service Innovation and when testing and implementing changes during the 'Change Development Lifecycle'. This will give the incumbent workforce and any new workforce the confidence that they are supported in the transformation journey to change the way in which things operate for the benefit of the business and themselves.

# What is business architecture

'**Business Architecture**' is often used to describe the practice of '**enterprise wide strategy and architecture**' in an organization. It is a practice comprised of the activities and behaviors that support an organization to join·the·dots across the the *five architecture layers of an enterprise* (p. 219-220). These layers must work cohesively while interacting with customers in the *experiential architecture layer* of a business to create value (p. 71-72) as the business navigates through the Five Stages of **THE STRATEGY JOURNEY**. This cohesion is how all the resources in an organization, especially its internal stakeholders, co-create the different forms of value with customers. It is also how optimal design and execution of business strategy through business transformation occurs. The enterprise is operating with a *culture of learning (p. 198)* and continuously striving to achieve optimal business agility (p. 235).

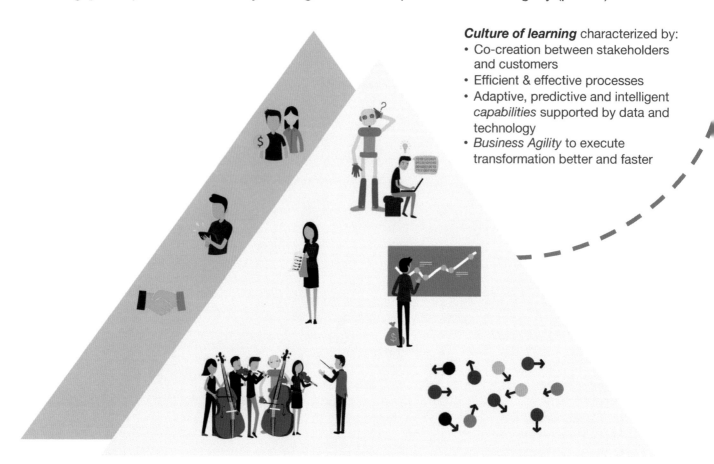

*Culture of learning* characterized by:
- Co-creation between stakeholders and customers
- Efficient & effective processes
- Adaptive, predictive and intelligent *capabilities* supported by data and technology
- *Business Agility* to execute transformation better and faster

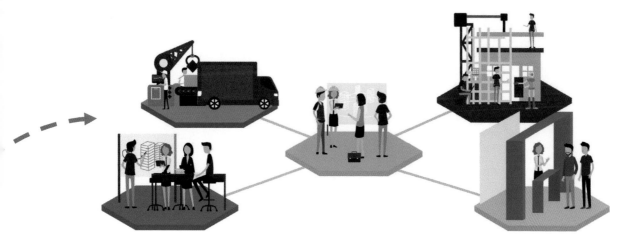

An organization may have different people who hold an organizational title called a 'Business Architect', but it is important that the responsibility of practicing enterprise wide strategy and architecture is not just limited to these people.

Continuous and sustainable *business transformation* that can produce and deliver increasing value, is achieved, when every internal stakeholder, is practicing strategy and architecture in some form as they go about their day-to-day activities. Everyone in the organization should understand their role in practicing strategy and architecture to successfully deliver business transformation, including digital transformation, that will provide the value-added outcomes desired and expected by all stakeholders and customers.

A disconnect between strategy and execution sets in when an organization is only practicing strategy and architecture including *business architecture* in silos and allows bureaucracy to create conflicts between different stakeholders, leading to *poor transformation culture* (p. 43) across the organization. The 'business architects' who are responsible for business design, that is 'business management', and the 'business architects' who are responsible for governing change, that is 'change management', should not overstep into the roles and responsibilities of other stakeholder groups.

**STRATEGY JOURNEY *Framework* TIP #15:**

Consider how you can apply a 'culture of learning' through practicing strategy and architecture or business architecture in your enterprise, by following the the dos and don't illustrated on page 231-232.

# The Dos And Don't Of Practicing Strategy & Architecture In Business

HOW an enterprise approaches or applies the practice of strategy and architecture in a business can tell us a lot about its successes and failures when it comes to business transformation and strategy execution. It is where and with whom the power lies and indicates the transformation culture in the enterprise. Does every organization need to practice business architecture? Should a business build central capability in business architecture? How? Where? When? By Whom?

## Five strategy & architecture practice approaches

We have summarized the do and don't across these five approaches that have been practiced consciously as well as unconscientiously by different organizations:

### Random & Sporadic Applications

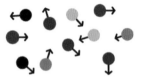

Strategy & architecture is practiced unconscientiously by random pockets of the organization across sales, operations, technology and customer servicing teams.

**Dos**
- Co-create transformation activities with other internal stakeholders to increase value creation
- Seek feedback from customers groups and share data with the rest of the organization
- Refer back to the organizations overall Mission, Vision and Values to align and account where possible to strategic objectives

**Don'ts**
- Apply transformation changes without understanding the implications to rest of the business, as well as operational risks to the overall organization
- Changes are not shared with other stakeholders, with no accountability, not supported by governance, and are not aligned to strategic objectives (ie. silo)

### Solution Led by Technology, Engineering or Operations

Strategy & architecture is led by technology, engineering and operations teams that are focused on solutions that do not match or need matching to actual business problems.

**Dos**
- Co-create through prototyping and testing with customers and other business stakeholders to understand what business problems need to be solved, what value can be added, and be prepared to change the solution
- Ensure that solutions produce outcomes that are aligned to strategic objectives

**Don'ts**
- Force transformation changes that do not add value through solving real business problems in the short and/or long term.
- Conduct innovation in isolation of other stakeholders across the organization, that is based purely on the latest technology hype, with no alignment to strategic objectives

## Change Management Led

Strategy & architecture is led by a central change management team, with a strong focus on planning and governance, to coordinate transformation activities and build capabilities, that are balanced across short and long term objectives.

**Dos**
- Transformation activities involve co-creation with appropriate level of responsibility, accountability, and contribution from the right stakeholders in the organization
- Transformation initiatives have clear outcomes that are balanced across multiple value measures and strategically aligned to Mission, Vision and Values

**Don'ts**
- Governance and bureaucracy, to ensure projects are conducted on time, on budget, with limited or no flexibility, stifles business agility
- Transformation initiatives lack sponsorship from senior executives, nor buy-in from other stakeholders with limited alignment to Mission, Vision and Values of the organization

## Business Management Led

Strategy & architecture is led by business management teams or individual executives in the organization with a strong sales orientated focus that grow and expand the organization.

**Dos**
- Co-create value propositions with customer groups, to maximize value and pivot where necessary
- Co-create value propositions end-to-end with engineering, technology and operations
- Value Measures are balanced and aligned to Mission, Vision and Values, with senior executive and buy-in from to stakeholders

**Don'ts**
- Develop value propositions in isolation of other internal stakeholders and customers
- Lack of accountability and deferral to third parties with different organizational values and agenda
- Bias sales focus that consciously compromises on other value measures, and conflicts with Mission, Vision and Values

## Strategically Driven Top Down and executed via Co-creation

Strategy & architecture is led from the top by senior executives, and driven into action through empowered co-creation by other teams who are supported by good communication, cohesive governance and investment in relevant capabilities.

**Dos** *RECOMMENDED*
- Clarify what actions and outcomes need to be taken and produced by different stakeholders in the organization in the short and long term with strategic alignment
- Support all stakeholder teams with the mandate and adequate levels of investment and training, to co-create value propositions and perform activities in cohesion

**Don'ts**
- Invest in transformation initiatives that are not aligned to the organization's strategic objectives, or are third party led and not co-created with internal stakeholders
- No or poor communication of strategic objectives, WHAT actions and outcomes need to be delivered through co-creation by different internal stakeholders

# EXAMPLE: How Singapore is transforming into a smart city that is using digital to connect the social needs of three generations

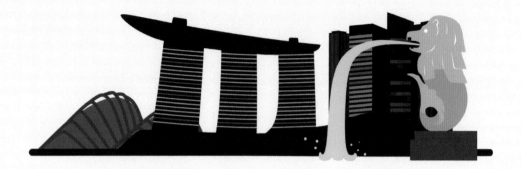

Singapore, is country of approximate six million citizen's as at 2018, that has transformed itself from a third world country to a modern city state in under one generation, since it gained independence from Malaysia through elections in 1954, lead by its first and former prime minister of eight successful terms, Lee Quan Yew. Lee is renowned globally as the architect of modern Singapore. As of 2020, Lee's son, Lee Hsien Loong continues his father's legacy as Prime Minister, but with his own leadership style that has transformed Singapore into a Smart City.

Singapore's government has been able to achieve its transformative successes through numerous economic lifecycles (strategy journey lifecycles), by developing the Five Models of **THE STRATEGY JOURNEY** *Framework*, to build the country's *business agility*, which it has become known for. The country has been smart with its investments in specific *capabilities* that developed an inherent transformation culture.

Continuous transformation through people power has been a core value of the Singapore Government since it began as the People's Action Party (PAP) in 1954. The city state has built high quality social housing that rivals many private properties, to house eighty percent of its population, one of the best and most efficient transport systems in the world, and focused on providing world class education services to ensure that it can compete on the global stage as an economic powerhouse through its availability of highly skilled labor, which has successfully served many manufacturers during the modern industrial revolution. Singapore was one of the first countries to provide fully supported mobile and broadband services, through its very modern telecommunications infrastructure provided by state-owned Singtel, which is now a global operator.

Many government or state-owned businesses have even led the world to offer some of the best quality services first, including Singapore Airlines with luxury air travel, and famous shopping districts including Orchard Road for high fashion and the Funan Mall for quality consumer electronics at cheap prices. Many global economists have come to refer to the city state, as Singapore PLC, to illustrate how the country has been run like a business. Of course, in winning so many elections, the Singapore government has used many *Persuasion Campaigns* to forward its agenda where required.

Singapore has been fast and early to embraced digital transformation, to innovate new services for its citizens and economy.

In June 2018, Singapore's Digital Government Agency, SMART NATION, launched its digital government blueprint* on how the city state would transform itself through digital transformation towards 2023 to become a fully digitized Smart City, with connected social and economic services, that would be both co-created with its citizens and businesses while being supported by the latest in digital technologies from big data to AI, AR and blockchain. As a digital or data driven Smart City, of course there are clear key performance indicators (KPIs), with many initiatives and projects already underway.

Services launched or being launch in 2019 as part of Singapore's Digital Government Blueprint, include:

- An urban mobility network with the appropriate grid infrastructure, and engineering talent for autonomous vehicles. This has led Dyson to relocate its manufacturing plant for self-driving cars to Singapore.

- Use of Augmented Reality to provide training in health services, including country wide first aid training for citizens over 60, and other community based and mental health related services for all citizens across all generations.

- A fully digitized real estate management and maintenance services for Singapore's social housing network of properties, known as the HDB (Housing Development Board).

  and many more …. which will be built as a set of capability building blocks to form Singapore's future **Operating Model**.

* Digital Government Blueprint Image and sources: https://www.tech.gov.sg/digital-government-blueprint/

# What does it take to operate …

*Business agility* is achieved and embedded within an enterprise, when it operates with a *culture of learning*, that enables the organization to continuously improve, innovate and transform itself through the five activities that build its transformation capability: access, architect, action, account and accelerate (p. 59-60). When an enterprise operates with this level of business agility, it can transform with speed as well as quality to capture, produce and deliver value during service delivery.

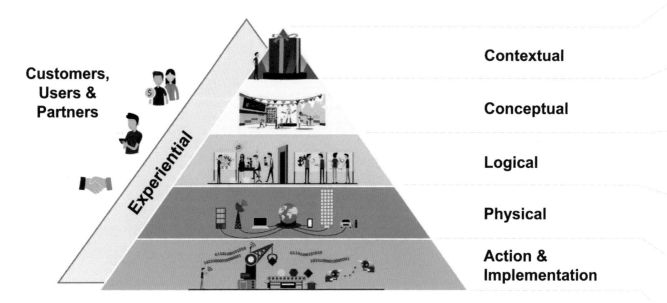

This 'agile' modus operandi is only possible when all the capabilities and component resources in an enterprise's **Operating Model**, including its transformation capabilities that can determine the success of its **Transformation Model**, are able to connect seamlessly and operate cohesively. They do this through effective and efficient *'processing of data'* in tasks, business activities and *value streams*, joining·the·dots across the *architecture layers* of the enterprise (p. 219-220) as it services and deliver its *value propositions* to customers and stakeholders.

Each of the five models in the **THE STRATEGY JOURNEY** *Framework*, is designed to support a corresponding *internal architecture layer* of the enterprise. Through connecting 'data' into optimized processes, the Framework offers a common language for an enterprise and all the resources including its systems and people in different locations, across *the five internal architecture layers* of the enterprise to operate and transform in cohesion, as it works to deliver value to external customers, user and partners through co-creation in the *sixth experiential architecture layer* of the enterprise.

# … at optimal business agility

**Mission Model**

The context by which an enterprise operates is defined in the value that it seeks to deliver through its *'value propositions'.* In the **Mission Model**, processes and data are focused on the specific S.M.A.R.T KPIs and metrics in the enterprise's value measures that define how its *'value propositions'* will serve the value added outcomes to customers and stakeholders.

**Business Model**

The concept of what value is delivered by an enterprise is defined in its *'value streams'* and organized in its *'value chain'.* In the **Business Model**, processes and data are focused on the specific components in the *'value streams'* that will deliver the value-added outcomes as proposed by the *value propositions* to customers and stakeholders, including costs, benefits and margins.

**Value Model**

The logic to deliver value that is unique and with a competitive advantage to customers and stakeholders is defined in the enterprise's *'capabilities'* in how they differentiate a service offering. In the **Value Model**, processes and data are focused on optimizing *value streams* with appropriate *'capabilities'* to deliver the a USP, that meets and exceeds customers expectations along their customer and user journeys.

**Operating Model**

The physical infrastructure supporting the *'component resources'* in an enterprise, including its assets are where the *'business activities'* that deliver the value are conducted. In the **Operating Model**, processes and data are focused on the *'business activities'* and the *'component resources'* that operate the *capabilities*, responsible for delivering the value add as defined by the *value streams* and *value propositions*.

**Transformation Model**

Value is delivered through *'tasks'* that are actioned and implemented by people and systems supported by technology. In the **Transformation Model**, processes and data are focused on the efficiency and effectiveness of *'tasks'* and that are carried out by people, as well as machines through lines of code, to ensure optimal operation and effective transformation execution of *business activities*.

*In the Strategy Journey Paths and process steps to business agility, you will learn HOW to join the dots and practically transform an enterprise as well as your career, as you follow the steps to build each of the Five Models of* **THE STRATEGY JOURNEY** *Framework.*

How

# Bridging the **strategy execution gap**

Enterprises big and small have tried many methods to successfully implement their new strategies, while transforming their organizations. However, this gap from strategy design to strategy execution remains a major challenge, with many projects that fail to deliver the value add desired by the business's strategic objectives, thus resulting in diminished ROI.

How can we change the odds from the 30:70 hit-miss record* that has remained unchanged for so many decades, as organizations navigate through their business lifecycles and along the minefield of disconnected projects that form their strategy journeys?

*The Five Models of* **THE STRATEGY JOURNEY** *Framework, can be joined into* **THREE GUIDED PATHS** *forming an end-to-end* **Methodology** *that enables an enterprise to cohesively bridge its strategy-to-execution gaps, and build its business agility, in an increasingly connected digital economy.*

**New Operating Model** *Reality*

**Current Operating Model** *Reality*

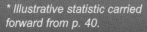

*\* Illustrative statistic carried forward from p. 40.*

# Three digital economy challenges …

In the fast changing digital economy, all businesses big and small are faced with three big challenges in addition to the *10 universal transformation challenges* (p. 9-10), as they navigate through their strategy journeys to adapt their **Operating Models** and innovate **Business Models** with solutions that become adopted by customers:

## Business Model disruption

When consumers are continuously changing the way they think, act and behave, this opens up a world of opportunities for innovations to become adopted quicker than ever before. Customer hyperadoption by some demographic groups (p. 126) has facilitated big bang disruptions through innovations from non-competitors (p. 103), increasing the need to compete through improved experiences. It is this constant change in customer behaviour that has and can continue to render many existing business models obsolete.

## Servicing relevant customer journeys

Businesses must learn to anticipate the changing needs and wants of customers through co-creation, and offer new services that form their customer journeys with improved connectivity and value add.

# ... in THE STRATEGY JOURNEY

*Customers adopt innovation delivered by new Business Model*

## Sustainable transformation

The increase rate and pace of change in the business ecosystem means an increase in costs to innovate and transform the operating model, in order to support the new business models of the future. Costs includes more time, resources and funds, and hence the potential for more waste too, if the transformation journey is not managed properly to deliver the best ROI possible.

# Paths are recipes for applying...

Enterprises traverse the *Five Stages of* **THE STRATEGY JOURNEY** differently based on their existing level of business agility and transformation maturity (p. 51-54) and the specific transformation challenges (p. 9-10) that they are facing at any point in time.

This means that they may have different *access points* or *starting points* depending upon their type of business transformation challenge. This is why enterprises should commence each end-to-end strategy journey with the guided-path that fits the problem they want to solve. Deciding what the challenge actually is, is as important as solving it using a structured and tested methodology. A higher level of transformation maturity will also provide more accuracy when executing a path.

## Three guided paths to traverse THE STRATEGY JOURNEY end-to-end

In **THE STRATEGY JOURNEY methodology**, there are three paths specifically aligned to the three digital economy challenges faced by a business:

### Business Model disruption

### Business Design for Disruption

How to address the threat of disruption to your business model, and make appropriate decisions on what strategies and tactics to undertake in the next phase(s) of your business.

### Servicing relevant customer journeys

### Transforming Operating Models with Service Design

How to design new services that deliver value according to customer and user journeys, and develop the new value stream and capabilities required in your operating model.

### Sustainable transformation

### Managing the Transformation Journey

How to deliver changes in your operating model using co-creation, and instill a culture of learning while improving operational efficiency and resources across geographies.

# THE **STRATEGY JOURNEY** *Framework*

## *What makes a Strategy Journey Path?*

The *Strategy Journey Paths* are constructed from the Five models developed in the **THE STRATEGY JOURNEY** *Framework*. A single path is supported by a subset of the models. The analysis approach in a model is used to gather and derive specific data which is then summarized in a **Strategy Journey Canvas** for each logical step of a path.

Joining the three paths in sequence enables a business to bridge the gaps between strategy and execution end-to-end and in doing so build, improve and achieve *business agility*.

***Individually the paths support business design, service-led transformation design and transformation execution.***

## *Which guided-path should your enterprise or project commence with?*

The three paths do not need to be taken sequentially and it may only make sense for new start-up businesses to navigate through the three paths in sequence from business design supporting a strategy to implementation.

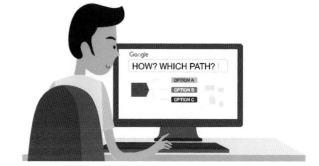

Choosing which path to commence with needs to factor in the following :
An enterprise's …
- Business transformation challenges
- Priority goals and objectives
- Immediate versus long terms threats that could cause disruption

You should also consider which part of the current **Operating Model** your project is operating within, your role within the enterprise and the implication of these to the **Target Operating Model** if it exists**.**

We have developed a tool to help you consider your needs in this respect and discover the Path with the best fit to get you started – in the **Strategy Journey Analyzer**.

*Assess our enterprise or project with the free* **STRATEGY JOURNEY** *Analyzer* *tool at:*
**https://strategyjourney.com/analyzer-tool**

# HOW to navigate the three paths

The three **STRATEGY JOURNEY Paths** enable a business and its organization to navigate from its **Current Operating Model** to a **New Operating Model** REALITY, while overcoming its big digital economy and wider transformation challenges. We illustrate how the Five Models of **THE STRATEGY JOURNEY** *Framework* span across the three paths to collect data, conduct gap analysis and infer as well as implement service solutions, that will enable a enterprise to achieve effective business transformation.

*Mission Model Blueprint*

**1** **Business Design for Disruption**

**Mission Model**

**Business Model**

*Customer Journey Map*

**2** **Transforming Operating Models with Service Design**

**Value Model**

## Current Operating Model *Reality*

How the enterprise runs and functions today, to support the business model that it currently deploys in the marketplace.

The three paths work together by connecting through data using the five **Strategy Journey Canvases.** Successfully traversing the paths will facilitate innovation and deliver the New Operating Model reality via transformation of the business. The paths employ the three data-driven approaches of value driven, customer co-created, and network connected to accelerate the speed of growth through digital transformation.

**New Operating Model**
*Reality*

*Digital Business Blueprint*

How the enterprise runs and functions at a point in time in the future, following successful implementation of business transformation, to support its new or changed business model, in the marketplace.

Operating Model

*Target Service Operating Model*

Transformation Model

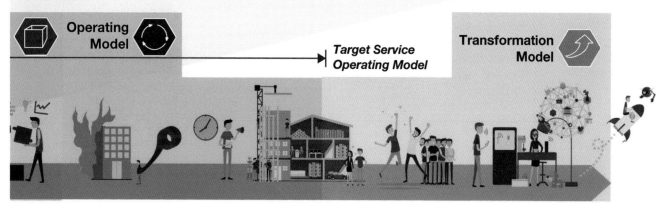

*Target Service Operating Model*

**3 Managing the Transformation Journey**

*Transformation Roadmap*

# Joining the dots with Service Innovation

A great many transformation initiatives that are undertaken fail partly or completely to deliver the intended business outcomes (p. 39-40). Businesses will readily undertake *Path 1* and revise their strategy and vision for a new business design feature or a revision to the existing design. Businesses with a low Operating Model maturity can tend to jump too quickly to *Path 3* and execute transformation to try to immediately realise the business design vision and associated benefits, without joining the dots in *Path 2*.

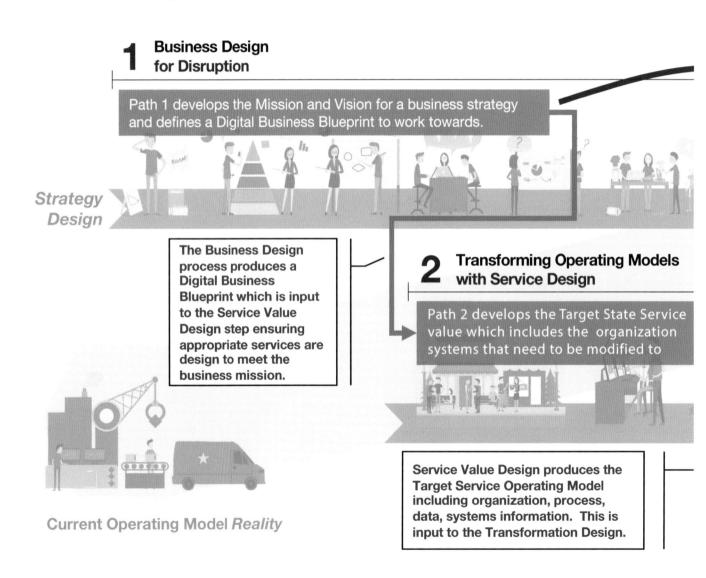

**1** **Business Design for Disruption**

Path 1 develops the Mission and Vision for a business strategy and defines a Digital Business Blueprint to work towards.

*Strategy Design*

The Business Design process produces a Digital Business Blueprint which is input to the Service Value Design step ensuring appropriate services are design to meet the business mission.

**2** **Transforming Operating Models with Service Design**

Path 2 develops the Target State Service value which includes the organization systems that need to be modified to

*Current Operating Model Reality*

Service Value Design produces the Target Service Operating Model including organization, process, data, systems information. This is input to the Transformation Design.

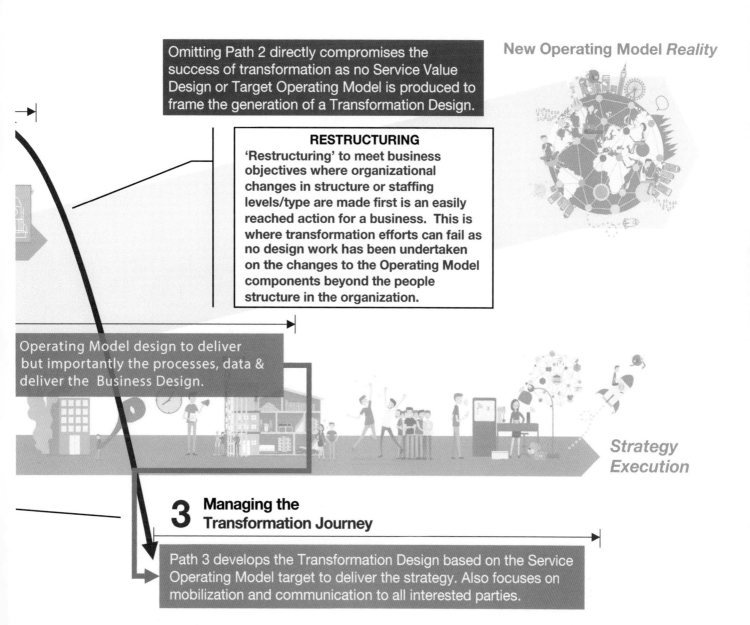

Omitting Path 2 directly compromises the success of transformation as no Service Value Design or Target Operating Model is produced to frame the generation of a Transformation Design.

New Operating Model *Reality*

**RESTRUCTURING**
'Restructuring' to meet business objectives where organizational changes in structure or staffing levels/type are made first is an easily reached action for a business. This is where transformation efforts can fail as no design work has been undertaken on the changes to the Operating Model components beyond the people structure in the organization.

Operating Model design to deliver but importantly the processes, data & deliver the Business Design.

*Strategy Execution*

**3** **Managing the Transformation Journey**

Path 3 develops the Transformation Design based on the Service Operating Model target to deliver the strategy. Also focuses on mobilization and communication to all interested parties.

# Joining the dots with data

The three **STRATEGY JOURNEY *Paths*** are enabled through specific data sourced from analysis prescribed by each model in the Framework.  In each path, data is collected in a structured manner using **THE *STRATEGY JOURNEY* Canvases** aligned to each of the models.  Key elements of data derived in an upstream path are used as inputs for following paths joining the dots through data.

**Five specially designed canvases,** one from each model, bring data together at key stages in the analysis of a path to aid decision making.

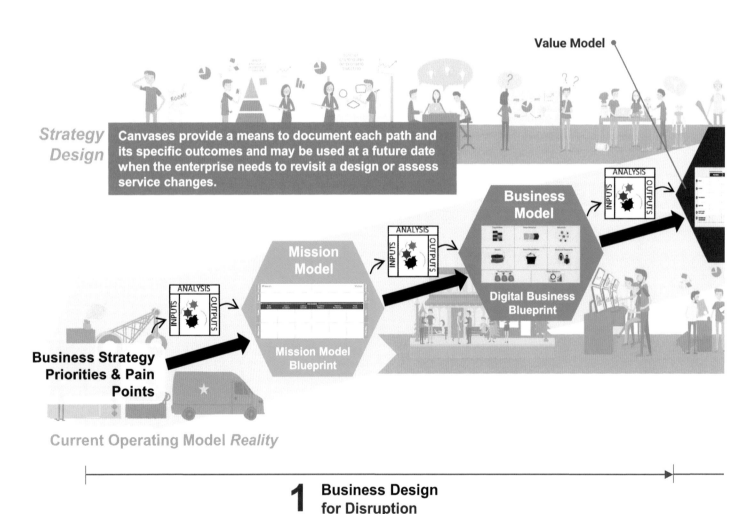

Value Model

*Strategy Design*

Canvases provide a means to document each path and its specific outcomes and may be used at a future date when the enterprise needs to revisit a design or assess service changes.

Business Model

Mission Model

Digital Business Blueprint

Mission Model Blueprint

**Business Strategy Priorities & Pain Points**

*Current Operating Model Reality*

**1 Business Design for Disruption**

Data capabilities are required in order to work through the data collection and analysis within a model as part of a path. The quality of data sourced or the maturity of data analysis undertaken will have an impact on the outcome of a model and the resultant outcome of the path.

New Operating Model
*Reality*

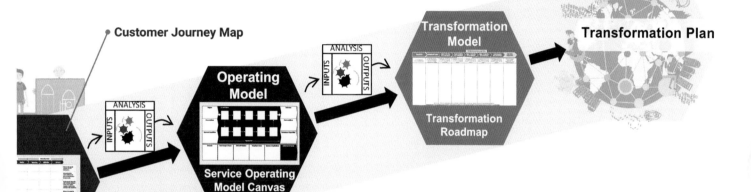

**Customer Journey Map**

**Operating Model**

Service Operating Model Canvas

**Transformation Model**

Transformation Roadmap

**Transformation Plan**

**Five Key Canvases**

|  |  |
|---|---|
| Mission Model: | Mission Model Blueprint |
| Business Model: | Digital Business Blueprint |
| Value Model: | Customer Journey Map |
| Operating Model: | Service Operating Model |
| Transformation Model: | Transformation Roadmap |

*Strategy Execution*

**2** Transforming Operating Models with Service Design

**3** Managing the Transformation Journey

# The Disruption-led path to business design

The *Business Design for Disruption* path is comprised of two phases: a **Mission Model Design** process that outlines a blueprint to lead and motivate an enterprise followed by a **Business Model Design** process that outlines the strategy to create, produce and deliver value.

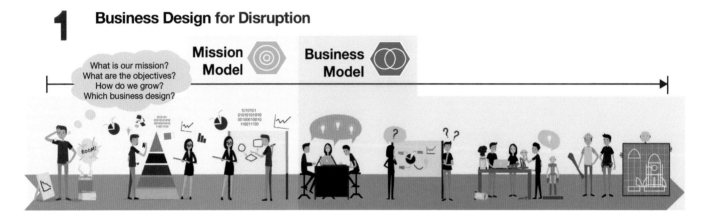

**1 Business Design for Disruption**

**Mission Model Design** analysis focuses on setting the direction of the business to fulfil its purpose with a 'mission blueprint' that outlines what the business wants to achieve over a period of time. The *Mission Model Blueprint* is comprised of the enterprise's starting position and desired outcomes so that the organization knows where the business wants to be and becomes motivated to support this journey.

**Business Model Design** analysis defines the 'business blueprint' by which the business will operate to achieve its goals and objectives in the **Mission Model**, through delivering the right value propositions to the right customers and users, and grow the value that the business creates, produces and delivers.

In today's digital economy, it has become essential to define a *Digital Business Blueprint* that will set up the business to operate as a data-driven enterprise, in order to support *business transformation* with *business agility* and maximize value.

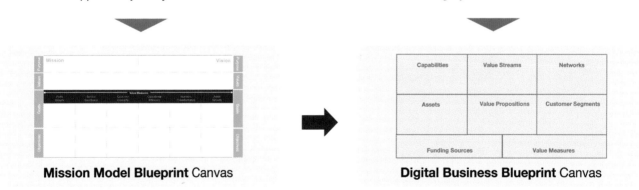

**Mission Model Blueprint** Canvas          **Digital Business Blueprint** Canvas

**Business Design for Disruption Path Outputs**

# When to use the Business Design for Disruption analysis path

The path should be triggered when an enterprise is faced with any of these transformation challenges (p. 9-10), which its leaders have prioritized for action:

- **Starting a new business**: It is vital to have a strategic blueprint that conceptualizes the full design (the Vision, Mission, Goals Objectives and Business Plan for the business) which can be continuously validated and tested to ensure value propositions are fit for purpose to a proposed target market, who will adopt and pay for the service offerings.

- **Digital disruption**: When a business experiences declining sales especially from using non digital channels, this is a sign of digital disruption. This can be addressed through a game plan that alters the Business Model to include use of digital networks and technology to support new or improved service offerings, including new digital service offerings, to customers and users, that they will adopt commercially.

- **Data driven scaling**: Big Data and especially customer data enables and empowers future value creation, so becoming a data-driven enterprise is almost mandatory in order to survive in the face of competition from players such as Amazon and Alibaba with their omni-channel marketplaces. Data can be used to drive innovation especially to identify niche opportunities. Businesses can connect with networks to reach not only more customers but leverage networks to serve customer and develop the customer relationship to increase Customer Lifetime Value (CLV) – powered by its data.

- **Build asset valuations**: Businesses exist to deliver value to customers, but also to its stakeholders and especially its owners and shareholders, who take the risk to invest in the business to help it grow. Overall business value or valuation which we witness through company sales and Initial Public Offerings (IPOs) is calculated from the assets that a business had built up, which hold their own value when sold, as well as driving future value through increase sales, future sales or licensing and subscription in the case of digital assets and other intellectual property (IP).

- **Local and Global Expansion**: Different networks and their services, local and global can be leveraged to increase an enterprise's operational capabilities to support business value creation and delivery. These external capabilities accessed via the networks can be used to speed the reach to and from a supply chain and to customers and users.

# Ten Business Design Path steps

The 10 step process to define the Mission, Vision and Digital Business Blueprint for an enterprise that will deliver value propositions aligned to market requirements, ecosystem influencers and customer problems using **THE STRATEGY JOURNEY** *Framework*.

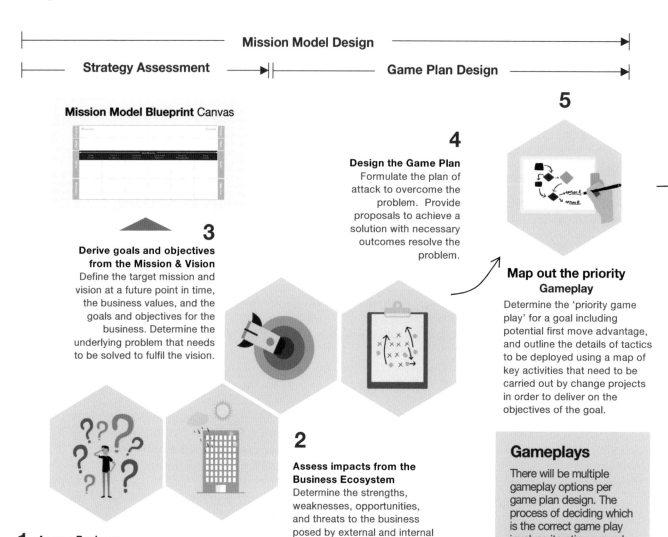

**Mission Model Design**

**Strategy Assessment** → | **Game Plan Design**

**5**

**Mission Model Blueprint** Canvas

**4**

**Design the Game Plan**
Formulate the plan of attack to overcome the problem. Provide proposals to achieve a solution with necessary outcomes resolve the problem.

**3**

**Derive goals and objectives from the Mission & Vision**
Define the target mission and vision at a future point in time, the business values, and the goals and objectives for the business. Determine the underlying problem that needs to be solved to fulfil the vision.

**Map out the priority Gameplay**
Determine the 'priority game play' for a goal including potential first move advantage, and outline the details of tactics to be deployed using a map of key activities that need to be carried out by change projects in order to deliver on the objectives of the goal.

**2**

**Assess impacts from the Business Ecosystem**
Determine the strengths, weaknesses, opportunities, and threats to the business posed by external and internal influencers

**1 Assess Business Priorities and Pain Points**
Agree and review priority problems including pain points impacting the business and where resources need to be focused to develop solutions and value-added outcomes.

## Gameplays

There will be multiple gameplay options per game plan design. The process of deciding which is the correct game play involves iterating around the challenge to assess each for its merits and selecting the most appropriate solution.

**Business Model Design**

**Value Proposition Design** → | **Growth Funding Design**

**10**

**9** **Assess funding sources**
What is the funding plan to accommodate the development of the propositions and manage the growth and scaling.

**Develop the Business Growth Plan** **8**
What is the expected growth proposed by the business, over the next three years through deploying the products and services.

**Digital Business Blueprint**

Complete the enhanced digital business model design summarized using the Digital Business Blueprint Canvas.

**7**
**Design the Proposition Proposal**
Define a proposition marketing plan that lists the system of products and services that will draw the target customers into ongoing value-driven relationships and transactions with the business. Include methods to digitize communications and interactions with customers via networks.

**6**

**Assess the market & customers**
Determine the customer journey data associated with being a buyer of the proposed service solution. Capture data associated with how the customer as a buyer of associated services, will think, act and behave along their customer journey.

**Digital Business Blueprint** Canvas

| Capabilities | Value Streams | Networks |
|---|---|---|
| Assets | Value Propositions | Customer Segments |
| Funding Sources | | Value Measures |

# Mission Model Blueprint Canvas

The **Mission Model Blueprint** Canvas is a viewpoint to illustrate the strategy of an enterprise at a point in time, and provides a 10,000 foot view of how the organization behind the business needs to operate. It is comprised of four main components forming a strategic blueprint of the enterprise: purpose, values, goals, and objectives. These provide everyone in or involved with the business and the organization that supports it with direction and alignment across the six value measures (p. 69-72) that define success for the enterprise.

**Purpose**
Comprised of the *mission* and *vision* of the business, and used to attract followers.

**Mission**
Why does your business exist and what will it do for customers that will make a difference?

**Goals**
Significant achievements and milestones that contribute to the *mission* and *vision*, balanced across the six 'value measures' of a balanced and sustainable business.

*\* The 'Mission Model Blueprint' canvas has integrated the Business Motivation Model (developed by the Business Rules Group - BRG and expanded by the Object Management Group – OMG) and the Balanced Scorecard (from Robert S. Kaplan and David P. Norton) to create an enhance strategy map that incorporates business and digital transformation.*

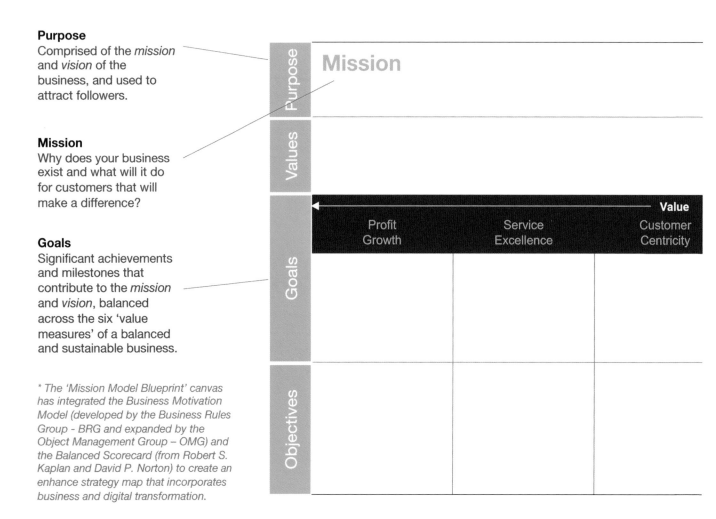

The **Mission Model Blueprint** Canvas should not be viewed as a static document, but rather as a dynamic model that needs to be changed and updated on a regular basis, ideally quarterly and at least yearly.

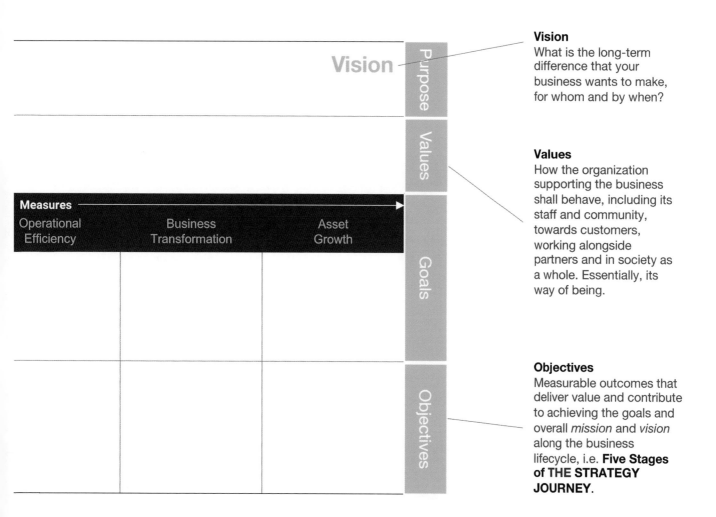

**Vision**

Purpose

**Values**

**Goals**

**Objectives**

**Measures**

| Operational Efficiency | Business Transformation | Asset Growth |
|---|---|---|
| | | |
| | | |

**Vision**
What is the long-term difference that your business wants to make, for whom and by when?

**Values**
How the organization supporting the business shall behave, including its staff and community, towards customers, working alongside partners and in society as a whole. Essentially, its way of being.

**Objectives**
Measurable outcomes that deliver value and contribute to achieving the goals and overall *mission* and *vision* along the business lifecycle, i.e. **Five Stages of THE STRATEGY JOURNEY**.

# EXAMPLE: Telsa's underlying Mission Model

Since launching in 2003, Telsa Inc. (formerly Tesla Motors Inc.) has shifted its mission beyond sustainable transport to sustainable energy. The company has introduced several new product and service lines that both complement and expand on its initial business strategy to develop a sports car and then make it more and more affordable, while in parallel also providing zero emission electric power generation options, including solar power to the world.

*In this case study example, we explore the company's goals and objectives at the start of 2019\*, which Entrepreneur CEO Elon Musk has touted as a 'pivotal year' for the company following its first full year of profitability in 2018, using the **Mission Model Blueprint** Canvas.*

*\* All information and data has been sourced directly or adapted from tesla.com or other publicly available sources to provide an illustrative example of Tesla's Mission Model as at 2019 - see References.*

*\*\* Unable to source concrete KPIs from Tesla or other sources*

## Mission

To accelerate the world's transition to sustainable energy (since 2016)

### Values

| | |
|---|---|
| Solving the world's most important problems to make the world a better place | Pace is fast, the work is stimulating, structure is limited, and innovation is expected |

### Goals

| Profit Growth | Service Excellence | Custome Centricity |
|---|---|---|
| Increase demand for car ownership in international markets – China & Europe | Further increase lead in batteries efficiency and costs | Being the custor go-to brand for transport / power |
| Launch ride sharing network to rival Uber, Lyft, etc… using autonomous vehicle fleet | Create fully autonomous vehicle fleet with data-driven AI learning capabilities | Enable energy pro owners to make m from generate electrical power su to energy grid |

### Objectives

| | | |
|---|---|---|
| Achieve avg. 19% gross margin across car models sold | Achieve a battery pack cost of $100 per kWh by 2020 | Enable Tesla own to make money vehicle ownersh with target price $4000 lease co |
| Generate profits through Mobility as a Service (MasS) using autonomous ride sharing cars, with target price of $4000, and 80% gross margins | Develop a self-driving capability that is 10X safer than manual via massive fleet learning at autonomous level 5 | Increase Tes Powerpack deployment and Roof installatior more sites\*\* |

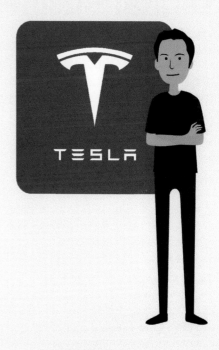

# Vision

**Vision** — Purpose

To create an entire sustainable energy ecosystem …
impacting our entire world to change the way we've produced,
stored and consumed energy for generations

**Values**

Agile, efficient and focused on excellence

Inclusive environment, with respect & support

...ures →

| ...perational Efficiency | Business Transformation | Asset Growth | |
|---|---|---|---|
| **Goals** | | | |
| Increase manufacturing efficiency and ...luce production costs through ...Gigafactory | First to market with Gigafactory able to scale mass production at affordable costs beyond existing capabilities | Continue to increase total assets valuation through innovation of patented technology in autonomous driving capability and sustainable energy generation & storage | |
| **Objectives** | | | |
| ...igafactory to ...luce up to 3,000 ...el 3s per week by ...end of the 2019, ...ding Stamping, ...lywork, Paint, & ...mbly Workshops | Build 3rd Gigafactory in Shanghai China with mass production by September 2019<br><br>Expand Buffalo Gigafactory to support increased production of Solar Roof and other energy products for 2019 sales growth** | Create own computer chip, with a 2,000% improvement over the next best chip supplied by Nvidia, and specially designed to power Tesla's autonomous vehicle fleets, and to work alongside Tesla's powertrain | |

*It is important to note that the **Mission Model** is a statement of intent with target KPIs that need to be achieved – functioning as a strategic blueprint or strategy map that provides the organization with a future direction. These strategies and tactics will need to be executed by the organization.*

*The **Mission Model Blueprint Canvas** should be a living document that charts a company's ongoing statement of intent, so it should be refreshed and updated at least yearly.*

# Digital Business Blueprint Canvas

The **Digital Business Blueprint** Canvas is comprised of eight 'architecture components' for constructing a **Digital Business Model**. It articulates the architecture foundations by which to build out a more detailed business plan for growing and scaling the value to be captured and produced by the digitally-oriented business, and to achieve ROI from investment funding.

**Capabilities** (p. 179)
The building blocks of resources required to operationally run the business, and carry out all its business activities end-to-end, to deliver value to customers and stakeholders.

**Value Propositions** (p. 97-100)
The vehicles or containers of outcomes by which value is produced and delivered to stakeholders, and in particular customers, in exchange for a payment. In the digital economy, it is necessary to have an ecosystem of propositions to manage customers along their customer journeys.

**Assets** (p. 149)
Any architecture components held and owned by the business, that holds value from being re-usable or re-sellable, and where the value held can potentially increase from appreciation based on future market conditions or a future use case.

**Funding Sources** (p. 145-148)
The mechanism by which funds are raised or drawn from, per amount that are required to pay for the different resources required to operationally execute the business activities that run the **Digital Business Model**.

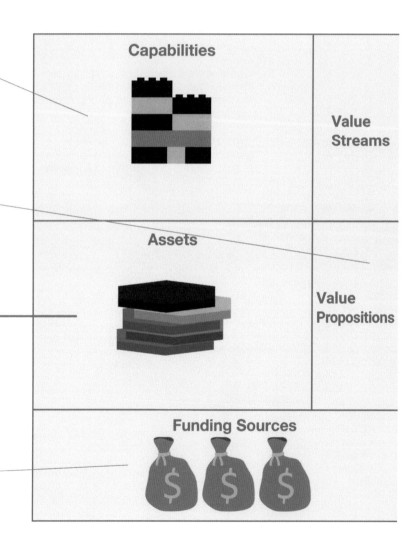

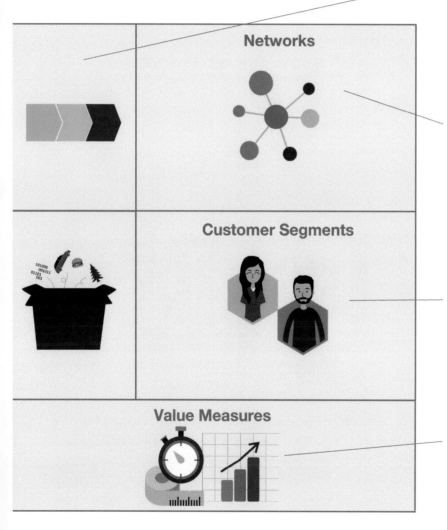

**Value Streams** (p. 154, 156)
The internal *value propositions* formed from sequencing different *capabilities* together to deliver value to stakeholders. They can also be converted to or used within an external *value proposition* for customers.

**Networks** (p. 133)
The mechanisms and platforms by which the business will interact and connect digitally or with support from digital technology with different customers and stakeholders. Includes people networks, information networks, energy or power networks, and any interconnectable group of things that can be used to support connectivity between the business and its stakeholders in the wider business ecosystem.

**Customer Segments** (p. 127-128)
The different segments of customers with a specific role who will interact with the business through the components of the **Digital Business Model**. Includes buyers, users, and partners such as sponsors, regulators, etc ... as well as internal stakeholders.

**Value Measures** (p. 71-72)
The different forms of tangible or intangible, but measurable value that is to be produced for and delivered to the different stakeholders of the business. 'Value Measures' are captured in a business's S.M.A.R.T business objectives.

# EXAMPLE: Udacity's strategic Digital Business Blueprint Summary

eLearning Unicorn Udacity has grown its revenues since launching in 2014 through its **Digital Business Model** where much of its services are operated through its Proprietary Learning Management System (LMS) that has been developed using the EdX Platform (an open source technology offered by MIT). The company has looked to extend revenues by increasing its enterprise services that blend a more traditional business model using business development to increase its learning services contracts with corporations. It has also remodeled its workforce by downsizing to improve efficiency of specific capabilities, while creating a Mentor marketplace and community services for students and professionals who could teach in order to create stickiness, while reducing costs.

*In this case study example, we use the **Digital Business Blueprint** Canvas\* to summarize the architecture components that form and sustain Udacity's Digital Business Model in 2019 as it sets out to scale-up towards achieving profitability.*

*\* Illustrative example reverse engineered by Stratability Academy based on publicly sourced data as at May 2019*

*\*\* See p. 183-184 for more detailed illustration of capabilities in the high education and MOOCs value chain*

*\*\*\* See p.149  for more detailed breakdown of Assets*

*μ See p. 152 for more detail of how Udacity's Proposition Bundles will support its Business Model to grow*

*^ See p. 127 for more detailed breakdown of Customer Segment data*

*Further sources available in the References section of this book*

## Capabilities**

Teacher & Mentor Management
Platform Management
Product Strategy & Curriculum Design
Consumer Student Marketing
Enterprise Business Development & Sales
Course Delivery
Infrastructure Management
Certificate Qualification Award Management
Course Content Creation
Student Enrollment
Student & Alumni Community Management
Software Engineering
Partnership Management
Innovation including R&D

## Value Streams

Career Development &
Support Services

Scholarship Services

Enterprise Training Services

Consumer Learning Services

Student Community Service

Teacher & Mentor Services

## Networks

Udacity owned & managed
Mentor Marketplace

Udacity owned & managed Code
Grading & Sharing Platform

Udacity owned & managed Student Hub
available on IOS and Android

Curriculum partnerships with Google,
IBM Watson, Facebook, GE, Amazon,
AT&T, Github, BOSCH, Uber ATG,
mongoDB, Mercedes-Benz, Autodesk,
Twitter, nvidia, cloudera, uranix,
Hubspot, BMW, Elektrobit, etc…

Infrastructure partnerships with
Github, Cloudflare (especially
China CDN Network), etc…

## Assets***

Proprietary network and multisided
platform

Student data – over 10 million
registered students

Over 200 enterprise partnerships

Content for its free and paid courses

Data on specific Industry skills
needed
Udacity Brand incl. leadership
by Sebastian Thrun

## Value Propositions$^\mu$

Approx. 237 free courses
(incl. 12 Career Courses in
collaboration with Google)

Approx. 35 active paid nanodegree
courses and certification programs

1.1 million funded scholarship
programs

Corporate Learning Management
System with content packages based on
existing free and nanodegree programs

Mentor Marketplace

Student Hub app

## Customer Segments^

Consumer Professional Learners that
want to upskill for the 'Future Of Work'

Mentors who provide teaching support
for learners including marking and
reviewing of course work, and CVs or
resumes. Some mentors are also
authors of course content.

Companies (mainly larger
corporations) that want to upskill and
maintain motivation in their workforce,
and thus sponsor scholarships that
pay for staff to learn through a Udacity
nanodegree

## Funding Sources

USD $165 million investor funding up to till 2015

Reinvested Revenue where available from $40 million in 2016,
$70 million in 2017, $88 million in 2018…

## Value Measures

Revenue from nanodegree course fees from consumers
Corporate contracts including scholarship funding
Cost savings from workforce & office consolidation in 2019
Customer stickiness from Mentor Marketplace & Community Services
Improved content and program content & delivery

# The Service-led path to business transformation

The *Transforming Operating Models with Service Design* path is comprise of two phases: a **Value Model Design** process that uses applied service design & innovation techniques to define new and improved service offerings that customers will adopt, and an **Operating Model Design** process that outlines what capabilities need transformation as well as how 'capability gaps' should be addressed.

## 2 Transforming Operating Models with Service Design

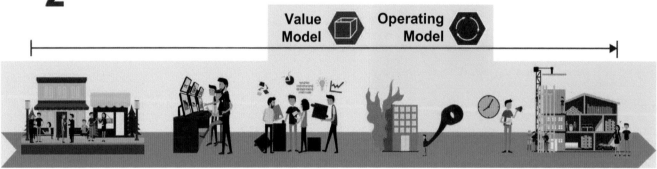

**Value Model Design** analysis focuses on understanding the problems, pains and gains faced by customers along their customer journeys to define new and improved service offerings that will meet or exceed their expectations. A **Customer Journey Map** is used to design new and improved services based how customers as buyers and users of service offerings think, act and behave, to create and build stickiness effects, along their journeys as they experience different value propositions.

**Operating Model Design** analysis is a 'transformation design' process that defines what 'capability gaps' exist in the enterprise's **Operating Model**, based on their current state of maturity and the gap to the desired target state which is required to realize the new and improved service(s) when business transformation and changes are executed. A new **Service Operating Model** is comprised of the inputs, components resources and outputs that will deliver the new and improved service offerings to customers, users and stakeholders.

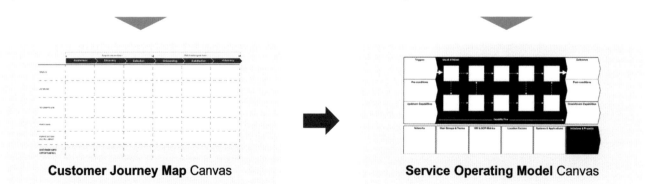

**Customer Journey Map** Canvas                    **Service Operating Model** Canvas

**Transforming Operating Models with Service Design Path Outputs**

## When to use the **Transforming Operating Models with Service Design** analysis path

The path should be triggered when an enterprise is faced with any of these transformation challenges (p. 9-10), which its leaders have prioritized for action:

- **Digital disruption service design**: As well as combating the threats of disruption, businesses may look to introduce their own service innovations that will disrupt the marketplace and gain market share. The business innovates new services using human-centred design techniques to ensure services are value-driven, customer co-created and network connected to in order to attract customers as well as introducing stickiness effects. This supports services to reach 'growth' as well as maintaining the enterprise in a continuously 'growth' state.

- **Building a strong brand by enhancing customer relationships**: Building long-term relationships with your customers, by managing their expectations and being intone with customers, and users can be achieved through development of sticky service experiences. Stickiness effects will create advocacy for a brand as well as increasing service adoption across a proposition ecosystem of products and services from an enterprise, to support continuous growth.

- **Business scaling in existing or into new markets**: There are many service innovation techniques that can enable a business to expand its market share at a global scale, especially with the aid of digital technology and virtual channels. Capabilities available from other players in the value ecosystem can be leveraged to support an enterprise to scale its services with improved business agility with speed to market, through integration with the existing value chain, and value streams in the Operating Model, when there are 'gaps'.

- **Adapting to ecosystem changes**: Regulations and other rules set at the global or government level with an industry, as well as other external factors can disrupt or impact the business and its operations requiring a lot of change. Examples include COVID-19, GFC, global warming, GDPR, and increasing threats from cybercrime. It is essential to identify the strengths and weakness in the business ecosystem to be able to adapt and make the enterprise more resilient to shocks and ongoing changes from its business ecosystem and the digital economy.

- **Operations inefficiency**: Inefficiency in production processes combined with the cost of the management of services and potentially a lack of speed of delivery in changing circumstances, can prevent a company from fulfilling its desired growth targets or capturing future market opportunities. An enterprise's services can continue on a path of decline along the Innovation Adoption Lifecycle when continuous changes in the business ecosystem, including changing customer and consumer behaviors take hold. They either do nothing and accept this or they can improve service innovation to introduce upgrades and develop the means to support 'growth'.

# Ten Transforming Operating Models Path Steps

Ten steps to define a **Target Operating Model** that increases Customer Lifetime Value (CLV) and provides a Return On Investment (ROI) from Digital Transformation using **THE STRATEGY JOURNEY** *Framework*. Covers four types of gap analysis, Customer Gaps, Service Gaps, Capability Gaps and Transformation Gaps.

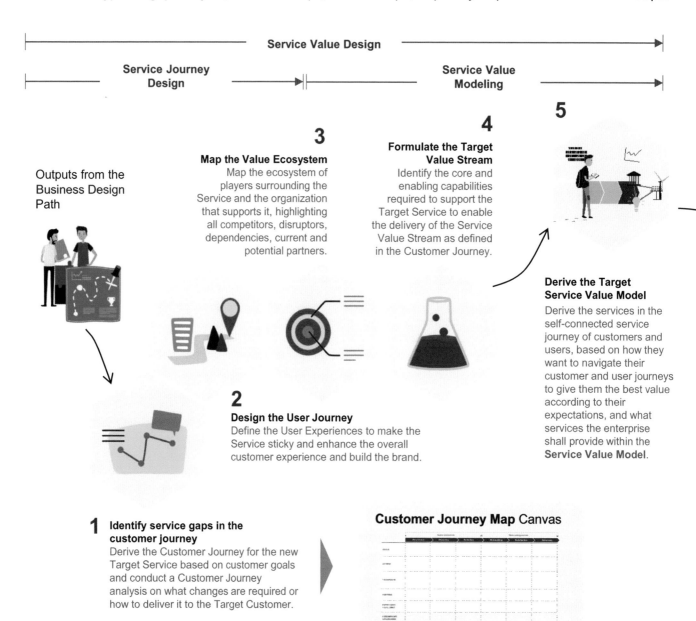

**Service Value Design**

**Service Journey Design**

**Service Value Modeling**

Outputs from the Business Design Path

**3**

**Map the Value Ecosystem**
Map the ecosystem of players surrounding the Service and the organization that supports it, highlighting all competitors, disruptors, dependencies, current and potential partners.

**4**

**Formulate the Target Value Stream**
Identify the core and enabling capabilities required to support the Target Service to enable the delivery of the Service Value Stream as defined in the Customer Journey.

**5**

**Derive the Target Service Value Model**
Derive the services in the self-connected service journey of customers and users, based on how they want to navigate their customer and user journeys to give them the best value according to their expectations, and what services the enterprise shall provide within the **Service Value Model**.

**2**

**Design the User Journey**
Define the User Experiences to make the Service sticky and enhance the overall customer experience and build the brand.

**1** **Identify service gaps in the customer journey**
Derive the Customer Journey for the new Target Service based on customer goals and conduct a Customer Journey analysis on what changes are required or how to deliver it to the Target Customer.

**Customer Journey Map** Canvas

**Operating Model Transformation Design**

**Service Transformation Design** → | **Service Architecture Design** →

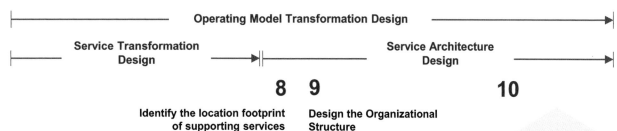

**8    9**

**10**

### Identify the location footprint of supporting services
Design the proposed location footprint for the new and value stream capabilities supporting the Target Service taking into account outsourcing and client/user servicing requirements.

### Design the Organizational Structure
Design the proposed organizational structure of the business or function aligned to the service and capabilities.

### Configure the Target Service Architecture
Define the logical blueprint of the capability components in how they will operate through joining the dots with data, to deliver the Target Service in the Target Operating Model.

**7**

### Derive the 'capability gaps' and their Operating Model components
Create Capability Definitions covering the process and data requirements for each of the capabilities in the new Target Service and the transformation initiatives and project actions that are required to deliver the new capability or bridge the gap to the Target Operating Model.

**6**

### Define the Target Operating Model
Derive the Target Operating Model for the new or Target Service based the Value Stream identified, indicating the inputs and outputs, operating model components and any impacted or new initiatives or projects.

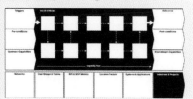

**Service Operating Model** Canvas

# Customer Journey Map Canvas

The **Customer Journey Map** Canvas enables you to establish how a buyer thinks, acts, and behaves along their buyer journey to solve their big problem and achieve their end-goal.

*We* provide *the following guidance to help you capture and translate data on the customer's behavior along the stages of their customer journey, to determine which customer gaps present as opportunities for improvement through service design of new service features or entirely new service offerings:*

| | Acquire new customer | | |
|---|---|---|---|
| | **Awareness** | **Discovery** | **Selection** |
| **GOALS** | | | |
| **ACTIONS** | | | |
| **TOUCHPOINTS** | | | |
| **EMOTIONS** | | | |
| **CURRENT EXPERIENCE EXPECTATION FULFILLMENT** | | | |
| **CUSTOMER GAPS OPPORTUNITIES** | | | |

Alter the naming of the customer journey stages as required to represent the language used, or actions and behaviors of customers, and not based on internal organizational processes that reflect the actions of operational staff.

*It is crucial to focus data capture on the buyer's perspective, and not resort to mapping internal processes based on staff perception. The customer journey is not the operational procedure of how to market, sell to, or serve customers.*

Retain existing customer

| Onboarding | Satisfaction | Advocacy | |
|---|---|---|---|
| | | | List the mini-goals of the customer based on their 'pains' and 'gains' as they attempt to solve their big problem and to achieve their end-goal |
| | | | List the activities that the customer undertakes to achieve their corresponding mini-goals on the customer journey. |
| | | | List all the places incl. online, mobile, media & social media, public places, services or travel, workplaces, communities… where the customer spends time on their customer journey. |
| | | | Indicate how the customer feels currently in trying to achieve the mini-goals on each customer journey stage. |
| | | | Outline customers' current experiences of how existing service options measure up to their preconceived expectations |
| | | | List all the ideal service solution features as desired and indicated by customers at each customer journey stage* |

*\* These may include complaints that lead to viable suggestions for improvement*

# EXAMPLE: Customer Journey of busy family home buyers

The busy growing family in Sydney Australia is a very lucrative target market segment for mortgage providers, including the Commonwealth Bank of Australia (CBA), who holds the greatest market share for home loans in Australia. CBA has managed to maintain this market dominance from its deep understanding of the customer journey, in how customers think, act, and behave when it comes to buying a new home, and has used this knowledge to innovate many services to meet and even exceed the expectations of its customers.

*In this case study example\*, we explore the customer journey for busy families looking to buy a new family home in Sydney Australia\* and who may need a mortgage to complete their purchase, covering how customers think, act, and behave as they solve their big problem using the **Customer Journey Map** Canvas.*

|  | **Awareness**<br>*Need to move house* | Acquire new customer →<br>**Discovery**<br>*Discover my options* |
|---|---|---|
| **GOALS** | • Upgrade home size<br>• Good schools<br>• Good commute<br>• Increasing cost of living<br>• Cost of education<br>• Build equity with home ownership | • Max purchase budget<br>• Mortgages available & suited to my financial needs<br>• Location & accessibility to amenities suits my family, work & lifestyle |
| **ACTIONS** | • Commuting and working<br>• School/nursery run<br>• Living in rented/temp accommodation<br>• Saving for future needs<br>• Learning about their kids' education needs<br>• Dreaming about future | • Searching online to find out more information<br>• Asking friends, family, colleagues for help<br>• Creating a checklist that includes family members<br>• Hiring a broker or advisor |
| **TOUCHPOINTS** | • Train, bus, roads, media<br>• Place of work & amenities<br>• School or nursery<br>• Home communication & entertainment<br>• Internet, social media<br>• Events with family and friends' local amenities | • Place of work & amenities<br>• School or nursery<br>• Internet, social media<br>• Family, friends & contacts<br>• Local amenities<br>• Brokers & advisors |
| **EMOTIONS** | • Annoyed/frustrated with long work/commute times<br>• Rushed school runs<br>• Uncomfortable space<br>• Financial worries<br>• Envy of others | • Worried/stressed about growing checklist of criteria<br>• Frustrated with research time and process<br>• Financial worries |

*Illustrative and inexhaustive example based on analysis conducted by Stratability Academy using publicly available data. Sources available in the References section of this book.*

Retain existing customer

| Selection | Onboarding | Satisfaction | Advocacy |
|---|---|---|---|
| Find & buy home | Moving in & settling | Living a great lifestyle | Share & expand experiences |
| • House is right size<br>• House is in good location<br>• House is in good condition<br>• House suits lifestyle<br>• House is affordable<br>• Mortgage suits my needs | • I have the right mortgage<br>• I bought the right house<br>• I can and know where to go to sort out new problems & issues quickly & easily<br>• My family is supported | • I am happy with our home<br>• My finances are fine<br>• Family is living the lifestyle that makes us happy<br>• Our experience has been good and unexpected issues were easily & quickly resolved | • I know where to go and what to expect if I had to do this again<br>• I can be helpful to someone else with the same problem & share my experience |
| • Searching for house<br>• Visiting schools<br>• Trialing local amenities<br>• Consulting with friends, family & contacts<br>• Gathering paperwork<br>• Finding/hiring solicitor<br>• Choosing a mortgage | • Property Handover admin<br>• Packing and removals<br>• Cleaning & fixing things in new house<br>• Buying new furniture<br>• Experience & learn about new environment<br>• Make mortgage payment | • Work/commute improves<br>• Kids are settled & doing well in school/nursery<br>• Living lifestyle, enjoying house & local amenities<br>• Mortgage admin<br>• Find new ways to growth wealth for future needs | • Enjoying free time<br>• Enjoying increase wealth<br>• Exploring lifestyle additions<br>• Exploring career enhancers or changes<br>• Saving to help children<br>• Building more assets |
| • Estate agents (online & local branches)<br>• School or nursery<br>• Internet, social media<br>• Family, friends & contacts<br>• Local amenities<br>• Broker & solicitor<br>• Banks & lenders | • Estate Agents, Broker & Solicitor<br>• Removalists<br>• School or nursery<br>• Home entertainment<br>• Family, friends & contacts<br>• Local amenities incl. govt<br>• Bank/lender channels | • Place of work & transport<br>• Education facilities & channels<br>• Home entertainment<br>• Internet, social media<br>• Events with family and friends' local amenities incl. govt<br>• Bank/lender channels | • Place of work & transport Education facilities & channels<br>• Home entertainment<br>• Internet, social media<br>• Events with family and friends' local amenities incl. govt<br>• Fintech channels |
| • Worried/stressed about picking house that ticks the checklist criteria<br>• Financial worries<br>• Frustrated with admin time | • Worried/stressed about moving and settling<br>• Financial worries about mortgage repayments<br>• Hope nothing goes wrong and future path is set | • Concerned about changes in family & kids' education<br>• Concerned about changes to work situation<br>• Annoyed with home maintenance/admin<br>• Enjoying new lifestyle | • Longing to give back & help others<br>• Concerned about children's finances<br>• Bored of lifestyle & inquisitive about new opportunities |

# EXAMPLE: How CBA identified a digital service opportunity to engage busy home buyers in Australia

The Australia Housing Market back by a strong Australia Economy grew significantly during 27 recession-free years up to 2018, with mortgages accounting for 80 percent of GDP, and house prices in Sydney, Australia's most expensive city, multiplying five-fold (x5) in value. Australian consumer expectations tend to be relatively high around housing related services including financial services or financial affairs management. Financial risk management, customer relationship management, and customer engagement from services and their service providers are three key customer expectation criteria along the home buying customer journey.

CBA has dominated and maintained its leading position in the Australia Mortgage Market, by offering award-winning services that leverage the latest in digital technology, focused on transforming customer and user experiences. As early as 2010, Mark Murray, general manager, consumer marketing, revealed: "We are leveraging new technology and continually innovating to deliver convenient, relevant, and real-time services to make buying a home easier..." as part of the banks' 2013 vision which included the launch of the world's first home buying augmented reality (AR) app, which was subsequently branded as 'The CommBank Property app.'

*In this case study example\*, we extend our analysis using the **Customer Journey Map** Canvas into customer gaps\* along the home buying customer journey, which led CBA to innovate several new digital services, delivered through the 'CommBank Property app', to support its **Omnichannel Business Model**.*

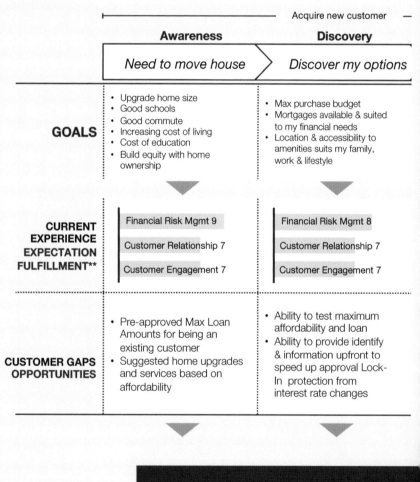

*\* Illustrative and inexhaustive example based on analysis conducted by Stratability Academy using publicly available data. Sources available in the References section of this book.*

*\*\* Illustrative example only using Customer Satisfaction Rating from 1-10 of three typical 'value measures' of importance within the Financial Services industry*

Retain existing customer

| Selection | Onboarding | Satisfaction | Advocacy |
|---|---|---|---|
| *Find & buy home* | *Moving in & settling* | *Living a great lifestyle* | *Share & expand experiences* |
| • House is right size<br>• House is in good location<br>• House is in good condition<br>• House suits lifestyle<br>• House is affordable<br>• Mortgage suits my needs | • I have the right mortgage<br>• I bought the right house<br>• I can and know where to go to sort out new problems & issues quickly & easily<br>• My family is supported | • I am happy with our home<br>• My finances are fine<br>• Family is living the lifestyle that makes us happy<br>• Our experience has been good and unexpected issues were easily & quickly resolved | • I know where to go and what to expect if I had to do this again<br>• I can be helpful to someone else with the same problem & share my experience |
| Financial Risk Mgmt 8<br><br>Customer Relationship 8<br><br>Customer Engagement 8 | Financial Risk Mgmt 8<br><br>Customer Relationship 8<br><br>Customer Engagement 7 | Financial Risk Mgmt 9<br><br>Customer Relationship 8<br><br>Customer Engagement 7 | Financial Risk Mgmt 8<br><br>Customer Relationship 7<br><br>Customer Engagement 6 |
| • Pre-approved Max Loan Amounts<br>• Fast 90min A/C opening<br>• Fast 48hr funding<br>• Membership access to additional exclusive services with discounts | • Moving home information packs & support services<br>• Packaged & discounted insurance from wealth membership | • Regular updates on customer wealth & credit score<br>• Automated reminders to maintain & secure personal data<br>• Ability to use personal data for other purposes | • Suggested opportunities to maintain/improve lifestyle through building wealth<br>• Further incentives & discounts based on membership |

**CommBank Property app**

# Service Operating Model Canvas

The **Service Operating Model** Canvas details how a service operates in its target state within the **Target Operating Model** of an enterprise, as an end-to-end process to deliver its proposed outcomes including experiences to customers and stakeholders as they navigate through the touchpoints of their customer and user journey. It enables you to conduct analysis on the inputs and outputs of the service, and define the **Operating Model** components required to support the Service Operating Procedures (SOPs) that will run the service in the future following successful business transformation.

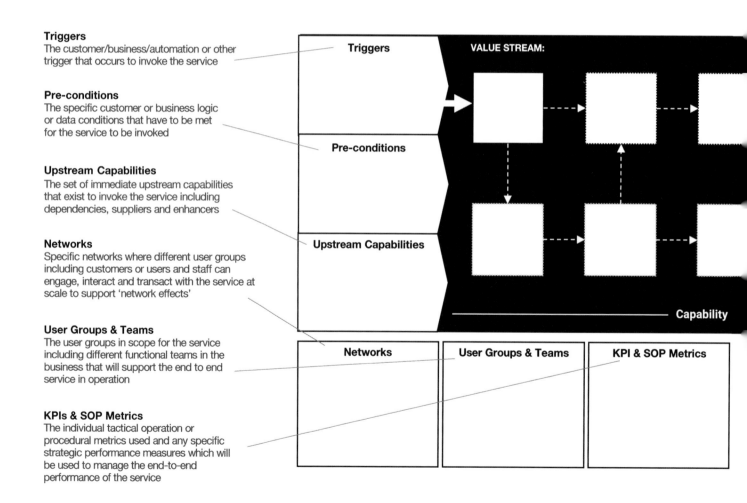

**Triggers**
The customer/business/automation or other trigger that occurs to invoke the service

**Pre-conditions**
The specific customer or business logic or data conditions that have to be met for the service to be invoked

**Upstream Capabilities**
The set of immediate upstream capabilities that exist to invoke the service including dependencies, suppliers and enhancers

**Networks**
Specific networks where different user groups including customers or users and staff can engage, interact and transact with the service at scale to support 'network effects'

**User Groups & Teams**
The user groups in scope for the service including different functional teams in the business that will support the end to end service in operation

**KPIs & SOP Metrics**
The individual tactical operation or procedural metrics used and any specific strategic performance measures which will be used to manage the end-to-end performance of the service

**Capability Flow**
The capabilities required and used by the enterprise to deliver the service through the value stream, which may occur sequentially or in parallel along different stages of service delivery & execution

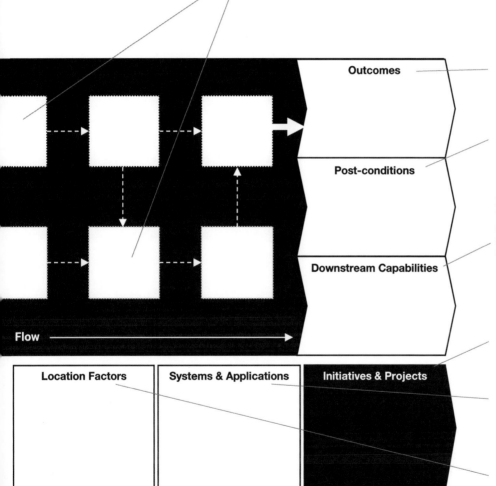

**Flow**

**Location Factors**

**Systems & Applications**

**Initiatives & Projects**

**Outcomes**

**Post-conditions**

**Downstream Capabilities**

**Outcomes**
The desired and/or required outcome(s) of the service to the customer and operationally in the business that result from invoking the service

**Post-conditions**
The specific customer or business logic or data conditions that are set at completion of this service to be carried forward to the next service

**Downstream Capabilities**
The set of immediate downstream capabilities that exist to receive the outcomes of this capability once it completes its operation

**Initiatives & Projects**
Currently active and new business initiatives and projects that are impact by and responsible for supporting the 'target services' and its inputs, outputs and **Operating Model** components.

**Systems & Applications**
The complete list of systems and applications required to support the end-to-end service, including dependent infrastructure

**Location Factors**
The complete set of factors from the business ecosystem including global and local regulations & customs… that are in scope with impacts to the level of service

# EXAMPLE: Behind Amazon's Alexa service

SMART SPEAKER ADOPTION* in the home has grown rapidly around the world reaching 20.7 million units sold and growth of 131% in 2019. The largest markets in the US and UK are forecast to rise to 55% and 48% respectively by 2022, while China overtakes the US as the fastest growing smart speaker market in the world accounting for 51% of global shipments in 2019. Voice-commence associated with speaker adoption is forecast to rise to $5B and $44B respectively by 2022.

Established global commerce businesses such as Amazon, Google, Microsoft, Apple, as well as Alibaba, alongside new offerings from Baidu and Xiaomi in China are striving to extend their **Digital Business Models** (p. 112) around voice services, to capture this growth where customers continue to desire voice assisted services as part of their user journeys and customer journeys, and clearly expect voice services to form a major component of their **Service Value Models** (p. 155).

*In the following case study examples, we shall conduct an analysis of current market leaders, Amazon who hold a market share of 70% in the US and 25% globally for Smart AI-based Home Speakers in 2019\*, using the five canvases in the Operating Model. The **Amazon 'Service Operating Model'** for the Echo device and Alexa assistant is an example of where value streams, capabilities and assets in the wider global **Operating Models** for the Amazon.com Marketplace and Amazon Web Services (AWS), have been used alongside newly acquired services, to create value propositions for customers and users, that are brought to market quickly, with quality and built to scale.*

**Amazon provides an ecosystem of *value propositions* comprised of connected or chained *value streams* such as Amazon.com shopping which encapsulates a web portal service & Amazon Web Services (AWS), search services, suggestion services, payment services and logistics to deliver bought items to customers.**

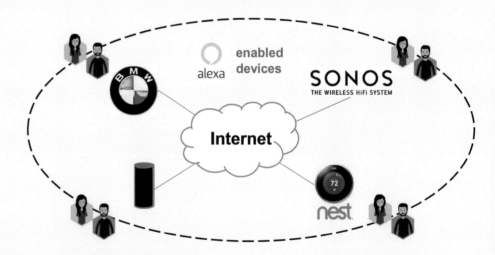

The Alexa 'Voice Service' also manifests itself as a network built by Amazon to increase its interactions and touchpoints with its customers generating a great deal of customer data which is then used to further improve the quality of all Amazon services in its vast proposition ecosystem (p. 135) – a circle of virtue and value.

## History of the Amazon Echo and Alexa assistant**

Back in 2011, Amazon was capitalizing on its market position by continuing to grow its emerging Omni-channel Marketplace and develop its push into consumer goods. Jeff Bezos had delivered the successful Kindle (project A) via Amazon's California research establishment, Lab126 and the unsuccessful Fire Phone (Project B). Project C was an augmented reality project which never came to fruition … however an offshoot of this (Project D) was the Amazon Echo and the Alexa AI voice assistant. Echo was originally launched in 2014 as purely a voice interface for Amazon.com and a music player.

Fortuitous timing brought Echo into contact with the world of home automation.  Bezos had not initially understood the value potential that existed across the ecosystem around the voice supported Amazon customer shopping and home music control experience. The smart home hub positioning has been a fortuitous accident of timing due to the state of evolution of the consumer technology market at the time. An Amazon engineer reportedly rigged an Echo up to control streaming TV services on a smart TV  and after this 'forehead slapping' moment, Bezos focused Echo on becoming the smart home control hub that it is today.

*Voice based commerce has been most successful to date in sectors where re-ordering of relatively low price point products previously purchased is undertaken.   Grocery is top of the list where relatively low and stable price point items are regularly re-ordered. Entertainment is second on the list fitting the low price point. Third on the list is electronics which does not fit the low-cost, consistent pricing or repeat purchase models. Electronics was listed at 17%, just slightly behind grocery at 20% and entertainment at 19%.*

Subsequently, Amazon has looked across the broader *value ecosystem* to understand that the convenience of voice interaction and the ability to request information or actions, not just shopping-related, has a myriad number of use cases resulting in the embedding of the Alexa AI assistant into cars, fridges, central heating controls that we see today.

Amazon has invested heavily to provide the Echo devices as a loss leader in return for data – the voices of the millions of customers (and in particular their self-connected **Service Value Models**) using the Alexa network.  This has provided significant value for the AI algorithms to dramatically improve the *capabilities* of the Alexa system making it more compliant with human interaction.

*\*Multiple data sources. See References section of this book for details.*

*\*\*See References section of this book for Amazon case study sources.*

# EXAMPLE: Amazon.com's Operating Model

Prior to the development and release of Amazon Echo and launching the Alexa Voice Service in 2014, Amazon.com's Operating Model was already a logistics powerhouse, but the company was smaller in comparison, with fewer subsidiaries and less mature *capabilities* in its *value chain*.

*In this case study example\* we illustrate the value chain, value streams and capabilities, including the organizational structure, that formed the Amazon.com **Current Operating Model (COM)** from using the 'Operating Model Canvas'. The example establishes the point of departure and the baseline that was built upon and scaled to grow the business through the Amazon Echo and Alexa Voice Assistant service since 2014.*

The Amazon *value chain* comprises a set of connected *value streams* handling the core elements of the **Amazon Business Model**:

- Sourcing goods for sale
- Marketplace and Infrastructure Operations
- Distribution Logistics
- Marketing & Sales
- Servicing

Organizationally, the **Operating Model** comprised of two geographical divisions, 'North America' and 'International', with a broad range of suppliers across the product categories, numerous country operating locations and a set of core applications and technology that enable the global and local operations.

## Indicative Amazon.com Operating Model Canvas (circa 2014)

### Suppliers

*Amazon fulfilled categories & third parties:*

| | |
|---|---|
| Books | Grocery |
| Music | Health |
| Electronics | Professional Services |
| Home & Garden | Luggage and Travel |
| Automotive | Sports |
| Baby | Toys |

### Value Delivery Chain / Processes

**Inbound Logistics**

- Integrated suppliers
- Decentralized Fulfillment
- Item replenishment
- Quality Control

**Operations**

- Marketplace operations
- Device and content creation
- AWS operations

### Organization

*Approx 500k people, approx. 100 business entities*
*Geographic Divisions:* North America, International

*International Consumer Business*
*Domestic Consumer Business*

*Global Functional Structure:*
Office of the CEO
Business Development
Finance
Accounting
Legal and Secretariat
AWS

*Functional Subsidiary structure:*
Zappos,
Kiva,
Quidsi

## Locations

Commerce locations:

| | | |
|---|---|---|
| Australia | Germany | Spain |
| Brazil | India | UK |
| Canada | Italy | USA |
| China | Japan | |
| France | Mexico | |

Key Business Locations:

Seattle – HQ
California – R&D
Cambridge UK – R&D

Amazon's *value streams* are supported by a core global business structure with global functional governance and a set of business functional subsidiaries where specialised sector businesses have been acquired. E.g. Zappos.com clothing.

### Outbound Logistics

- Order fulfillment
- Order Management
- Invoicing

### Marketing & Sales

- Customer centric/prime
- Hassle free returns
- Customer services
- Promotions
- Customer Tracking

### Service

- Order tracking
- Warranty and support
- Education and training
- Issue management

## Information

Amazon.com

Amazon Web Services:
- AWS Lambda
- AWS WAF
- Amazon S3
- AWS Shield
- Amazon ECS
- Amazon EC2
- Amazon Cloudfront

Amazon Route 53

Other web sites:
Zappos.com
Wholefoodsmarket.com
Souq.com
Audible.com
Exchange.com

Amazon logistics system
Amazon Warehousing system

CRM data
Product data

*\* Produced based on analysis conducted by Stratability Academy using publicly sourced articles written at the time of 2011-2014 or since to retrospectively provide a view on how Amazon looks today. It may not represent the exact Operating Model of Amazon at the time. All sources listed in the References section of this book.*

# EXAMPLE: The voice supported Amazon.com customer journey

The end-goal of customers who use the Amazon.com service is to discover and purchase specific goods that add value to their lifestyle including what books they want to read, home appliances, game, gadgets, gardening products, clothing and fashion accessories, skins products… that support this lifestyle.

*In this case study example the* **Customer Journey Map** *Canvas is used to record the Goals, Actions, Touchpoints and Emotions that a typical Amazon customer might have recorded through a customer journey investigation such as an interview highlighting what the service would have to do to be fully adopted. It highlights how customers think, act, and behave as they solve their problems as buyers of goods… including the desire for different experiences that make up their customer and user experiences.*

| | Awareness<br>*Shopping ordering convenience* | Discovery<br>*Discover my options* |
|---|---|---|
| **GOALS** | • Reduce time & effort to search for information and products/services.<br>• Integrated control experience with home technology. Complete shopping transactions more easily. | • It's a responsive and intelligent service<br>• It Reduces my effort and enhances my experience for information sourcing, home automation, shopping<br>• Easy to use/learn |
| **ACTIONS** | • Web searching to purchase books, music electronics<br>• Reading on-line reviews about service | • Investigating the Amazon service offering<br>• Attending web-based information sessions<br>• Understanding the charging and delivery service and reviewing |
| **TOUCHPOINTS** | • Blog Posts/Review sites<br>• Advertising<br>• Email/SMS<br>• Social Media channels | • Amazon Website<br>• Blog Posts/Review sites<br>• Advertising<br>• Email/SMS<br>• Social Media channels |
| **EMOTIONS** | • Frustration with time required for competitor physical shopping, product exchange with competitors, Small product choice, having to use multiple shop portals for different categories of product | • Intrigued with the prospect of on-line order and deliver value proposition across breadth of product categories.<br>• Impressed with the promise of the order and returns process |

Acquire new customer

*Illustrative and inexhaustive example based on analysis conducted by Stratability Academy using publicly available data. Sources listed in the References section of the book.*

Retain existing customer

| Selection | Onboarding | Satisfaction | Advocacy |
|---|---|---|---|
| *Investigate voice channel & services* | *Buy device & service & using for tasks* | *Living made easy by having device/service* | *Share & expand experiences* |
| • Devices are affordable<br>• Service is affordable<br>• Service suits needs and is controllable<br>• Service is extensible | • Service reduces my effort and replaces tasks in day to day life – communication, home control, shopping.<br>• I have used the service for new tasks successfully | • I used the service as a core part of my day to day life making my life better<br>• I have explored the new partners bringing more value to the service through 3rd party skills | • I Understand the new service approach and value it brings<br>• I can be helpful to someone else pondering the same transition to using voice services |
| • Signing up for a trial account.<br>• Attending web-based information sessions<br>• Trying some free on-line books, music and assessing product choice, order and deliver service | • Signing up for full account<br>• Ordering books, music and electronics through core Amazon services<br>• Using reviews to assess best product selection | • Expanding to add further product services from full site<br>• Grocery ordering<br>• Using Account as login for other services<br>• Actively leaving reviews for purchased products | • Active user of Prime for shopping across all categories and for Amazon streaming audio and video<br>• Promoting the services to friends and family<br>• Active on social media about the Brand service |
| • Amazon Website<br>• Blog Posts/Review sites<br>• Advertising<br>• Email/SMS<br>• Social Media channels | • Amazon Website<br>• Blog Posts/Review sites<br>• Advertising<br>• Email/SMS<br>• Social Media channels | • Amazon Website<br>• Blog Posts/Review sites<br>• Advertising<br>• Email/SMS<br>• Social Media channels | • Amazon Website reviews<br>• Blog Posts/Review sites<br>• Advertising<br>• Email/SMS<br>• Social Media channels |
| • Happy with the initial trial portal and app, Pleased with the product choice available, Happy with the delivery service process<br>• Confident with the security and with the level of communication and transparency | • Confidence with search and purchasing across main product categories<br>• Happy with the easy of order, delivery and exchange/refund via website and app | • Confident with expanded purchasing across broader product categories<br>• Elated with Prime membership delivery time benefits and choice<br>• Happy with purchasing further service products in video. | • Excited to share experiences with friends and family / work colleague<br>• Social media active on good experiences |

278

# EXAMPLE: Using the customer journey analysis to identify features for the Alexa Voice Service and Echo device

Alexa and the Echo was originally launched in 2014 as purely a voice interface for Amazon.com and a music player. Subsequently Bezos stumbled upon home automation control integration and this spawned a set of use cases supporting an ability to request information or actions, not just shopping-related. Through the skills development framework Alexa has evolved to support myriad applications resulting in the embedding of the Alexa AI assistant into cars, fridges, central heating controls that we see today.

*In this case study example the **Customer Journey Map** Canvas extends to include consideration of third-party skills and home automation integration requirements from an ecosystem analysis at the time of conception of the Alexa Voice Service.*

|  | **Awareness** | **Discovery** |
|---|---|---|
|  | Shopping ordering convenience | Discover my options |
| **GOALS** | • Reduce time & effort to search for information and products/services.<br>• Integrated control experience with home technology. Complete shopping transactions more easily. | • It's a responsive and intelligent service<br>• It Reduces my effort and enhances my experience for information sourcing, home automation, shopping<br>• Easy to use/learn |
| **EXPECTATION FULFILLMENT** | • Intrigue at learning about the possibilities of voice only interaction with Amazon services | • Amazement at first experience of how voice service enhances Amazon services<br>• Intrigue at the provision of third-party skills<br>• Impressed with the ability to control home automation. |
| **CUSTOMER GAPS OPPORTUNITIES** | • Position voice services to fully automate the Amazon buying process<br>• Extend to provide access to 3rd party offerings (skills)<br>• Integrate with home automation devices to control these via voice activation | • Build a developer model like the Apple app store to build a base of 3rd party skills to further enhance the customers experience during investigations.<br>• Demonstrate house automation ecosystem. |

Acquire new customer

Retain existing customer

| Selection | Onboarding | Satisfaction | Advocacy |
|---|---|---|---|
| *Investigate voice channel & services* | *Buy device & service & using for tasks* | *Living made easy by having device/service* | *Share & expand experiences* |

| | | | |
|---|---|---|---|
| • Devices are affordable<br>• Service is affordable<br>• Service suits needs and is controllable<br>• Service is extensible | • Service reduces my effort and replaces tasks in day to day life – communication, home control , shopping.<br>• I have used the service for new tasks successfully | • I used the service as a core part of my day to day life making my life better<br>• I have explored the new partners bringing more value to the service through 3rd party skills | • I Understand the new service approach and value it brings<br>• I can be helpful to someone else pondering the same transition to using voice services |
| • Elation at the convenience and enhancement to their life given a deeper understanding of the value and convenience of voice controlled services | • Happiness with the ease of access to existing Amazon Services and new services offered via 3rd parties via Skills. | • Excited to use the service for new experiences given the positive outcomes for existing Amazon services.<br>• Seeks out new skills and experience across the voice controlled ecosystem. | • Delight with how the service enhances own life and experience when accessing online services.<br>• Active with friends, family and via social media to promote |
| • Provide the hardware technology at a reduced price to promote multiple purchase to build momentum commercially. | • Use customer anonymized voice data to enhance the the NLP algorithms in the AVS.<br>• Enhance the voice understanding with the customer over time to make the customer believe the device is building an intimate relationship | • Provide integrated experience via the voice device with notifications about deliveries on purchases and control of streaming media services.<br>• Capture data from the customer for personalization opportunities | • Utilize the social media data where recommendations are made to offer platform/services or recommendations on skills and additional services to existing and new customers |

## Alexa Voice Service and Echo device

# EXAMPLE: The Service Operating Model for Amazon's Alexa

The Alexa Voice Service enabled *value stream* is not significantly different in how it operates through its *capability flow* to the Amazon.com Marketplace with all of its channels across its *omni-channel network*. However it does utilize new capabilities to enable voice interaction and language understanding, and significantly, this is where it has been able to build a first mover competitor advantage.

*In this case study example\*, using the **Service Operating Model** Canvas, we highlight how Amazon's exploration into the voice interface following several unsuccessful projects, including Project C, an augmented reality project that never came to fruition, was what led to an offshoot service that became the Amazon Echo and Alexa Voice Assistant.*

Echo was originally launched in 2014 as purely a voice interface for Amazon.com and a music player. As Amazon began to study and understand its data of customer usage patterns, and through innovation and co-creation with customers, the service began to evolve to incorporate a skills library, that has since expanded through integration with IoT devices, and the Alexa Marketplace into the Home Automation market and more…

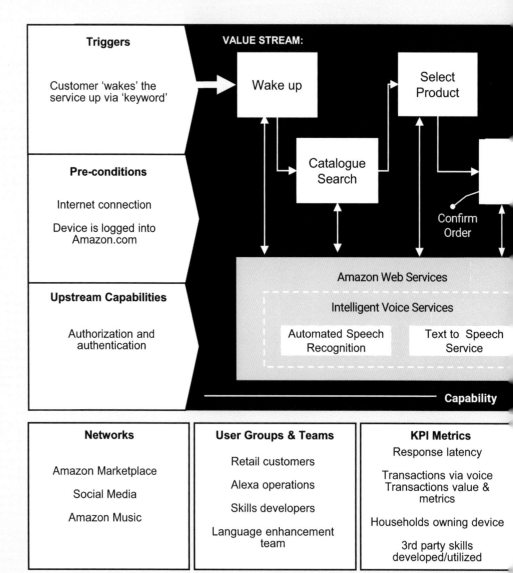

| Triggers | VALUE STREAM: |
| --- | --- |
| Customer 'wakes' the service up via 'keyword' | Wake up / Select Product |

**Pre-conditions**

Internet connection

Device is logged into Amazon.com

Catalogue Search

Confirm Order

**Upstream Capabilities**

Authorization and authentication

Amazon Web Services

Intelligent Voice Services

Automated Speech Recognition

Text to Speech Service

**Capability**

| Networks | User Groups & Teams | KPI Metrics |
| --- | --- | --- |
| Amazon Marketplace | Retail customers | Response latency |
| Social Media | Alexa operations | Transactions via voice Transactions value & metrics |
| Amazon Music | Skills developers | Households owning device |
| | Language enhancement team | 3rd party skills developed/utilized |

*Amazon Alexa case study sources and references are listed in the References section of this book..*

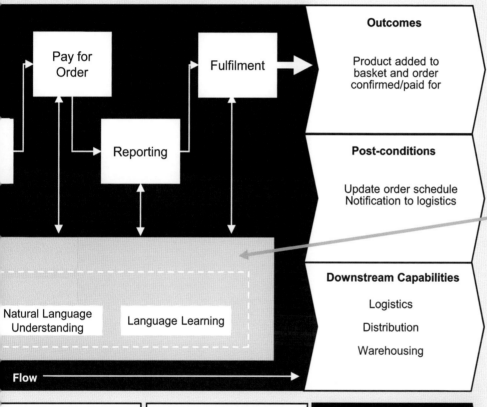

| | Outcomes |
|---|---|
| **Pay for Order** | Product added to basket and order confirmed/paid for |
| **Fulfilment** | |
| **Reporting** | **Post-conditions**<br>Update order schedule<br>Notification to logistics |
| Natural Language Understanding | **Downstream Capabilities**<br>Logistics<br>Distribution<br>Warehousing |
| Language Learning | |

**Flow** →

| **Location Factors** | **Systems & Applications** | **Initiatives & Projects** |
|---|---|---|
| Data privacy laws | Voice recognition AI | Project C – Augmented reality |
| Language variances including local slang | Natural language processing AI | Project D – Amazon Echo & Alexa Voice Assistant |
| | Text to Speech | Alexa Venture Fund projects incorporating IoT and AI |
| | Language Learning | |
| | Alexa API | |

## Accelerating Intelligent Voice Service Capabilities and Gaps

The sub-capabilities within the Alexa Intelligent Voice Service, interface with existing core capabilities that operate the buyer journey supporting the Amazon marketplace including:

- Product Catalogue
- Product Search
- Recommendations
- Product Selection
- Order Management
- Reporting
- Fulfilment

Amazon's goal is to expand on these capabilities addressing any gaps in service as demanded by customers along their customer journeys from the data gathered by Alexa, with the addition of AI. This enhances its predictive capabilities on buyer behavior and future sales through the Amazon Omni-channel Marketplace.

In 2017, Amazon launched its Alexa Fund, a $200 million venture capital fund to encourage developers and other Technology Services from third parties especially those with IoT devices to build new Alexa Skills that would expand the capabilities of its Intelligent Voice Service, as it continues to gather the data to further develop its AI capabilities.

# The Outcomes-led path to change execution

The **Managing the Transformation Journey** path is comprised of a process that supports an enterprise to execute the necessary changes in how it operates to achieve its **Target Operating Model** where value-added outcomes from its new and improved service offerings to customers and stakeholders, aligned to the enterprise's strategic goals and objectives in **Mission Model**. It is the process to design and implement the **Transformation Model** using **THE STRATEGY JOURNEY** *Framework*.

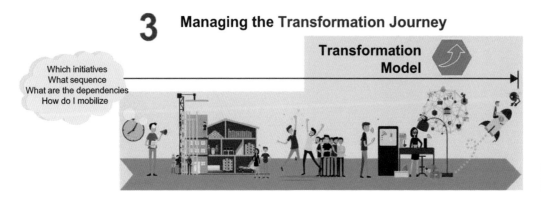

**3** Managing the Transformation Journey

Transformation Model

Which initiatives
What sequence
What are the dependencies
How do I mobilize

*Strategy Execution*

**Transformation Model Design** analysis focuses on defining, coordinating, communicating and governance all the business transformation activities that need to be executed by an enterprise, in order to implement changes, scale and upgrade the capabilities required to deliver the value-added outcomes from its target service offerings in its **Target Operating Model**.

A **Transformation Roadmap** is used to structure the activities into stages that will join·the·dots to deliver to specific milestones goals, and achieve the targeted outcomes outlined in the S.M.A.R.T. objectives defined in the enterprise's Mission Model and game plans. It is a joined up plan, that will shape, prioritize and mobilize the enterprise and its organization forward with agility, accountability and action – including how, where and when to invest funds to ensure the best possible return on investment based on the point of departure and the 'transformation gaps' to the target state.

This includes investing in the right resources and skills including people, systems and technology, through partnerships where required, to build up the enterprise's business agility, while instilling a 'growth mindset' culture where co-creation and service innovation can flourish.

Once mobilized, monitoring of the 'Transformation Roadmap' performance during transformation execution is supported through an agile governance structure, where the enterprise adapts as required.

**Transformation Roadmap** Canvas

**Managing the Transformation Journey Path Outputs**

# When to use the **Managing the Transformation Journey** analysis path

The path should be triggered when an enterprise is faced with any of these transformation challenges (p. 9-10), which its leaders have prioritized for action:

- **Transformation Culture**:  Business transformation activities performed in the enterprise cannot be attributed to value creation. This is primarily caused by a negative culture with resistance to change and lots of duplicate and redundant activities from people fighting for ownership of activities, rather than performing their activities to the best of their ability, or hiding their activities, as they are unable to justify their activities.

- **Consistent Failure to Deliver Transformation**: Very little or no value is achieved in the outcomes delivered by an enterprise's business transformation activities. Transformation projects are constantly started, but then stopped from a lack of outcomes delivered, while costs surpass original estimations, leading to poor Return On Investment (ROI). Despite numerous transformation initiatives and projects, including several attempts at change, there continues to be a lack of alignment between the desired Business Model that will deliver new and improved services to customers, and the operational activities that are being performed in the Operating Model. Monitoring of changes implemented show very little improvement or changes to productivity, and capacity, as well as sales, because these outcomes are not connected to transformation activities through the capabilities that they are supposed to change or improve.

**Execution of the Transformation Journey should update the other STRATEGY JOURNEY Models, to enable the next and future business lifecycles.**

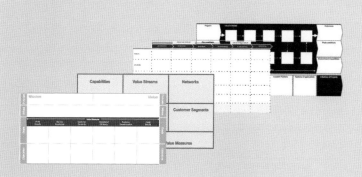

The *Transformation Journey is shaped by data contained in the key canvases of the upstream **Strategy Journey Paths**. Once a transformation has been executed the roadmap and tracking data is also fed back to the Mission Model Blueprint to update the goals and objectives, so that new paths can commence to forward the enterprise on its next and future strategy journeys.*

# Five Transformation Journey Path Steps

Five steps to assess, prioritize, co-create, mobilize and monitor a **Transformation Roadmap** to deliver a **Target Operating Model** for a new and improved services through business and digital transformation.

## Transformation Journey Design

Outputs from the Business Design and Transforming Operating Models Paths

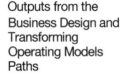

### 3
**Indicate how resources will co-create through projects**
Indicate the different resources, including people in teams as well as technology systems and their RACI roles across the activities of the transformation journey to support collaboration and co-creation.

### 4
**Mobilize the roadmap with communications**
Review the level of influence and interest of stakeholders and develop a communications plan that will run parallel with the Transformation Roadmap to mobilize the stakeholders into action, with accountability as well as influencing a more transformative culture of learning.

### 2
**Sequence activities in the Roadmap to deliver outcomes**
Analyse and prioritise the capability gaps in the Target Operating model and compare these with the Backlog Priorities to produce the set of activities, and the projects that will execute them in the *Transformation Roadmap*

### 1
**Assess pain points backlog & prioritize activities**
Draw together the existing set of transformation programs/initiatives and the backlog of requested change work into a consistent form for review and consideration by a Design Authority or other government structure.

## Prioritisation Analysis
Assessment of all transformation activities is undertaken against the strategic objectives of the business to produce an ordered set of initiatives or projects that form a roadmap for transformation execution.

**Transformation Journey Execution**

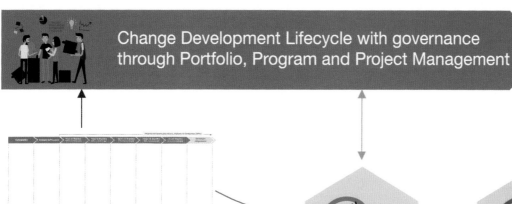

Change Development Lifecycle with governance through Portfolio, Program and Project Management

**Transformation Roadmap indicating what activities will be co-created by project teams, and communications from leadership and governance to mobilize resources**

## Transformation Governance

Monitoring and ongoing review of the performance of all transformation activities is undertaken against the strategic objectives of the business, and new ecosystem influencers, to update and adapt the initiatives and projects in the roadmap, while ensuring the best possible ROI is achieved.

## 5

**Strategic Progress Tracking**

Regularly track and report in a structured manner the performance of transformation activities and the outcomes realized by them. Adapt and adjust Transformation Roadmap activities to inform decision makers as well as other teams of required and approved/funded changes.

# Transformation Roadmap Canvas

A **Transformation Roadmap** Canvas is a plan that details the initiatives or projects that an enterprise has committed to execute, in order to transform its capabilities and deliver its new and improved services over a period of time, as it transitions to its **Target Operating Model**.

*We recommend an effective 'roadmap' that describes the activities that will be performed to implement specific capability changes, including the outcomes targeted by the enterprises strategic objectives. Sets of activities should be organized into budgeted or proposed projects (as described by their commitment levels), that span over at least an 18 month period, and up to a longer term period of 36 months, based on their milestone stages with different levels of commitment\*. Key communications to motivate and influence stakeholders based on their RACI (p. 221) roles along this transformation journey should also be included.*

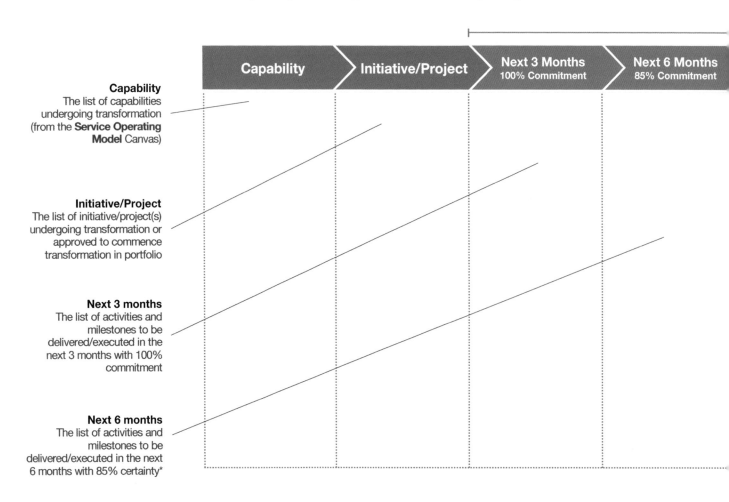

**Capability**
The list of capabilities undergoing transformation (from the **Service Operating Model** Canvas)

**Initiative/Project**
The list of initiative/project(s) undergoing transformation or approved to commence transformation in portfolio

**Next 3 months**
The list of activities and milestones to be delivered/executed in the next 3 months with 100% commitment

**Next 6 months**
The list of activities and milestones to be delivered/executed in the next 6 months with 85% certainty\*

Capability | Initiative/Project | Next 3 Months 100% Commitment | Next 6 Months 85% Commitment

Initiative and projects are likely to have interdependencies that require management. Use arrows to indicate the relationships between capabilities, activities and milestones, as well as strategic alignment of objectives, and across initiatives and projects in the roadmap.

*\* Commitment level refers to the scope for change requests that could influence, impact and hence force further changes. Eg. If there is a 50% commitment, then approximately 50% of the activities are likely to change based on the need to be flexible to influencers and disruptions from the business ecosystem.*

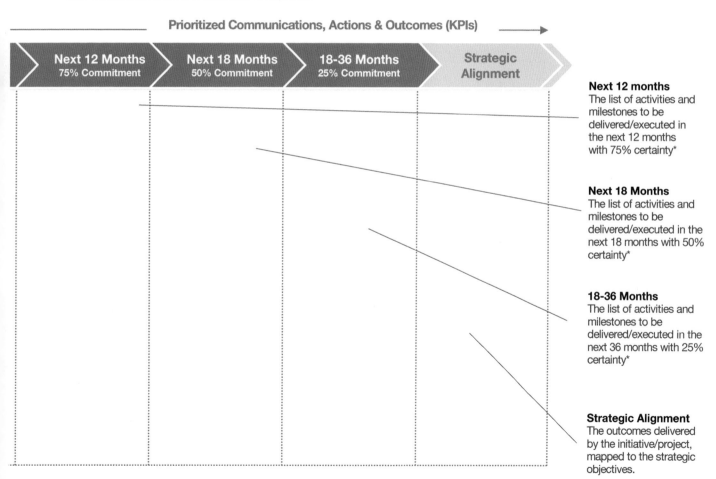

**Prioritized Communications, Actions & Outcomes (KPIs)**

| Next 12 Months 75% Commitment | Next 18 Months 50% Commitment | 18-36 Months 25% Commitment | Strategic Alignment |

**Next 12 months**
The list of activities and milestones to be delivered/executed in the next 12 months with 75% certainty*

**Next 18 Months**
The list of activities and milestones to be delivered/executed in the next 18 months with 50% certainty*

**18-36 Months**
The list of activities and milestones to be delivered/executed in the next 36 months with 25% certainty*

**Strategic Alignment**
The outcomes delivered by the initiative/project, mapped to the strategic objectives.

# EXAMPLE: Behind Apple's global operations

Apple provides a thorough example of how managing your strategy journey end to end reaps rewards.

Apple is one of the most valuable companies in the world, that has achieved success from manufacturing top quality products and software services designed with user experience and customer satisfaction as core principles. Over several decades, the Apple brand is has become known for innovating in the consumer electronics business to change the way people live and behave through the Mac, iPod, iPhone, and Apple Watch products built around the Apple Ecosystem.

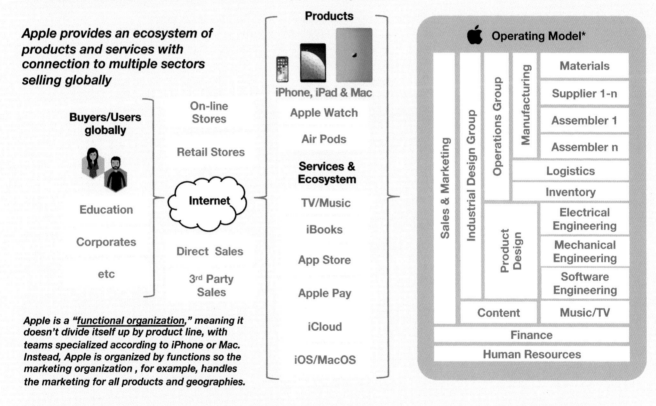

*Apple provides an ecosystem of products and services with connection to multiple sectors selling globally*

*Apple is a "functional organization," meaning it doesn't divide itself up by product line, with teams specialized according to iPhone or Mac. Instead, Apple is organized by functions so the marketing organization , for example, handles the marketing for all products and geographies.*

However, Apple has gone through growing pains in its recent past as it struggled to manage the supply chain efficiency and manufacturing scale required to support the large volume sales given the popularity of its products.  These Operating Model issues were at the heart of rational for Steve Jobs hiring Tim Cook from IBM in1998. Jobs realized that this fundamental aspect of the Apple business had to be addressed in order to successfully grow further.

Under Cook,  Apple transformed its operating model between 1998 and 2005 (when Cook became COO), retaining the design and product manufacturing process intellectual property in California whilst outsourcing manufacturing operations into Asia, rationalizing to fewer carefully chosen strategic suppliers, optimizing its supply chain and inventory processes and leveraging economies of scale.

## A brief history of outsourcing Apple Operations*

When Steve Jobs returned to Apple in the 1990s he wanted to concentrate on doing what he loved best – creating new products with designer Jony Ive. Tim Cook joined Jobs in 1998 to focus on Apple operations and is credited with being the main architect of the giant manufacturing and logistical operation that has made Apple a mature and successful company. Today, the Apple focus is not just about the products, but also about logistics. An efficient supply chain, distribution service, finance operation and marketing are not high profile aspects of the business but they have shaped the success of the past decade.

When Tim Cook joined Apple in 1998, Apple was suffering with low inventory turn rates and held relationships with100s suppliers and assemblers in a myriad of contractual arrangements. In the early days Cook focused on procurement, reducing the number of key suppliers from hundreds to twenty-four and introducing a bidding process to get better deals. He convinced many to locate next to primary assembly plants and closed ten of the company's nineteen warehouses. By reducing the places where inventory could pile up, he de-facto reduced inventory*. By September 1999, Cook had reduced the inventory shelf time from two months to two days. By 2013, Apple was dealing with 154 key suppliers and only one central warehouse optimising distribution operations with 250 stores.

Given the product strategy, Cook knew that scaling and efficiency would be issues for the high volume consumer product lines coming in the early to mid 2000s (iPod, iPod Mini, iPod shuffle, iPod Nano and the advent of the iPhone in 2007). The sheer volume of products that Apple would require to shift to support this strategy greatly surpassed the existing levels of Mac computer units produced and meant outsourcing would be a key to success. Cook looked to Asia, as the number of human workers required to operate production lines to meet the required scale was not available in the US.

Devising the correct outsourcing model with your partners is critically important. Apple's operating model for scale produced one of its of its greatest competitors*. For 10 years Samsung used to make components for Apple products. However, Samsung decided the profit Apple made on phones was highly attractive and that it could design and manufacture phones based on the Android OS. This brought about the patent legal case in 2011 between Apple and Samsung and the parting of the companies. Apple had to think again about its operating model.

*Foxconn, a strategic partner for many years, has approx. 800,000 employees in a 2.3km square factory in Foxconn Shenzhen most of which are assigned to Apple. These sorts of numbers of manual workers used in product assembly at this scale are not available in the US or other developed parts of the world. Today, It is estimated that Foxconn is to be able to produce 750000 iPhones in a day. To give an idea of the scale changes in business terms, when Cook joined in 1998, Apple was transacting $6B of business a year - today it does that in 10 days.*

*Apple case study sources and references are listed in the References section of this book..*

# EXAMPLE: Devising the Transformation Roadmap for Apple

Cook's initial focus looked to procurement optimisation to simplify the suppliers and inventory management. Beyond this he would have undertaken structured thinking on the Apple operating model in those early years, analysing and devising an appropriate target operational state aligned to Apple long term strategy. The target model incorporated a move away from US based manufacturing to outsourcing to Asia to achieve scale. In concert with this was a move to rationalise suppliers to fewer strategic players who would share risk with Apple in terms of setting up dedicated manufacturing sites and tooling.

**R&D Design & Marketing**
- Develop new technologies
- Market and product research
- Product and process design
- Concept testing
- Strategic Marketing

**Sourcing**
- Sourcing of Materials & Services
- Supplier Management
- Subcontracting
- Fierce Supplier Competition

**Manufacturing**
- Manufacturing of Components
- Assembly of Components

**Warehousing**
- Product Storage
- Inventory Management
- Supply Chain Management
- Light Manufacturing & assembly

**Distribution**
- Distribution & Delivery
- Online Store
- Retail Stores
- Direct Sales Force
- Wholesalers, Retailers, Network, Carriers

**Apple's operating model core activities**

Given the scale of the transformation envisioned, several Apple upstream functions including Industrial Design Group (IDG), Product Design (PD), Operations itself and a significant number of strategic partner operations organisations, existing and new, would have to be taken on the transformation journey. Clarity of vision and a clear roadmap created through co-creation with these Apple functions and partner organisation would be required. Appropriate communication and mobilization would be paramount in order for a successful migration to a simple outsourced operations model. The cost of errors at this scale could be large. Not transforming to a model sufficient to meet the business strategy would be highly damaging to Apple. Other corporations who have suffered from poor transformation can pay the ultimate price as evidenced by Yahoo in the race with Google (p. 295).

With an outsourced operations model devised, Cook would have developed a transformation plan to achieve it – and then mobilized this starting in 1999, executing it over the subsequent years . Many items would have to be taken into consideration in this plan including the existing project backlog and the product release schedule so that the operations transformation roadmap would marry up and support the business product launch schedules and existing book of business change activities.

# Further transformation of Apple's Operating Model

The Apple Operating Model in place as of 2019 is more sophisticated than that delivered in the transformation of the early/mid 2000s. Innovation and continuous process improvement has delivered constantly improving operations processes. However, due to the experiences with the 10 year strategic partnerships with Samsung and Foxconn and the subsequent legal battle Apple decided it required transparency and intimate control over the manufacturing process. This required some changes to the operating model and subsequent transformation.

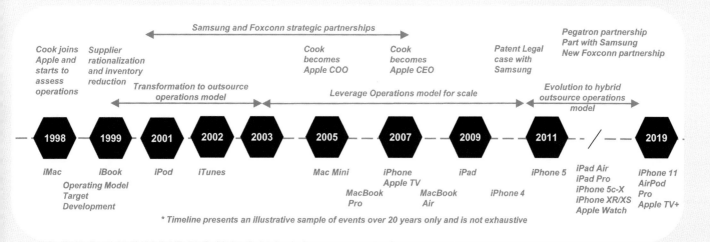

**Timeline of product and operating model changes in Apple**

Apple Operations evolved in design to a 'hybrid' outsource model wherein Apple actually has a much more intimate role in the operation of the outsourcing. Apple provides tooling and financing to some of its contract partners, buying the manufacturing equipment that is put into their factories. Apple owns the manufacturing equipment and has Apple staff on the ground in the manufacturing facility, but the supplier owns the factory and the workforce**. This allows Apple to engage and monitor the manufacturing process end to end looking for improvements and fast issue resolution whilst minimising the leakage of intellectual property (reducing the risk of another Samsung type issue).

Since evolving to this new hybrid operating model and taking on the CEO role in 2011, Cook has aggressively expanded Apple into new markets, especially China. This would not have been possible without the big, efficient operations and supply chain to feed the massive growth.

*** Apple case study sources available in the References section of this book.*

# EXAMPLE: Apple operations transformation roadmap*

Tim Cook's transformation of Apple's operations took place over a multi year period of orchestrated change to achieve the envisioned outsourced model that was developed. It also aligned to Apple's move to higher volume personal consumer products strategy. This Operating Model has since evolved to its current 'hybrid' outsource state supporting the business in 2019 achieved through continuous improvement based on feedback on the efficiency and effectiveness of the model.

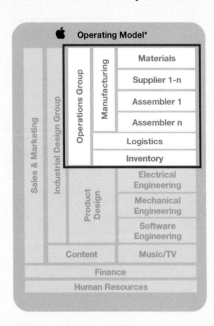

*The **Transformation Roadmap** Canvas has been used to illustrate Apple's indicative roadmap of how the company might have broken down the challenge. It is representative of what the journey may have looked like as Tim Cook embarked on the global transformation of Apple Operations. Further details would have been included in each set of activities and a well structured and timed communications plan would have been used by Tim Cook to mobilize the teams of engineers and marketers at Apple into action.*

| Capability | Initiative/Project | Next 3 Months 100% Commitment |
|---|---|---|
| Component Manufacturing and supply | Supplier Rationalization | Component supplier due diligence |
| Product Assembly | Strategic Assemblers Relationships | Product assembler due diligence |
| Quality Management (QM) | QM for scale | Develop new QM process |
| Process Design & Automation | Process Optimization for Operations | Detailed operations process design with Apple functions and strategic operations |
| Supply Chain | Optimization | Design detailed supply chain model |
| Operations Process Management | Systemization of process management | Design detailed OPM system |
| Logistics | Strategic logistics partners | Perform due diligence on new logistics providers |
| Inventory Management | Inventory Optimization | Due diligence on warehousing and inventory supply lines |

## Priority Actions & Outcomes (KPIs)

| Next 6 Months 85% Commitment | Next 12 Months 75% Commitment | Next 18 Months 50% Commitment | 18-36 Months 25% Commitment | Strategic Alignment |
|---|---|---|---|---|
| Select strategic partners and setup model | Rationalize to <100 suppliers and implement | Optimize the delivery time and scaling factor | Rollout across global operations | Cost, Quality – fewer more dependable strategic suppliers |
| Select strategic partners and build operating model | Migrate core product lines to new assembly | Scale up product assembly for all lines | Continuously improve to increase yields | Cost, Efficiency – scale relationship with 2-3 core assemblers |
| Prototype QM process | Implement QM across new product processes | Scale across all product processes and feed back into assembly | Continuously improve to increase yields | Quality – quality to improve yields and reduce returns |
| Implement across retained strategic partnerships | Implement as part of new product process across all new partners | Scale across all product design and automation lines | Optimize across global operations | Agility – operations scaling, integration with Apple functions and automation |
| Develop new supply chain process and systems | Implement to support new product process | Scale to all suppliers for all product lines | Rollout across global operations | Efficiency – reduction of time to supply globally |
| Integrate with key processes | Implement for new product process | Scale to all product lines globally | Continuously improve to increase efficiency | Agility – instrumented build and supply |
| Tender and secure contracts | Operationalize to support new product process | Operationalize across all product lines | Continuously improve to increase efficiency | Cost, Efficiency – fewer more dependable logistics partners |
| Begin warehouse rationalization | Rollout optimized process and rationalize warehousing | Migrate to single logical warehouse globally | Migrate to single logical warehouse globally | Cash Management – reduced inventory holding |

*Publicly available information was used to build this roadmap describing the Apple operations transformation journey. All sources are available in the References section of this book.*

# EXAMPLE: How Google won the game for Search Supremacy over Yahoo*

## *Poorly devised and executed transformation kills a business*

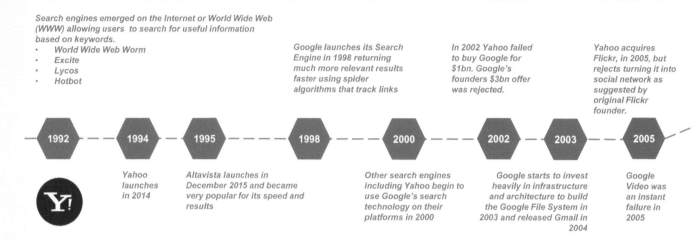

Search engines emerged on the Internet or World Wide Web (WWW) allowing users to search for useful information based on keywords.
- World Wide Web Worm
- Excite
- Lycos
- Hotbot

Google launches its Search Engine in 1998 returning much more relevant results faster using spider algorithms that track links

In 2002 Yahoo failed to buy Google for $1bn. Google's founders $3bn offer was rejected.

Yahoo acquires Flickr, in 2005, but rejects turning it into social network as suggested by original Flickr founder.

1992 — 1994 — 1995 — 1998 — 2000 — 2002 — 2003 — 2005

Yahoo launches in 2014

Altavista launches in December 2015 and became very popular for its speed and results

Other search engines including Yahoo begin to use Google's search technology on their platforms in 2000

Google starts to invest heavily in infrastructure and architecture to build the Google File System in 2003 and released Gmail in 2004

Google Video was an instant failure in 2005

*Timeline presents an illustrative sample of events over 27 years from 1992-2019 only and is not exhaustive*

After more than 20 years since the first *Search* engines appeared on the Internet in 1992, the search engine industry is dominated today by Google. No-one questions that Google's *Search Engine* algorithm is superior to all others providing it with a far superior product. But we all know that it takes a lot more than a great product to succeed as a business.

So how did Google really do it? What did Yahoo do wrong?

Co-founder Sergey Brin's original vision clearly illustrates the underlying strategy at Google that has played a big part in its success.

Larry Page's launch of Alphabet via the domain abc.xyz again shows the firms values and objectives to continue with a long-term strategy, while letting their leadership team run operations to execute product and service delivery at the highest quality.

> *"My vision when we started Google… was that eventually you wouldn't have to have a search query at all. You'd just have information come to you as you needed it"* -Sergey Brin

It is this long term view and building up slower initially through investment in their architecture and infrastructure that allowed Google to overtake Yahoo as the leader in the Search ecosystem.

While Yahoo was busy growing market share but outsourcing all of its infrastructure to Netapp with a short term view on go to market rather than long term agility and costs management, Google was busy building its Google File System over four years from 2003 to 2006. This provided it with an agile operating model to support its future ambitions for rapid product development and continuous transformation.

In 2006 – just a year after its launch – Google acquired YouTube, a crucial early move with the rise in popularity of video.

Google Wallet (launched in 2011) fails to take off. Google wanted to take data from banks to use for ad targeting but banks weren't keen.

Despite warning in 2008 about MD5 encryption technology risk, Yahoo fails to change and suffers security breach with 1 billion email accounts hacked in 2013

2008 was also the year that Google launched Android. Whilst not received as an instant hit it now has 88% of the recorded market by 2016.

**What & where next?**

**2006**  **2008**  **2011**  **2012**  **2013**  **2016**  **2019**

Yahoo fails to buy Facebook for $1bn in 2006

Google launches Chrome in 2008. With a minimalist look and so many extensions it was an instant hit.

2005 investment in Alibaba brought in profits to Yahoo by 2012, but CEO Jerry Yang leaves.

Yahoo acquires Tumblr in 2013 but still has no clear strategy for the platform.

In 2016 Yahoo was sold to Verizon having had 24 different mission statements in 24 years and 6 different CEOs over the years.

Google AI, Home automation, autonomous engineering, machine learning …

Yahoo kept operating with a pipe business model whilst Google played the long game and focused on the journey ahead creating the agility it needed to support its platform business model (p. 111). Yahoo lost the race as early as 2000, when it realised it was too late to innovate a new way to deliver *Search*, and instead became a partner using Google's *Search* technology on its own platform. Unlike Apple who builds in switching costs to its business model with the IOS and Apple App market, the main rival to Google's Android market, Yahoo focused on customer acquisition and less so on customer retention to drive sales and with little focus on costs and hence profits. During their partnership, Yahoo customers were easily able to switch to Google and its products. Of course, it helped that many Google products were much better from a user experience (UX) perspective, as illustrated and demonstrated to this day, through Google's simple Search page. Yahoo's recent email security breaches in 2013 is evidence of its poor operating model and lack of investment in the right architecture. It has also experienced massive changes in governance with six different CEOs in its history. In 2015, just past 20 years after it launched, Yahoo posted a loss of $4.36 billion compared to Google's profit of $16.35 billion.

Google's failures and successes reflect its strategy as a product centric organisation. It is constantly trying out new innovations and discontinuing what doesn't work while improving what does. Famously discontinued products include Google Wallet, Google Video, Google Glasses, Google Notes, and Google Plus to name just a few.

Today, Google is no longer a start up and it has the funds and the resources in its agile operating model to support pivoting through its failures. Google Video has pivoted into YouTube through acquisition in 2006.

Google Chrome replaced Microsoft's Internet Explorer's 18 year reign as the most used browser in April 2016. Android surpassed 80% market share in 2016 amongst all smartphone operating systems.

All three platform solutions support the Google success story helping it to amass almost 90% of its revenue in 2016 from advertising.

In 2019 Google, valued at $800B, is no longer just about search as it is a powerhouse in Artificial Intelligence – a topic at the heart of Google's development from its inception.

*All sources for this case study on Google and Yahoo are available in the References section of this book..*

# Building Quick Win Business Agility...
## ... to fast track digital transformation

***Is there a simpler, better and faster way to build business agility?***

As we have seen from the case studies in this book, it took Jeff Bezos more than a decade to nurture and build **Amazon** to be a leading business and two decades to grow it into the powerhouse that it is in 2020. **Apple's** reinvention and disruption of the mobile phone market using smartphones took eight years and it wasn't until Tim Cook joined and changed Apple's Operating Model that the company started to really transform how it functioned using insourcing and outsourcing of services to complement Apple's USP in design. Since 2018 and into 2020, **Tesla** has focused on its *business agility* to deliver its cars to customers on time, by really scaling its Operating Model after more than 15 years.

Whether you run a small business or a large enterprise, the **BIG QUESTIONS** most business owners, shareholders and stakeholders have are:

- Where do you **start**?
- What are the **priority capabilities** to build on a tight budget?
- Is there a way to **fast-track** your strategy journey?

There are four *priority capabilities* to focus on, where you should start and how you can fast track your transformation journey to achieve digital transformation and build an **AGILE OPERATING MODEL**:

**Technology Infrastructure (using Digital Services)**

**Data Intelligence (readiness for data science)**

**Service Design & Innovation**

**Digitally Skilled Workforce**

*Go to strategyjourney.com/tools to download the practical guide and business agility checklists to help you fast track digital transformation in your enterprise*

## Technology Infrastructure (Digital Services)

**Automate key business functions, processes or business activities that can be better performed with technology and digital services through the cloud, with the ability to support data collection and building future value in the business.**

Going digital for SMEs is all about using digital services or SaaS applications in the cloud to support the operations of the business. It is more than just having a website. A static website that isn't SEO enhanced will barely be seen by anyone, no matter how much design effort you put into making it look great. Investing in this capability involves replacing specific processes or business activities, with a software application, so essentially automating these with software, that is managed by a third-party and licensed for use in the business.

For smaller businesses there is currently a wealth of platforms at attractive price points;

- Payroll and accounting via XERO or Quickbooks
- CRM via ActiveCampaign or Salesforce
- Affordable advertising via Facebook and Youtube to promote your business via video,
- Project Management using tools like Notion and Trello
- Customer rea-time communication via Calendly to book meetings on ZOOM or Skype
- E-commerce capabilities for payments using Woocommerce, Shopify, Wix or Squarespace
- Marketplace platforms such as Amazon, Teachable, Udemy, Deliveroo, Upwork
- Self-service FAQ/knowledge base and support services for customers through Zendesk
  …and more

Many of these software applications can be chained together passing data between them to deliver business services more effectively and efficiently. Using SaaS apps to automate process and integration across apps and with processes performed by staff, is how any business can begin to scale its Operating Model to support more capacity and increase productivity, without the massive software and infrastructure maintenance costs.

Most larger businesses and corporations, including our listed case studies, have invested in enterprise systems and technology to support their business activities and this is how they have scaled their operations. It is with these systems and digital infrastructure that they have been able to build competitive advantage and grow their business. These enterprises use software apps as part of their process and operating procedures, including core banking platforms, books and records platforms, finance systems, CRM applications, and more bespoke developments. Many of these enterprise-scale applications require a significant investment as they offer more specialist functionality, support many hundreds of users or are specifically customised for a corporation.

Often SaaS application providers offer different tiers and pricing packages based on the needs of each client business. For example, you can license Salesforce.com software for less than $100 a month or your business might be paying an undisclosed and customized amount under the 'tier' called 'Enterprise Services' on their website.

## Data Intelligence (readiness for data science)

**Gather existing data and collect more data from many sources about your customers, transactions and performance. Analyze the data against business activities, competitors, and cross industry, to gain insights on what to change and improve in how the business operates and create value add in the business and for customers.**

Data and information are the most powerful tools in a business's arsenal – provided you know what data to collect, and then how to use it. Data intelligence is about being smart through data collection and analytics, which are necessary steps before further investment in a data science capability.

There's a great deal of free data available via the Internet if you know how to search for it. You don't necessarily need to invest in extremely expensive Artificial Intelligence (AI) to become smarter with your data. Many of the apps listed earlier in the Digital Infrastructure capability come with the data analytics and AI included. This level of functionality is already accessible for smaller businesses via the providers' middle pricing tiers. e.g. Some SaaS CRM software has predictive emailing and smart reporting, as well as providing APIs programmatic access. With the right data, you'll be able to gain insights and make more intelligent decisions. This is the approach pursued by Amazon. Jeff Bezos asked his Chief Data Officer to define 500 data attributes about customers and Amazon is tracking our behaviors with every tool they offer us either via Amazon.com or the Alexa Voice Assistance Service.

## Service Design & Innovation

**Ensure service offerings are relevant to customers, and their customer journeys, where they have problems that need solving and use cases... can make services sticky. Enhance or adapt services accordingly to possible demand. Deploy methods to influence demand for your services.**

Expectations are rapidly changing in the digital world. Millennial and post millennial customers demand less friction and more features and integration to enable their lives.

This is why Service Value Design & Innovation is so important in business. Constant innovation and reinvention of services will ensure they deliver on their promises as well as keep your customers (and employees) interested. This is important given the barriers to switching to another provider are often low. As a business, you need to keep learning and improving what you offer. Build those new skills and capabilities to support your efforts to offer that remarkable 'sticky' service which your customers are willing to pay for and continue to use. Service Design & Innovation skills guide the interaction with and capture of data about your customers, and their behaviors. Practicing these will inform the best way to serve customers creating the most value for you and them. This is the capability that Apple has so effectively mastered through their sticky ecosystem of Apple and IOS products and services that people are willing to pay premium prices for.

# Digitally Skilled Workforce

**Improve an enterprise's capabilities through training to improve the skills of your people and systems, so they can perform business activities and transform to improve the enterprise better and faster, when needed. Support the development of a growth mindset culture.**

How good or bad a business is at transforming is often forgotten because it is so busy just trying to make the changes and deliver the solutions right away (changes were required 'yesterday').  Most businesses invest in the activities to deliver specific solutions, but fail to learn how to transform effectively especially in how to operate as a data-driven enterprise through the principles of being value-driven, customer co-created and network connected.   They miss the fact that digital transformation through a digitally skilled workforce is a 'capability' that needs investment.

Upskilling and involvement in the innovation process, can motivate staff more than than just financial rewards.

A digitally skilled workforce that will support the enterprise to fast track its digital transformation efforts requires support from:

**Organizational Culture:** Mindset and attitude play a big part in how a business is able to change. Are staff resistant to change, and of a fixed mindset? Or is the organization orientated around a growth mindset and always learning to be better at what it does and what services they can offer to customers?

**Structure and Governance with an understanding of different benefits versus costs:** All the activities in the transformation journey can be methodically executed with speed and efficiency while delivering quality, or they can occur randomly based on who shouts the loudest.  Overly vocal or dominant stakeholders can skew the focus during transformation. Investment funds and limited cashflow can so easily be wasted on the wrong things to transform, if the wrong decisions are made. Governance might sound quite hierarchical or even bureaucratic, however it is important and applies in any business. Small businesses need to be disciplined in how they spend their money as well as large corporations, perhaps more so.  This is why some structure, be it using a checklist or a spreadsheet or a some product management software capability with a Kanban board will go a long way to providing an appropriate amount of governance around transformation.

Being able to **Manage the Transformation Journey** so that it provides the best ROI, comes down to HOW you made decisions on what actions to take. This requires data especially on customers behaviors and how existing services from a business as well as competitors are performing. It also requires staff to understand the cost of activities and their actions, including lost opportunities, and always doing the right thing for their enterprise and team. These problem-solving skills need to be continually developed, so that staff have the experience to identify what changes to make and then define HOW, WHERE and WHEN changes are made in the Operating Model. These skills ensure that market leading solutions are developed for customers.

# Example: Business Agility in banking and financial services

In 2020 the world's universal banks are still saddled with legacy processes, systems and data infrastructure which hamper their competitiveness in the rapidly innovating digital financial services world. Banks such as Deutsche Bank, HSBC, Barclays clamour to improve with major investment in transformation programs focused on creating sustainability and cleaning up thousands of legacy systems and data. Whilst this is on-going, smaller more **business agile** competitor banks and new start-up banks from the Financial Services Technology (FinTech) scene are forging head with digital strategies eating away at the market share the big banks used to enjoy.

Digital banking services are developing quickly and becoming more and more sophisticated. A web site or mobile app is considered a basic services in todays market. Internet banking started from humble beginnings in the 1990s when the first set of challenger online banks started to launch. These included UK's Egg, which was subsequently acquired by Citigroup and became Yorkshire Building Society. More traditional UK banks of the time such as Midland Bank also launched internet based services through the internet bank FirstDirect (subsumed into HSBC after the Midland acquisition in 1992). E-Trade brought online trading services to the public back in 1982. Online foreign or currency exchange services have also been around since early 2000.

FinTech has had an increased public profile since 2010 due to the myriad number of new challenger bank and sophisticated on-line service launches. However, FinTech actually started as early as the 1950s when much of the technology infrastructure supporting today's credit card payments was put in place. FinTech has become a marketing buzzword for what is really a new digital era in technology across the Financial Services industry, where the race is about new business models supported by new agile operating models built using digital technology and infrastructure.

The differences between banking services for everyday customers versus institutions and large corporates will widen in this digital age. Driven by increasingly digitally savvy customers, consumer and retail banking services are being developed in a **highly agile** manner with a focus on enabling customers in their lives through user or customer experience friendly processes supported end to end by technology. These agile banks will be able to scale to serve customers from anywhere without new infrastructure overheads, effectively commoditising banking services. Independent start-up banks operating entirely on Digital and Mobile technologies such as Monzo and Atom in the UK and Fidor in both Germany and the UK have emerged from the Digital revolution and challenge the established names.

DBS, a Singaporean-based medium sized bank that won the inaugural best digital bank award in 2016 from Euromoney, has already succeeded in implementing a full digital strategy starting from 2009.

The bank has managed to move from having one of the lowest satisfaction ratings in Singapore to having the best by introducing new metrics to measure success such as 'the customer hour' to eliminate waste. This cultural change and its focus on digital innovation has allowed DBS to move one step further by becoming an invisible bank through the launch of Digibank in India, one of the world largest unbanked markets. Digibank is an entirely mobile-centric banking service, with no branches.

In customer terms strong encouragement for the agile approach has come from a survey of over 10000 millennials over three years in the US (known as the Millennial Disruption Index) which reported that nearly half of them were counting on tech start-ups to overhaul the way banks work and 73% being more excited about new financial services offerings from Google, Amazon, Apple and PayPal. Tech giants like Apple, Google and especially Facebook already have access to billions of consumers currently using their mobile operating systems and social network applications have the ability both in capital and liquidity as well as digital knowhow to play in the banking space.

With the rise of digital banking, business agility is paramount for an institution, large or small, to be a dominant force in the future financial services ecosystem.

## Digital wallets will drive business agility

According to the 2019 Future of Digital Banking Report*, by 2030 the banking value ecosystem as we know it will look very different with the 'Platformication' of services, as consumers opt for an autonomous banking experience*. In this world of the autonomous banking experience, customers will take control of their finances through their digital wallets to form their own value chain of self-connected services involving different traditional and digital currencies and assets using the Cloud. This will drive the sub-services and capabilities offered by banks and other financial services providers to undergo further unbundling and rebundling into value streams that are directed by the customer journey and a customer self-designed user journey.

Banks and other financial services providers will be expected to use data including what a customer chooses to share from their digital wallet to predict and provide the most relevant and value-added personal financial management services, tailored to the customer's needs and wants and according to their customer journey problems. Agility will be key to success in this scenario.

With future supply and demand economics being driven by the data available in a customer's digital wallet, future **Business Models** and **Operating Models** will need to be integrated with the digital wallet service.

Currently, the digital wallet has become a major focus of the Financial Services industry with banks including CBA, DBS, Barclays and more… rushing to upgrade their Internet Banking services with digital wallet features, while the latest neobanks, such as Revolut and Monzo, offer a digital wallet service as their core *value proposition* alongside traditional banking products such as deposits and loans.

*2019 Future of Digital Banking Report (KPMG and Commonwealth Bank of Australia)

** Illustrative and inexhaustive example inferred through analysis conducted by Stratability Academy.

# EXAMPLE: How Harvard still leads as a data-driven enterprise

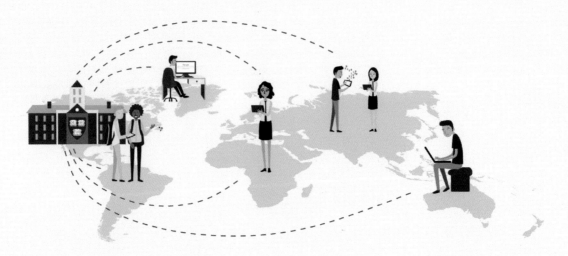

The rise of social networks and freely available information from the internet has challenged and transformed the media industry. These factors are driving change across many education institutions, in particular the private Higher Education market, but also institutions protected by government regulation where government grants continue to shrink. The Coronavirus/COVID-19 pandemic with its social distancing requirements to keep people safe, has simply accelerated this disruption in an industry that was already under siege.

Many universities around the globe have continuously increased fees at alarmingly unaffordable rates over the past two decades since the late 1990s in order to keep their existing Business Models afloat. However, undertaking a university degree at such high cost must come with a corresponding customer or user experience that meets and even exceeds students expectations with appropriate value – a return on investment (ROI). Unfortunately, the trend for the higher education experience is one where a significant portion of graduates are burdened by high student debt and a reducing likelihood for employment due to an oversupply of graduates without the appropriate practical or technical skills required by industry employers. This is reducing the uptake of traditional university and similar college education learning models. As the gig economy continues to grow, there has also been a shift towards entrepreneurship and creative industries where education and training require a more practical learning model than those traditionally available through universities (with the exception of medical industry). These alternate career paths have also reduced the pull of students.

*So how has Harvard University, one of the most traditional of universities, and the Harvard brand avoided the emerging and predicted decline in uptake of traditional higher education services, whist other universities are beginning to feel the effects of their degrading Operating Models from increasing costs and lower demand for their services?*

Universities and other college education institutions around the globe are fighting for a declining pool of traditional learning model students and funding, by trying to offer better content and research facilities. They face stiff competition from alternate digitally disruptors that have recently entered the education market especially E-Learning Platforms ranging in different content, value return and costs, such as Udacity, as well as incumbent online competitors such as the Open University, which has gained in recognition, as well as offerings from non-profit professional bodies.

However a Harvard Education and the ever popular Harvard Business Review (HBR) publications continue to offer a highly valued network of services to a very wide audience. There is no doubt that the Harvard brand has helped its business models to stand the test of time. However, what Harvard does well through the design of its Business Models and services is to engage strongly with the prospective customer community and importantly the past customer alumni community. The Harvard brand is comprised of many assets that are high in value and continue to drive value. Co-creation with customers and users, use of latest digital techniques for learning and engagement and being network connected are key to the value provided in their services. From its beginning, Harvard has invested to create very strong Student and Alumni Networks that are open to co-creation, to continuously increase value for all stakeholders involved, including strong partnerships with industries.

Harvard is recognized for giving birth to new networks including the largest social media network in the world, Facebook, which was founded by Harvard student Mark Zuckerberg, and originally a closed Harvard only social network.

Instead of being overtaken by other networks and communities that have used digital technology or social media to provide more value through better content services, better connectivity services, better employment services … Harvard has evolved its **Business Model** and **Operating Model** through digital transformation. It has used the latest technologies including social media along with the latest adaptive learning techniques that utilize AI and AR technology, to enhance its value propositions. By engaging and co-creating with its network of customers and users the **Business Model** supports these communities well and Harvard's service offerings are readily adopted because of the **Value Model** offered.

Additionally, HBR is now comprised of several digital services from e-books, to an online magazine and regular podcasts. This maintains and continuously improves the overall quality of Harvard education related value propositions.

Ongoing Operating Model investments in its digital platforms and digital service offerings has made Harvard a Data-Driven Enterprise with appropriate business agility to provide a relatively smooth transition to a 'learn at home' model during the COVID-19 pandemic crisis. Equally data-driven higher education businesses, such as sister school Cambridge in the United Kingdom and rivals MIT and Stanford who have always been seen as Science Technology Engineering and Mathematics (STEM) colleges have also experienced similar business agility, and the ability to pivot their Business Models with relative ease.

*Based on observational research conducted by Stratability Academy*

# Winning the game by joining the dots ...

## *How to execute strategy to deliver transformation value*

In the three **Strategy Journey Paths**,

- **Business Design for Disruption**
- **Transforming Operating Model with Service Design**
- **Managing the Transformation Journey**

... we have shown you **HOW** to 'play the game' of business, by joining the dots, to execute **business strategy** through **transformation** that delivers value.

A business that is able to traverse a path with speed and quality of outcome is an *agile data-driven enterprise*. **Business agility** including use of fast track digital transformation techniques enables a business to be nimble and effective in responses to the transformation challenges (p. 9-10) of the digital economy.

Building **Business agility** in an enterprise should be one of it's 'key' goals. Agility is not only about analysing the required response, it's about delivering the necessary changes to a business's Operating Model quickly and effectively. Agility is what gives a business its 'speed to market' and 'speed of execution', and enables it to adapt quickly to different influencers & disruptors within its operating markets.

Businesses build agility organically over time through continuous transformation and learning with strategic quick wins. There are five key steps to focus on to build business agility...

## 1 ASSESS your customers

Conduct customer modeling and *service design*, to understand customer problems and behaviors including their current and desired future experiences along their customer and user journeys.

*Assess different customers using the 'Mission model', and the 'Customer Journey Map'*

## 2 ARCHITECT your services

Evaluate the *capabilities* and services in the *value ecosystem* surrounding your services, define new improved target services that meet and exceed customer expectations, and what are the gaps in your *capabilities* and *value streams*, that need to be overcome to take them to market.

Review existing *capabilities* and services and define the target services. Conduct a gap analysis and use the Service Operating Model Canvas to detail the target service

## 3 ACTION your business transformation activities

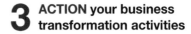
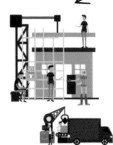

Determine what transformation activities you will undertake, when, and how, to overcome different gaps based on priority, strategic alignment, and ROI ... and mobilize the organization and its resources into action to support execution.

*Define the specific steps in the transformation journey using the 'Transformation Roadmap'*

# ... to achieve business agility

## 4 ACCOUNT for your value-add performance

Measure and review the performance of outputs and outcomes from services, *capabilities*, and resource components, and the specific changes applied during transformation , to understand if and how they work and explore what needs to be improved or adapted.

*Continuously review and evaluate the data to validate specific strategies and tactics and transformation activities to determined if objectives are met, and identify improvements and next steps,*

## 5 ACCELERATE transformation with improved business agility ... keep innovating

Deploy alternate **Business Models**, update and adapt current strategic and tactics, and keep innovating current and new services into new markets, while exiting those in decline, as you continue to improve and adapt capabilities in the **Operating Model** to support more growth in value through new services.

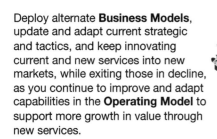

*Update and adapt the canvas used in the Business Model, and move into the next business cycle... Assess your customers...*

Application of data science provides a more valuable level of business intelligence to support decision making. Data provides clarity on which gaps to address, why, with whom, when, and where, to optimize value-add, while overcoming risks (p. 19-20, 51, 125, 207-216)... across **THE STRATEGY JOURNEY** and business lifecycle.

Data is a 'potent' ingredient which acts as a 'power-up' in the game. However, data is not the be all and end all in...

You have to play the game to learn and improve your gameplay. Importantly, you have to be equipped to take a shot in order to have an opportunity or chance to 'win' – you can't get stuck over analyzing.

Much is learnt from making a play to understand how good your data and capabilities are. In reality, you may have to take multiple 'shots', to build up a score and start to lead against the competition. What is clear is that, in the digital age, an enterprise has to keep improving and stay agile to adapt to disruptions. Being agile will sustain your winning momentum and carry you towards whatever is your Mission and Vision.

The game of business and the gamification process is all about gap filling – to be better and faster than the competition in finding these gaps and resolving them through 'joining the dots', and creating a *'culture of learning'* (p. 44, 198), that keeps the momentum of winning.

# The Digital Target Operating Model in ..

*In the digital age, deriving and delivering a market leading Operating Model to realize a Digital Strategy is paramount for business success.*

The goal of this book is to provide the motivational context, an explanation of the business challenges and the imperative behind why businesses have to develop an effective digital future as part of their Strategy Journey. It has also provided some insight into the complexities of the business environment today. Organizations are complicated evolving systems of people, processes, systems and data, all built on the collective ambitions and talents of real people. Mixed with the dynamics of ever evolving business culture and an increasing reliance on complex new technologies such as big data and machine learning, it is no wonder that enterprises have struggled to map out an effective future.

This why we created **THE STRATEGY JOURNEY** *Framework*, to provide a practical, formulaic, data driven means for businesses to navigate their digital transformation challenges. The framework guides all components of the **Business Operating Model** (organization, process, data, systems, location) and supports development of a more effective future enterprise, as well as the path to achieve it.

Today's businesses must start on their strategy journeys toward a new and better future by building their **BUSINESS AGILITY** and **DIGITAL OPERATING MODEL MATURITY** to gain operational resilience.

**THE STRATEGY JOURNEY** *Framework* provides a guidance system to enable an intelligent, relevant and valuable **DIGITAL TARGET OPERATING MODEL (DTOM)**, a considered and costed digital transformation path and the capabilities to then go on and deliver the necessary changes to the enterprise quickly and effectively to realise its goals, objectives, mission and vision.

**BUSINESS AGILITY** brings the skills and experience to apply the Paths and Framework to developing future states. Different levels of developed agility present different levels of value;

- **Tactical agility** enables distinct elements of a business's Operating Model to be designed and developed in cycles to deliver evolutionary step changes in line with strategy.
- **Strategic agility** enables the generation of a full Digital Target Operating Model for a business and supports continuous transformation aligned to a dynamic business strategy.

In a fast changing world that is increasingly driven by a digital economy, businesses are at different maturity stages on their journey to a **Digital Operating Model**. Those that are mature, such as Amazon or Apple, are thriving. Those that are not mature, are challenged and at risk of disruption.

# ... the digital economy

## DIGITAL OPERATING MODEL MATURITY

We have seen the effects *of Business Transformation* (p. 81) and *innovation* (p. 109) in the Fourth Industrial Revolution (p. 13-16) in evolving new **Digital Business Models** (p 111). The **Operating Models** that sit behind the **Business Model** have also evolved in their capabilities not only to operationally support the business but also to support its transformation and its operational resilience.

- **Traditional Operating Models** tend to be business operations focused and are developed and used to derive **Economy of Scale** based transformations aligned to distinct business case driven transformation programs or needs. These Operating Models are supported with tactical levels of business agility delivered through low maturity transformation capabilities.

- **Digital Twin** based operating models bring a level of expertise in modeling the current state operating model and presenting a context of the strategic objectives to drive how different business capabilities that exist currently should be transformed. **Digital Twin** is supported through a medium level of business agility providing a more consistent approach and structured cycles of transformation.

- **Digital Operating Models** are highly developed with a dynamic data-driven **DIGITAL TARGET OPERATING MODEL** used to steer all transformation investment. Strategic business agility supports the continuous transformation that is undertaken as the business reacts to change.

## Evolution of the Business Operating Model

### Economies of Scale

Focused on elements of business operations. Used to optimize costs through distinct business case-based transformation. Lean process analysis, process offshoring & automation and organization rationalization is used to improve the cost-to-service ratio.

*e.g. Some traditional retail and corporate banks are still cost driven and remain focused on drive processes offshore with basic automation support.*

### Digital Twin

Focused on the enterprise and customer. End to end process led analysis and transformation delivering evolutionary steps to fulfilling strategic objectives. Transformation is driven in cycles through structured processes and consistent approaches that leverage digital technology and services via a twin organization or Digital Twin.

*e.g. Securities processing businesses, Wealth Management companies ...*

### Digital Operating Model

An ecosystem of integrated services supporting customers and users, realized through a platform. The Digital Operating Model is continually being updated dynamically through use of data and AI, based on customer experience, market opportunity or changes, disruptive market entrants, technology advances, ecosystem evolution and regulatory driven changes.

*e.g. Amazon Marketplace, Disney, VIP.com, Apple ...*

# Next

# Steps

# How to continue your learning journey

To win in the 'game of business', you have to keep learning to play the game (practice and apply) to take your shot.

**Here are some resources and tools to dive deeper into...**
**THE STRATEGY JOURNEY Framework and Paths... to help you accelerate your Career Growth... and resolve your business challenges.**

Enroll in the
**Strategy Journey Kickstarter Masterclass Series**

This 4 step mini-course with WORKSHEETS and a private community is **included** as part of owning this book.

## THE STRATEGY JOURNEY BOOK

Discover your
***Strategy Journey Path***

https://strategyjourney.com/kickstarter

# Level up with the
# STRATEGY JOURNEY Accelerator

Do you want to accelerate your growth and level up your Career Journey with **access to the special techniques, tools and guidance, including mentoring** from the authors and other practitioner experts who together have many 100s of years of cross industry experience along the 5 stages of **THE STRATEGY JOURNEY**?

Want to learn how they applied their craft to **become industry and domain leaders**?
Want to steal their secrets and techniques to buildup your own experience, and personal brand inside your Career Portfolio to **increase your opportunities and income by many multiples**?

With a growing set of case study examples including lead author Julie Choo's Career Strategy Journey...
How did Julie get promoted to a 6 figure salary within 2 years post graduation, despite being made redundant at 23 following a major global industry and economic disruption?

Discover her strategy journey to VP and Director, independent consultant advisor and strategist to the C-Suite of many multinational Fortune 500 companies including big banks. Follow her journey to entrepreneur and founder of her own company as well as speaker and coach capable of charging up to 10000 USD per day for her time.

Get both the **technical business skills and the non-technical 'soft' inter-personal skills in the one place** to transform your career and **fast-track your transformation to your dream career**, and especially if you are currently stuck, want to switch out of your 'nightmare' or 'non-existent' career, and looking to find your passion.

## https://strategyjourney.com/accelerator

# The STRATEGY JOURNEY ❯

❯ ## Extended FRAMEWORK with 25 Canvases

The Five Models of **THE STRATEGY JOURNEY** *Framework* can be extended from 5 Canvases into 25 structured design thinking tools for practicing strategy and architecting your business and career, to empower transformation in the digital age.

Learn more at https://strategyjourney.com/extended-framework

Customer Journey Map ·
User Journey Designer ·
Value Ecosystem Map ·
Value Stream Designer ·
Service Value Model ·

**Value Model**

**Mission Model**

**Business Model**

Mission Model Blueprint ·
Priorities & Pain Points ·
Ecosystem Influencers Map ·
Game Play Map ·
Game Plan Designer ·

· **Digital Business Blueprint**
· Target Market Validator
· Proposition Ecosystem
· Business Growth Plan
· Growth Funding Map

## Transformation Model

## Operating Model

- **Transformation Roadmap**
- Backlog Priority Planner
- Co-creation Journey Map
- Transformation Analyzer
- Strategic Performance Tracker

- **Service Operating Model**
- Capability Definition
- Location Footprint Designer
- Organizational Design Map
- Service Architecture

314

Printed in Great Britain
by Amazon